GENRE AND VOID

Developing a reading of some of Beauvoir's and Sartre's most influential writings in philosophy, Max Deutscher explores contemporary philosophy in the light of the phenomenological tradition within which *Being and Nothingness* and *The Second Sex* occurred as striking events operating on the border of the modern and the post-modern. Deutscher traces the shifts of genre that produce their gendered philosophies, and responds in terms of contemporary experience to the mood and the arguments of their works. Drawing upon the writings of two contemporary critics in particular – Michele Le Dœuff and Luce Irigaray – Deutscher reworks this part of philosophy's history in order to advance thinking in contemporary philosophy, generate renewed philosophical reflection on consciousness, freedom and one's relation to others, and to return a look still cast in our direction from an earlier time.

T0372809

ASHGATE NEW CRITICAL THINKING
IN PHILOSOPHY

The *Ashgate New Critical Thinking in Philosophy* series aims to bring high quality research monograph publishing back into focus for authors, the international library market, and student, academic and research readers. Headed by an international editorial advisory board of acclaimed scholars from across the philosophical spectrum, this new monograph series presents cutting-edge research from established as well as exciting new authors in the field; spans the breadth of philosophy and related disciplinary and interdisciplinary perspectives; and takes contemporary philosophical research into new directions and debate.

Genre and Void

Looking Back at Sartre and Beauvoir

MAX DEUTSCHER

Macquarie University, Australia

LONDON AND NEW YORK

First published 2003 by Ashgate Publishing

Reissued 2018 by Routledge
2 Park Square, Milton Park, Abingdon, Oxon, OX14 4RN
711 Third Avenue, New York, NY 10017, USA

Routledge is an imprint of the Taylor & Francis Group, an informa business

Publisher's Note
The publisher has gone to great lengths to ensure the quality of this reprint but points out that some imperfections in the original copies may be apparent.

Disclaimer
The publisher has made every effort to trace copyright holders and welcomes correspondence from those they have been unable to contact.

A Library of Congress record exists under LC control number: 2002027771

ISBN 13: 978-1-138-70959-1 (hbk)
ISBN 13: 978-1-138-70957-7 (pbk)
ISBN 13: 978-1-315-19948-1 (ebk)

Contents

Acknowledgements

This work owes most to the critical enthusiasm and hard work of students –
from first year undergraduates to advanced postgraduates – at Macquarie
University. They had to bear with my experiments during the period when
my teaching Sartre, then Beauvoir, Le Dœuff and Irigaray, was part of the
process of my own learning how to read them. And, going far beyond
bearing with these difficulties, they responded with intelligence, scholarly
application and imaginative invention.

Amongst the many colleagues who have been generous with criticism
and encouragement, I should mention, in particular, Luciana O'Dwyer who
brought from Italy – with her wide experience in German and English
philosophy – a living paradigm of rigorous scholarship and creativity in
recent European philosophy.

Genevieve Lloyd and Paul Crittenden have each read entire versions of
this work, and the result owes a great deal to their close and critical
attention and to their suggestions about structure and presentation. Phyllis
Perlstone, Isabel Karpin, David Ellison, Penelope Deutscher and
Marguerite La Caze have made valuable criticisms and suggestions about
various chapters, and about the work as a whole.

I am also grateful to the reader for Ashgate Publishing, whose critical
comments, while causing me a good deal of extra work, so finely
comprehended what I was trying to achieve that I was encouraged rather
than deterred. Kristen Thorner at Ashgate, and an unnamed proof-reader,
not only radically improved the state of the text but also made numerous
thoughtful and welcome suggestions about points of clarity and expression.

I read a section of this work 'in progress' while a visiting scholar at the
University of Tasmania, and I also wish to thank the philosophers at the
University of Warwick for inviting me to present part of the work as a
seminar there. Macquarie University has generously supported my work –
both in terms of study leave and then by expediting an early 'retirement' so
that I could take up writing full-time.

Abbreviations

'BN' is used throughout for Sartre's *Being and Nothingness* (Sartre 1976)

'SS' is used throughout for Beauvoir's *The Second Sex* (Beauvoir 1983)

Introduction

In this work I develop a reading of some of Beauvoir's and Sartre's most influential writings in philosophy. My aim is to work upon ideas to be found (not exclusively) in Sartre and Beauvoir, so as to keep them in motion as part of contemporary thinking, not rendered *passé* by structuralism and post-structuralism. I do not wish simply to make some reading of their works, even if a novel one, merely to 'explain what they mean' and thus to consign them to a place in the museum of 'worthy and esteemed' philosophical constructions. Nor would I read their tradition of philosophy as merely a (dead-end) branch line of analytical philosophy's railroad of concern with the eternal triad – dualism, idealism and materialism.

To conduct contemporary philosophy in the light of the phenomenological tradition within which *Being and Nothingness* and the *The Second Sex* occurred as such striking events, requires that one find idiomatic ways of reading 'being', 'nothingness', 'being-in-itself', 'being-for-itself' and 'being-for-others' ('*L'être*', '*le néant*', '*l'être-en-soi*', '*l'être-pour-soi*' and '*l'être-pour-autrui*'). Beauvoir's debt to these terms is less continuous and less intense. I hope to show that in making more connections with biology, economics, history and social circumstance and, not least, sexuality and sexual difference, her use has already shifted a good deal more towards a flexible idiom.

Not wishing to take a new reader by the ear and haul them through the whole of *The Second Sex* and *Being and Nothingness*, I do not consider the works in the same order as they were written. Though I feel more sympathetic with the general tenor of attitude and opinion in *The Second Sex* than in *Being and Nothingness*, I have worked more closely with Sartre's work, and for longer. It came as something of a surprise to have a critic of a late draft of the present work observe that '*[though] the voice is distinctive, the discussion is full of insights, and the argument draws one into thinking about the issues ... Sartre [remains] at a remove, a shadowy figure*'. Some readers may find the Sartre of this work not so remote, but for others my 'Sartre' may speaking to them as if he were a shade amongst a philosophers' company in Hades. Since there is no life everlasting, even in the literary sense, I can live with this. There is, after all, a dark irony in John Keats' avowal, hope, or dread, voiced in his '*I think that I shall be amongst the English poets when I die'*. Michèle Le Dœuff, the critic through whose reception of Sartre the reader will first discover his philosophy in this work, has written, indeed, of a time when *'we spoke fluent existentialese'*. Though I announce the bold hope of making some of Beauvoir and Sartre's ideas work within the contemporary scene, I do not expect those times to return. No writer has the power to recreate them.

*   *   *

There are other particular reasons, deriving from problems of translation of language and of thought, why even a sympathetic reader may find the well-known Sartre a 'shadowy figure' within these pages. (It seems less of a problem with Beauvoir because she, or her narrative persona, makes the reader privy to her difficulty in situating herself. There is less of the 'omniscient author', more of the 'situated subject'.) For example, as the reader may know full well (or shortly will discover), after the modes called *'being-in-itself'* and *'being-for-itself'*, the key term in *Being and Nothingness* is *'l'autrui'*, usually translated as 'the Other'. The capital letter works to inspire some awe and to indicate that one is not merely referring to some specific person or other, identity unspecified. In Sartre's uses, *'l'autrui'*, this 'Other', works as an elusive, or evanescent figure. This challenge is far greater than solving a problem of adequate translation from French to English. And here we must look more generally at the problem of language, and of languages.

Sartre's French is already a 'take' on the German of Hegel and of Heidegger. And that, in its desire and willingness to write of *being* and of *non-being* was already a 'take' on the Greek philosophy of Plato's *Sophist* and *Parmenides*. Unless the reader of the work-in-English called *Being and Nothingness* has their attention drawn to these facts, he or she is placed in the position of being required somehow to divine a meaning that is surrounded by an *aura* (as you like it) or a *fog* (if you don't). Though Sartre sets up his position, overtly, in relation to the René Descartes of the *Discourse* and the *Meditations*, there has been little awareness of the fact that Sartre can assume a currency for the problem of *'l'être et le néant'* directly from that famous French predecessor. Having introduced his method of doubt simply as a strategic device, Descartes writes as one who has found himself *'as though [he] had suddenly fallen into a deep sea, and could neither plant [his] foot on the bottom nor swim to the top'* (Descartes 1954: 66). Having merely 'imagined' that he might have no body, he 'discovers' that he is entirely separate from it, and might well exist without it. And yet we shall find him insisting, within some pages, that he *'is not lodged in his body like a pilot in his vessel'*. What am I then, and where, in relation to matter, and any science of it? In a line that ought to be as famous as '*Je pense, donc je suis*', he declares, '*Je suis dans un milieu entre l'être et le néant*': 'I am in a situation as if between being and nothingness'.

It is downright curious that whereas Descartes' concern with *le néant* is profound, he is never thought of as a philosopher of nothingness. Thinkers, whether attracted or repelled by his famous 'dualism', have been too impressed by his insistence that the 'I' that cannot doubt itself is a thinking *substance*. This 'I' that thinks differs from matter in being a *spiritual* substance. But Descartes' only explanation of *spiritual* is *immaterial*. Now, to *be* immaterial is no more and no less than *not to be* material. That is, the nature of this 'I' as an especially curious and remarkable *thinking thing* is thus to have a *non*-nature. To think is *not to be*. That we might understand thinking in terms of *not being* rather than as a special kind of being is thus (perhaps inadvertently) already encapsulated within Descartes' *Discourse* and his *Meditations*.

It is not the issue of some unacknowledged Sartrean 'debt to Descartes' that concerns me. The point is that the 'mysteriousness' of mind and its relation to body that has been such an obsession within philosophy is that of *non-being to being*, of '*not (merely) being a thing*' to '*being (merely) a thing*'. The history of philosophy of 'mind' has been a history of the insolubility of a dilemma that I would express thus: '*Defining thinking in purely physical terms is an always unsuccessful reduction*' but '*Not defining thinking in purely physical terms is to turn thinking into a process that is a perpetual mystery to science*'.

The names of six philosophers since Descartes – Leibniz, Spinoza, Husserl, Wittgenstein, Ryle and Sartre – signal the most creative attempts to understand this problem. First Leibniz, with the 'neutral' *monad* in which mind arises as a complex series of folds of matter upon itself, and then Spinoza for whom 'mind' becomes the body's own idea of itself. Then Husserl returns to the scene of the crime. He examines afresh the clues regarding Descartes' separating mind from body. Husserl is the first to locate Descartes' wrong turning in losing sight of the 'transcendental' nature of the doubt, and thus the 'transcendental' rather than substantial nature of the 'I'. That 'I', as Husserl puts it, 'brackets' (rather than doubts) all the objects it can perceive or think. The 'I' that 'transcends' – the 'transcendental ego' – is *not a thing*. It is the point that subtends all intentional relations that give meaning to the objects of perception and thought. So, if anything that could be a 'thing' is always already within the sights of this 'I', then this 'I' itself cannot, in turn, be a thing.

Reading Husserl but desiring a domestic idiom for philosophy, and influenced by Wittgenstein's conceptual phenomenology, Gilbert Ryle made his own return to the Cartesian primal scene. In a series of strategies that differently map the Husserlian territory, he too dares to say that we cannot find this 'mind' or its 'inner process' called thinking, not because it is a mysterious thing but because there is no such 'thing'. There is no 'place' in which this 'thinking' may occur. And yet, though there is no such *thing* as mind, it is no less important that we '*Mind out!*' or that we '*Mind our own business!*'.

It is in such contexts, then, both of historical turnings that signal the possibility of Sartre's strategy, and in terms of the resources of contemporary idioms that deal in 'nothing', that we can continue Sartre's project of *recognising being conscious without making a thing of it*. At that point we can hazard a glance at the Gorgon's head that has transfixed or repelled thought that deals in Sartrean terms: the verb '*néantir*', constructed by Sartre (Sartre 1943) from the established noun '*néant*', meaning as a nominal, 'nothing' as in 'of no account' as in '*gens de néant*'. As a noun, '*le néant*' means a thing of no value. It also takes on a cosmic extension, as in Pascal's '*un néant à l'égard de l'infini*' ('insignificant from the point of view of the infinite') or Racine's '*Il voit comme un néant tout l'univers ensemble*' ('He sees the universe as a whole as of no account'). As we have remarked, Descartes already uses it in this existential sense to convey the intensity of his doubts about the very existence of things, '*Je suis dans un milieu entre l'être et le néant*'. Bergson gives '*néant*' a narrower sense simply derived from negation – '*Le néant est la négation radicale de la totalité de l'existant*' ('The void is the radical negation of the totality of existence'). In contrast with Sartre's '*néantir*', '*anéantir*' ('to destroy utterly') derives from the 12C (*Petit Robert*: 68).

From time to time I shall give an idiomatic reading of '*néantir*' as '*to make nothing of*'. This has as an idiomatic variant, '*to make light of*'. This reading goes with Sartre's attack on the 'bad faith' of posing things as if given in their essence – of receiving them in the 'spirit of seriousness'. My homely reading may seem to make too little of the metaphysical force of *néantir*', but the noun 'nothing' and the verb '*néantir*' are always set up to be used in an already established context. Nothing is ever absolutely nothing.[1] On the reading of '*néantir*' that will be at work in this present project, it is an already structured and motivated 'being-for-itself' that 'makes nothing of' some already describable and specific situation. It is

---

[1] There is a parallel between Heidegger's '*Das nichts nichteit*' ('the nothing noths') and Sartre's suggestion that it is only a conscious being that can 'nihilate'. A conscious being has taken *le néant* into its heart.

true that these homely 'nihilations' which bring about the countless little *négatités* – the 'little nothings' of everyday life – suggest the occurrence[2] of some absolute *nihilation* of a featureless '*being-in-itself*' in itself.[3] But this 'writing before the trace', as Derrida would diagnose the temptation of thought, is impossible. Nonetheless, there is a constant attraction in metaphysics towards recognising reality prior to our recognition – endemic just because of its tantalising impossibility. Like the child's peeking very quickly at the adult as if to try to catch what the adult is when not seen.

When applied to all specific uses that describe situations of perception, feeling and choice in *Being and Nothingness* we shall create at least one very satisfactory and revealing reading if we hear '*to nihilate*' as '*to make nothing of*', or '*to make light of*'. And in the same vein, we shall make at least one equally satisfactory reading of the *nothingness* that lies within the heart of *being*, as, quite simply, the 'nothing' with which one replies to 'What did you find in the room?' (Or what did you find in your heart?). I find *nothing* of any interest or consequence for myself in my project, or in connection with the intentions of my questioner.

It is in the same spirit that I often alternate 'living for oneself' with the more familiar and orthodox 'being-for-itself', and I supply 'living for others' in place of 'being-for-others'. One of the advantages of this reading is to remove the strange hypostatisation produced by an over-literal translation of '*l'être-en-soi*', '*l'être-pour-soi*' and '*l'être-pour-autrui*'. After all, the definite article before the verb 'to be' in French is a formality. It is a slight straw that is asked to support a whole ontology of a variety of kinds of *being* that somehow stand in place of my, your, or our doing, feeling and perceiving what we do. At least one generous reading of *being* here is that of a *mode*. Sartre, like Locke and, of course Heidegger, is taking the category of *modes of being* as ontologically vital. Modes are not 'things', nor are they to be reduced to the 'things' that 'have' them. So it is poor thanks to Sartre to raise up those modes as if they were independent entities of their own sort – agencies at work and at war within us.

I shall not press, remorselessly, these new inflections of reading and translation. Out of respect for established scholarship and communication with other readings I often use the customary hyphenations – *being-in-itself*, *being-for-itself*, *being-for-others*, and even the more risky definite article – '*the* in itself', despite the obvious danger of reification. But unless at least we shift between such readings and more idiomatic variants, we

---

[2] This 'occurrence' might be thought of as a once only originary event, or as a continually repeated, renewed, creation.
[3] My elaboration, catching a line of thought generated by Sartre's notion, '*being-in-itself*', as always discovered as it is For Us, not as it is In Itself!

simply have no way of avoiding a hypnotic effect of reification. This hypnosis has the effect of either a mind-numbing acceptance of the Sartrean (gigantic) construction, or else of a violent wrenching of oneself out of the mesmerism by rejecting it as 'obscure', 'mysterious', even 'irrationalist'.

One of the questions posed to Sartre in the Schilpp volume is whether '*being-for-itself*', for instance, takes the plural. Are there are a lot of little '*beings-for-themselves*' that dart about the cosmos? Sartre is amused by the enormity of the misconstrual. To be for oneself is a mode, not an entity. To use a touch of Merleau-Ponty, it is a way I 'comport' myself. And yet it is, for reasons if only of grammar, difficult to avoid raising up *being* as if it were an entity. One establishes a theme, the theme word is part of a theme park, the word goes up in neon lights and 'Lo and behold!' one has a title and therefore, apparently, an entity to stand behind it.

*   *   *

There is another reason why a 'Sartre' as now 'Other' for us, should figure as elusive when we attempt to rework his writings. Theorists have firmly established the literary distinction between human bodily author – the one who sweats at the desk and may be paid on some rare occasion for doing so – and the narrative voice of the author's novel, play or poem. In philosophy, this is not so. Those who read in a philosophical mode are much more liable to identify the 'Descartes' that is the narrative voice of the *Discourse* and *Meditations* with the man who was born in Le Havre, who had a child, and died while in Sweden at the request of a royal person. In writing of Sartre in terms of his *philosophical* productions, there is the same tendency to permit a coalition between the persona, the 'I' of *Being and Nothingness*, and the young Jean-Paul Sartre. He who formed the book while killing time in a prisoner of war camp. And so this man, this Sartre, tends to haunt the pages of the book – indeterminable – and yet connected with the voice of the 'I' that narrates it.

In the late 80s and 90s a number of important books have appeared that place Beauvoir beyond dispute as a serious philosopher. I have assumed much of this work as a platform from which to begin my own, and have chosen to make my contribution by examining some relatively limited sections of her writings in detail, including many citations. This is part of the process of receiving her work with the same critical thoroughness that has been extended to Sartre's. In Part I, Beauvoir's work gets more close attention than Sartre's does. In Parts II and III, Sartre's is more often the text subject to examination. In Part IV, the work of two contemporary feminist inheritors and critics of Beauvoir's legacy is brought to bear on

Sartre. I am keenly aware that all of this still falls well short of doing full justice to Beauvoir's contributions – in particular to the themes of freedom and of reciprocal regard. After all, it is she who immediately challenged Sartre's view of objectification as inevitable. It is she who, by more concrete analysis and description, challenged Sartre's apparently inevitable cycle of a rebellion against domination that only reinstates domination.

I work with the ideas of *Being and Nothingness*, and the most theoretical passages in *The Second Sex* as lying within the traditional problem of the inconsistent and apparently irresoluble triad of dualistic realism, idealism and solipsism. Nevertheless, the aim is not to 'make Sartre or Beauvoir clear' by showing how their theory fits a standard tradition, but rather, to show how they figure amongst those who deconstruct that triad. True, neither is a Derridean 'deconstructionist' – a mythical persona of the culture wars that peaked in the 80s of the last century. But their (differently) idiosyncratic appropriations of Husserl's phenomenology[4] succeed in bringing about an irretrievable shift and fluidity in the meaning of the terms of that triad. Metaphysics is domesticated – *'one can write philosophy about anything'*. Equally, the domestic takes on a metaphysical aura, and to discover that best, one would read *Nausea* along with *Being and Nothingness*.

Beauvoir, Sartre and Hegel

In their use of the concepts of *'being-in-itself'*, *'being-for-itself'* and the *'Other'*, both Beauvoir and Sartre have their debts to the nineteenth-century German philosopher George Hegel. They recognise that *'Hegel's brilliance is to make me depend on the Other in my being,'* so that *'the Other penetrates me to the heart'* (BN, 237). Hegel recognises another's 'otherness' as enabling my self-recognition, but for Beauvoir, the Other can perform this role of mediation only if he has a life beyond his role in enabling self-understanding. Sartre's Other appears on the scene to shock me out of my self-centred wits. He sets out from the immediate experience 'I' have of being critically regarded by another, observable, conscious being. He writes that this *'look has set us on the track of our being-for-others and has revealed the indubitable existence of this Other'* (BN, 282). But, aware that that this 'look' cannot show how a *reciprocity* of conscious subjects is possible, realising that something crucial has been left out, he tries to *'examine the fundamental relation of Me to the Other'*.[5] He wants

[4] And, to a lesser extent, Heidegger's appropriation of it in his *Being and Time*.
[5] This 'Other' cannot be present as an individual, it would appear.

no part of what he sees as Hegel's reduction of the Other to another (necessary) part of 'Spirit'. He wants to maintain that

> what [the certainty of '*I think*'] reveals to us here is just factual necessity ... [as is the fact that] our being, along with its being-for-itself, is also for-others. [M]y being-for-others as the surge of my consciousness ... has the character of an absolute event ... an historicisation (BN, 282).

Sartre admits that this effort of 'I' and 'Other' to achieve a totality by mutual and challenging recognition indicates my vain effort to re-apprehend myself as if in the mode of what has being simply 'in itself'. Strictly, the existence of self and Other as structures of one and the same totality of being should allow each of us to recognise a 'we' who perceive and interact. We exist at any moment when we share intentions and a common consciousness of things. So even though 'my selfness and that of the Other are structures of one and the same totality of being', the Other as physically present is part of the larger totality that includes both of us. As internal partner the other has the independence of role of another character on stage. The Other as immediately present by 'internal negation' is not thereby some facet of myself.

But Sartre criticises Hegel for presuming to take a point of view from outside this totality of 'self and Other'. What Sartre terms, in a biological metaphor, the 'scissiparity'[6] of self and Other as 'moments' created by Spirit as a totality is available to *no* individual consciousness. To mix Jean-Paul Sartre's vision with Gilbert Ryle's, Hegel's 'Spirit' is like the child who scampers to place their foot (*of their own transcendence*) on their own shadow (*of their objectity*) (Ryle 1949: 195–196). As Sartre puts it, '*the recovery fails*' because the putative 'totality' itself, like any being in that mode, exists 'as a whole' as '*being-for-itself*'. 'I' have no vantage point from which to consider it 'as a whole'. Totalisation fails, and this is to say that I can never be 'at home' with myself – or with another.

Edmund Husserl's 'Bracketing Out' of What We Perceive

Edmund Husserl re-established[7] the tradition of phenomenology for the twentieth century, in 1900 and 1901, with the two volumes of *Logical Investigations*. A work that greatly influenced Sartre, *Cartesian Meditations*, appeared in 1929 (Husserl 1970a). During his period of study

---

[6] 'Scissiparity' – reproduction by fission – schizogenesis.
[7] Hegel had published his *Phenomenology of Spirit* in 1807 (Hegel 1967).

in Germany in the 30s, Sartre would also have encountered the ideas that were to appear in Husserl's final great work, *The Crisis of European Sciences and Transcendental Phenomenology*.[8] Phenomenology aims at rigorous philosophy by means of systematic and close *description* of the world as experienced, rather than by searching for abstract 'foundations' for knowledge. Husserl recognised Descartes' systematic *doubt* about experience[9] as the inspiration for his idea of 'bracketing out' the objects of experience so as to regard our manner of experience. This method, called a 'reduction', was to be the key to a new kind of objectivity that incorporated subjectivity rather than combating it. We have Beauvoir's legendary vignette in her *The Prime of Life* about a meeting with Raymond Aron upon his return from Berlin in 1932:

> We spent an evening together at the Bec de Gaz in the Rue Montparnasse. We ordered the speciality of the house, apricot cocktails; Aron said, pointing to his glass: 'You see, my dear fellow, if you are a phenomenologist, you can talk about this cocktail and make philosophy out of it!' Sartre turned pale with emotion at this. Here was just the thing he had been longing to achieve for years – to describe objects just as he saw and touched them, and extract philosophy from the process (Beauvoir 1965: 135).

In 'bracketing out' the objects of experience, Husserl thought he had discovered a 'transcendental ego' – a pure point of origin of experience – and in his *La Transcendance de l'Ego*, Sartre attacked this as outside any description of experience (Sartre 1936). Nevertheless we can understand the debt Sartre owes to Husserl even in the way he criticises how Husserl handles the Other – how a 'transcendental ego' could relate to another became a principal problem for Husserl. This 'Other' is present

> not only as a particular concrete and empirical appearance, but as a permanent condition of its unity and of its richness of experience ... the veritable guarantee of the object's objectivity (BN, 233).

Sartre claims that Husserl has no resource for relating transcendental egos. Husserl's 'ego-pole' subtends the world of experience in lying 'beyond' it – a condition of intelligibility of the Other. Husserl makes *knowing* the primary relation between us, but our articulated knowledge would produce

---

[8] Because Husserl, as Jewish, was debarred in the 30s from teaching in any German university, and, with further publication of his writings prohibited, this work was not generally available until after the Second World War, in the 50s.

[9] This 'doubt' is expressed in his *Discourse on Method*, in 1637, and in the *Meditations* in 1640 (Descartes 1954).

immediacy of co-presence only if each *knew* the other as s/he *knows* themselves. Though marked by 'an exteriority of bodies', the distinction of Other and self does not stem from that, but from the interiority of experience that excludes another's knowledge. For Husserl the 'Other' is revealed as an *absence* within concrete experience. In seeing another as a centre of experience one *sees* what one *cannot* experience in the Other.

We shall see (in Part III of this volume) that Sartre draws upon this image of 'absence', but still he nags at Husserl about it. How does Husserl recognise such 'absence'? Sartre declares that, for Husserl, '*the Other, on principle, refuses himself to us, and flees*' (BN, 235)! Sartre himself tries to show that while the 'Other' as such is simply 'not-me', any 'Other' can confront me, appeal to me, and be confronted by me. We can respond directly to what we cannot know by abstract or detached means. The Other *may* 'flee' – *particular* people may flee reciprocal 'upsurge' – whereas for Husserl, however, the Other can be only the

> empty [intentional object of experience][10] which corresponds to my [attention] towards the Other [when] he appears concretely in my experience (BN, 235).

Husserl declares that '*we are as sure of the Other as we are of the world*', to which Sartre makes the caustic rejoinder that 'a solipsist would say as much'. Equality in their *lack* of assurance! As Sartre insists, '*my affirmation of the Other [would] demand ... the existence beyond the world of a similar transcendental field*' (BN, 235). An 'existence beyond the world', that is, as it is specifically for him from the point of his interiority. Husserl recognises the Other as an irreducible phenomenon but, Sartre argues, does not '*prove that my consciousness is affected in its being by the other consciousnesses of the same type [as mine]*' (BN, 235).

Sartre agrees with Husserl that *my world is a world 'for others'*. Sartre notes a submerged precondition, however, that

> the Other confers a particular type of objectivity on the objects of my world because he is already in this world [as] an object (BN, 272).

This is a keen point, but it raises a question or two. First, about the meaning of this 'objectivity'. Like 'objectivity' in English, Sartre's '*objectivité*' has the sense either of something's own existence apart from being perceived, or of the human quality of impartiality. He coins the useful term '*objectité*' ('objectity') to catch the 'objectness' of what we perceive. Even a

---

[10] What Husserl, followed in this by Sartre, calls a 'noema'.

conscious person, perceived as such, is thus perceived *at least* in its '*objectité*'. Let us agree then that this 'Other' can perform the familiar condition recognised by Husserl of signifying how much more than what I glimpse is attributed to something as 'object of perception or thought'. Even heeding Sartre's other caution that the Other must be already in this world as object, the question still remains: 'Is he there as only an object *for me*? Rejecting a 'proof' of the existence of others as no part of philosophy, Husserl chooses to *describe* the ways in which the Other appears to me. He connects one ego with another in terms of the *meaning* each has for the other, but Sartre protests that the 'Other' I encounter is more than such 'a series of meanings' that 'I' confer. For Husserl others appear implicitly within my experience, since '*each object appears in my experience as possessing systems of reference to an indefinite plurality of consciousnesses*' (BN, 233). We find this approach reflected in Sartre's own descriptions of seeing a *person* amongst the objects in a park. To see *someone* amongst the objects appears as an enriched dimension of the park imagined as observed by this other being. Sartre would also bring the Other into 'immediate presence' by recognising that the Other before whom I am ashamed is the 'being' of my shame rather than an external condition of it. This is an inviting move. Nevertheless, we shall see how it stores up a problem of relating to any individual other, this 'Other' who lies indubitably within my distress.

Martin Heidegger's 'Being-in-the-World'

Sartre visited Germany in 1933 and 1934 to study Husserl's and Heidegger's phenomenology, and also Scheler's and Jaspers' explorations.[11] He welcomed Heidegger's notion of *Dasein* – the modes of 'being-there', but declared that it cannot supplant what is raised by '*I think*'. Heidegger does insist, himself, on the 'mine-ness' (*jemeinigkeit*) of any being in the world but, Sartre replies, his language of '*being-in-the-world*', while descriptively rich, still does not recognise the relation of one specific individual to another. Sartre says of Heidegger's '*mit-sein*' (being with) that '*we have indeed been given what we asked for: a being which in its being implies the Other's being*'. But, he says, this does not enable us

> to pass from 'being-with' to the concrete experience of the Other ... as when from my window I see a man walking in the street (BN, 247).

[11] Beauvoir claims that Sartre did not study Heidegger seriously until 1939. See the Introduction to *Understanding Phenomenology* (Hammond 1991: 1).

This criticism of Heidegger strikes home. To describe being in the world cannot silence questions about one's own life as one lives it and as it is observed. Nonetheless, Heidegger's strategy has the advantage that any number of individuals may share a 'mode of being', differently. This sharing averts the traditional divisions of 'subject' and 'object', 'I' and 'Other'. The approach through 'being in a world' emerges within Sartre's adaptation of Husserl, in his own principle that *'all consciousness [posits an object] ... [it] transcends itself ... to reach [the] object, and exhausts itself in this positing'* (BN, xxvii). If I am caught up in what I am conscious of, rather than by my being conscious of it, then the investigation of consciousness *is* the investigation of its worlds. Nevertheless, Sartre insists that even in the 'very heart' of involvement, we are 'still alone'. He says, *'Human reality at the very heart of its ekstases*[12] *remains alone'* because the Other is a *'contingent and irreducible fact. We encounter the Other, we do not constitute him'* (BN, 250).[13] But 'aloneness' is not absolute if my being for others is beyond my power of denial. Sartre's position is unresolved.

Sartre's 'nothing' differs from Heidegger's. His *'néantir'* (to 'nihilate' or to 'void') has the idiomatic sense 'to make nothing of' something. That, in turn, is to 'make something' of something else. Now, Heidegger's epigram *'Das Nichts nichteit'* ('the nothing noths') is like Sartre's *'The void nihilates'* in bringing out that 'being nothing' is 'to make nothing of oneself'. This *nothing* is not static or merely 'void'. It is more like a faint or self-effacing action – coughing apologetically. Or nodding dozily – letting one's mind go to sleep to avoid a situation. 'Nothing' is a pseudo-object. The reality is the activity of *no-thing*. It is *to void* an undifferentiated aspect of existence. 'Nothing' is not a strange something – 'there' with the obdurate solidity of a boulder.

For all that, Heidegger's formulation is not intimate enough. He boldly constructs the active *'nichteit'* (*'noths'*) but doesn't express the bodily fact that it is he (or his readers, when it comes to their turn with the text) who 'noth'.[14] He distances his own perception from himself, as for his readers, so that it appears as an abstracted *nothing*, given as the framing condition of a world, which *noths*. Sartre rejects this strain in Heidegger, insisting

---

[12] Sartre, like Heidegger, borrows from Greek. We can borrow back from our English 'ecstacy' – caught up in the experience of something – forgetting oneself.

[13] This Other is 'present' to make an object of me when I am alone. Is it *I*, then, who constitute this Other?

[14] We should recall his claim for the neuter(ed) nature of *Da-sein* – not masculine, not feminine, and not simply by reason of an intended use of the expression as for each or either sex, without discrimination.

that any *no-thing* must arise 'within the heart of being'. But we should inquire of Sartre how specific this nihilating *being* must be, in order to do what is required. The human is already an acculturated, sexed and gendered being. For Sartre, certainly, it is nothing other than the human body (for itself) that is conscious. But his language gives some readers the impression of freedom and consciousness as an origin without an origin – without context or culture.

In making his critique of Heidegger (BN, 244–251), Sartre sketches a story of how 'I' can be perceived by another, and can see another as a conscious being. Though Heidegger's 'being-in-the-world' improves on dualism, not dividing one person from another by the gulf of body and mind, Sartre objected that *being-with* does not recognise 'being with' *some specific individual*. Nevertheless, we shall find (in chapter 6) how Sartre's own narrator runs into trouble in encompassing this phenomenon once he gazes at a 'specific individual'. The 'subjective object' he needed for the 'I' and the 'Other' refuses to remain stable between subject and object.

Individuals must be able to form '*a plurality of subjects which ... simultaneously apprehend each other as subjectivities*' (BN, 413), says Sartre, reminding us of co-optive uses of 'we' that do not signify a conjoint subject. I say to the waiter, '*We are very dissatisfied*'. Another demurs, '*But no, my dear, speak for yourself*'. '*I*' legitimately declares '*we*' only on the basis of shared experience – shared grimaces as we tasted the dish or discussed reactions as we dined. It is, thus, all too easy to adopt a formal 'we' that lacks experiential content, negotiated consensus or a new frame of mind. 'We' then signifies only the speaker's arrogance.

This use contrasts with the 'we' of exchanged opinion, shared interest and creative relationships, whose intention must be described within the terms of a shared mind within which each thinks, feels and acts in ways beyond the power or skill of each separately. Despite Sartre's efforts to efface the 'we' he first evoked, his writing raises the possibility of a shared outlook, even as he guides the reader so as to skirt its many pitfalls. He calls attention to the many ways in which 'we' form, as subject and as object, but assumes that because at each moment each makes a separate contribution, any 'we' fragments into a plurality of 'I's.

In *Being and Nothingness* Sartre co-opts Hegel's structure of 'self' and 'other' and locks it within Husserl's transcendental turning of Descartes' scepticism. He fuses that with Heidegger's ways of 'being-in-the-world'. The metaphysical surrealism of Sartre's style and stories broke the ice in Husserl's and Heidegger's descriptions. Their inhibitions and halts are thrown into relief by his intrusion of sexual themes, and he forms a work with which Beauvoir could interact in writing *The Second Sex*.[15] In fact, Simone de Beauvoir used a system of phenomenology that in Husserl's and in Heidegger's hands was blind to sexuality and in Sartre's, biased against women in its imagery, structure and anecdote. In a *tour de force* she laid hold of these images, theories and stories to bend and enlarge them into a structure with extensive foundations of its own in biology,[16] history, literature and mythology. What she created had the strength and scope to inspire, and act as a reference point for a new wave of feminist action and writing. She inflected lines of thought from Kant, Hegel, Kierkegaard and Husserl. She worked in critical collaboration with Merleau-Ponty and Sartre. Her writing makes this 'partial identification' with systems of ideas partly alien to her interests.[17] The result of this friction was a particularly vigorous and powerful form of philosophy. '*Reading* The Second Sex *taught us ... to look at the social world with a critical eye, instead of looking at ourselves for some hidden cause of our incapacity*', as Le Dœuff put it (Le Dœuff 1991: 57). For decades after its production women recognised in Beauvoir's descriptions the limitations of their position in the home and society, and became adept in deciphering the ways in which men regard them. They learned to recognise how they are liable to regard themselves and each other. Beauvoir's 'ambiguity' about femininity played its part in revealing the extent to which women had absorbed the pre-emptive claim of the needs and ambitions of men.

The phenomenology of *The Second Sex*, now often attacked as reflecting 'masculinist' attitudes to women and the female body, described women as having ambiguous attitudes to femininity. 'One is not born, but becomes a woman', and the attitude becomes internalised that as a woman one is feminine and as feminine one may be adored or may be despised, but never taken seriously. Beauvoir makes a play of abdicating from formal responsibility for the philosophy upon which she and Sartre had been combatively collaborating: '*I would leave the philosophy to Sartre*' (Le Dœuff 1991: 135–139, 162–167, 170–172). This strategy leaves her free to create concepts and philosophy in a different style. She is then free to *tort* (to create a neologism) Sartre's language of the *Other*. My neologism – *to tort* – derives from the *tort* in *dis-tort*, *re-tort*, *con-tort*, and the 'tort' of the

---

[15] Sartre's mutated bird in the hand was turned into an iridescent two in the bush when Beauvoir wrapped up existential phenomenology in current literature, sociology and everyday observation within her revised phenomenology.

[16] Beauvoir does not see the gender bias that can form part of scientific theory. For all that, her including scientific theory within phenomenology was vital to transforming its spirit.

[17] There is a rich source of literature on this matter: Bergoffen 1997, Fullbrook and Fullbrook 1993, Fullbrook and Fullbrook 1998, Lundgren-Gothlin 1996, Moi 1990, Moi 1994, Simons 1995, Vintges 1996.

'Law of Torts'. To *tort* involves *torsion* – twist, strain, the resilience of the stuff you twist. You can't set up torsion in plasticine. Sartre *torted* Hegel's language of an *Other* who first terrifies, then becomes victim, and operated Hegel's language of 'geist' within a kind of materialism where it is the body that does the work of 'spirit'. In turn Beauvoir 'torts' existentialist concepts and principles.

Theory too has tensile elasticity. Sartre *torts* life into metaphysical melodrama. In contrast, Beauvoir used her lively and accurate perceptions to deconstruct the system of ideas that expresses the male fear of women. She re-*torts* this *Other* into a specific social product. It is men's desire for control that makes women the 'Other', just as national chauvinists make an 'Other' of those of other nations. Upon contact, contempt oscillates with reverence; adulation and rejection rhyme without reason. Exoticism is the name of the game. Where in Sartre's hands the system of *'being-for-oneself'* as against *'being-for-others'* conveys a sense of a threat to myself, Beauvoir built what became a feminism from within such a framework. In describing woman as man's 'Other', she diagnoses an error based in confusion and men's self-interest. The 'threat' in being observed by another ceases to be intrinsic to the difference between 'myself' and an 'Other', becoming an object of critical scrutiny – sometimes farce.

For all that, Beauvoir is perhaps too closely implicated with Sartre in the theory through which she interprets these images. Le Dœuff, for instance, thinks she has taken on metaphysical and anecdotal cargo biased against a feminist philosophy (Le Dœuff 1991: 55–64, 88–92). But Beauvoir does challenge the idea that we are free simply in being conscious, which would cause the distinction of a liberating and an oppressive situation to fall away. To be sure, Sartre recognises the reality of social, political, bodily or economic powers, but in assigning 'bad faith' to the waiter he does not take into account that his boss, who can sack his employee for not acting his part, is party to this play.

Sartre does describe oppression in making a theme of treating another as 'object' and this makes existentialist ideas useful to a proto-feminist such as Beauvoir – with the risk that she too can deem the victim guilty of 'bad faith' in 'consenting' to their status (SS, 29). (Sartre and Beauvoir agree that in refusing that objectual status the victim can 'turn the look' back upon their oppressor.) So, in following a position worked out jointly with Sartre, Beauvoir does sometimes lay the weight of responsibility only on women as authors of their own oppressed position. But she challenges Sartre when he says outright, *'It is senseless to dream of complaining, since nothing alien has decided for us what we feel, what we live, what we are'* (BN, 554). She argues that one's situation may make this impossible.

Women must act and go beyond a status of subjection, but others may abuse their power and nullify the possibilities for freedom. My freedom lies also in the hands of others.

Luce Irigaray

I use some recent writing by Luce Irigaray in Part IV of this work to illustrate a contemporary line of criticism of Sartre's treatment[18] of one's relation to an 'Other'. Irigaray is a Belgian philosopher, feminist theorist, linguist and psychoanalyst who both uses and disturbs the traditional language of philosophy. She holds that a *work* of sexual difference is required in order to reform the language of 'I' and 'Other'. In words that recall Beauvoir's Introduction to *The Second Sex* she writes that we must

> [begin] with the way in which the subject has always been written in the masculine form, as man, even when it claimed to be universal or neutral (Irigaray 1993a: 6).

Like Beauvoir before her, Irigaray analyses the way in which the fabrication of a 'neutered' subject has displaced or suffocated the sense of difference that inspires creative thought and feeling. She is critical of the way that religions have neutralised the difference between men and women through the notion of 'husband and wife' – as 'one flesh', or as 'children of God'. Furthermore, the religious treatment of woman as a 'sex for man' and as a 'mother of his children' neutralises her sexuality as for herself. This theme connects with the present work in examining the sources and meaning of the dualism of consciousness and matter. For Irigaray, as for Beauvoir, denial of sexual difference is connected with the *'dissociation of body and soul'*. Either the sensational materiality of sexuality is denied by a 'spiritual' elevation, or, cynically, sexuality is reduced to the banal 'materiality' of sexual commerce. This abuse merely reverses the claims of 'spirituality', and the ambivalence is the typical result of puritanical or 'spiritual' attitudes to sexual difference.

Unlike Beauvoir, however,[19] Irigaray has a utopian vision in which perception and the formation of theory would be revised in every detail, as a 'transition to a new age'. To negate existing systems is only to reinstitute the old structures within the new. The answer, Irigaray thinks, is to revalue

---

[18] Beauvoir took issue with Sartre's depiction of this difference as essentially *hostile*. One can read Irigaray as developing Beauvoir's suggestions, though in a very different style.

[19] I am not here taking sides in the disputes about the values and hazards of utopian thinking.

and reform the old systems from within. So she *uses* the language of philosophy, science, and even religion, while subverting and changing its imagery, assumptions and its tacit elevation of 'masculine' values. The urgent mood of her writing suggests that to do anything to change the understanding between the sexes and the understanding of consciousness and matter requires that everything be rethought at the same time. She constructs an abstract language, charged with the tones of the everyday, so as to evoke diverse fields of phenomena.

While Irigaray rejects a transcendent and 'masculine' 'God', she would have *us* 'divine' the world in all its differences, including the irreducible differences of the sexes. She criticises the religious idea that only as God's creation' is the world an object of wonder – we can wonder at it in itself. Women and men may 'divine' each other across their differences, but not to spiritualise the materiality that makes us discernible objects of wonder. From such concepts she develops an account of 'my' encounter with an 'other' (chapters nine and ten of this work) that works from, but finally contrasts with, what Sartre and Beauvoir have written.

Like Beauvoir, she sees 'woman' as being not born but constructed – assimilated to a 'masculinised' world that she subjects to a radical critique in order to make her own place. The 'masculine' has never worked out *its* own proper place, either, having traded upon the ambiguous role of woman who 'contains' the child and creates a living space for man. In combating such co-options of the 'Other', Irigaray evokes the phenomenon of *wonder*. We can feel wonder at what we perceive, rather than summoning up an unknown 'God' as a guaranteed object of wonder. We thus discover the beings around us in all their differences as objects of wonder. There are successful transactions between men and women despite irreducible differences, of course. Irigaray suggests a new use of Aristotle's idea of the 'common place' (Irigaray 1993a: 34–58). 'Man' and 'woman' might 'occupy the same place' though they see they do not occupy the particular place each has in virtue of being their own sex.

Despite her attacks on the damaging effects upon women (and men) of traditional religion, Irigaray observes that we never succeed in banishing 'God' from the language that forms us. That language returns to haunt science in the form of its ideal of a 'God's eye' vision of the world as if from outside it. Evidently the ghost of God also moves in the disputes about the 'subjectivity' or 'objectivity' of morality and law. And the 'God's eye' project that would surpass impartial, local or transient knowledge remains part of the internalised ideal self of philosophy, affecting in particular its fixation with the problem of consciousness and matter. These last concerns are at the heart of the issues that arise within the present work.

It is in consequence of such considerations that at one stage (Irigaray 1993b: 55–72) Irigaray proposed that we go on using the word 'God', not to stand for a *being* but as a genre of discourse and perception. In one sense this is a radical atheism since the language of 'God' is that which assigns paramount value to the concerns of those who can control it. In this spirit she even proposes that women must create a 'God' of feminine gender. Also, in attacking a dualism of mind and matter, and of 'masculine' and 'feminine', Irigaray attempts to use religious language even while attempting to subvert and to appropriate it. She thinks that the language of the 'divine' can lend gravity to our common experience of not 'comprehending' what we know most intimately.

It is problematic whether Irigaray – or anyone else – can appropriate the language of religion to her own ends. In the end, after all, its hold on society, language and the common imagination is far more powerful than any force her subverting language can muster. And this difficulty may mark even her use of 'divining' each other and the things in the world. This issue is explored in this work. In another example of her strategy of appropriating religious language, Irigaray takes up the trope of the 'angelic'. She considers the figure of the 'asexual' child as the 'neutral innocent' made to serve as the 'common ground' for a 'man' and 'woman'. This, Irigaray argues, is abuse of the household 'angel' that leaves no proper place for child, woman, or man. The problem of 'place' is one of Irigaray's constant concerns, and she can surprise the reader in the way she places 'mourning' – for lost place – as of central significance within philosophy. The idea that philosophy is driven by a sense of loss of place – an 'always already' lost place, casts an oblique light across the smooth surface of its writing and reveals a more varied texture. 'Woman' (and therefore 'man' too) mourns being only a marker for someone or something else. We mourn what has never been – that it has never been.

False divisions – and homogenising solutions – to the need for reciprocal relations between the sexes, adults and children, and between people of different races, nations and cultures are of the same kind as the false divisions – and false compromises – between 'creative consciousness' and 'inert matter'. In this, Irigaray also follows to a surprising degree[20] the path set by Beauvoir in *The Second Sex*. In its opening chapters this work will follow Beauvoir in arguing that the creation of an 'inessential Other', stripped of its own life and reality, is an operation as much of economics, race and the desire for status as it is of some pure sexual prejudice.

---

[20] A 'surprising' degree because Irigaray's feminism of 'difference' has come to be regarded as the antithesis of Beauvoir's attack on the myth of sexual difference as a device that serves established masculine powers and conventions.

Michèle Le Dœuff's Critique of Beauvoir and Sartre

The problems in reading *The Second Sex* as philosophy, and *Being and Nothingness* in a seriously critical vein, were shifted considerably by Michèle Le Dœuff's terse 'Operative Philosophy' (Le Dœuff 1979). She was amongst the first to show how Beauvoir's writing amounts to a significant and generous inflexion of the 'transcendentalism' of existential phenomenology, whose abstractions of 'being', 'nothingness', the 'for-itself', the 'in-itself' and 'being-for-others' interact with the sexual imagery and anecdotes to generate a philosophy that appeared essentially misogynist. Le Dœuff conjectured that *'the verbal violence it evinces may be a counterpart of a far more everyday violence in domestic situations'* (Le Dœuff 1991: 195). Le Dœuff took Sartre seriously, reading his text as 'meaning what it says'. Le Dœuff also challenges the terms of Beauvoir's analysis of the position of women. She asks whether it is *'really necessary to use the concept of transcendence to bring women's oppression to light'* but decides that *'it is fairer, and far more instructive, to read Simone de Beauvoir's essay as it is'* (Le Dœuff 1991: 56). Le Dœuff shows how Beauvoir uses phenomenology as a form of language for her concrete analyses of the *'world where men force [women] to assume [themselves] as the Other'* (Beauvoir, cited Le Dœuff 1991: 56).

Le Dœuff uses a strategy of disconnection, contrasting Beauvoir's sociological and literary case studies with the fantastical anecdotes and imagery by which Sartre gives distorted life to existential abstractions. Sartre writes as if he could speak of the conscious life of those in his stories by the same right as he projects his own consciousness of a situation. In contrast, Beauvoir makes her own subjectivity manifest, not confusing it with the position of those she describes. She can thus describe what is terrible without making the reader part of it, as if just they were bound to be in the same position.

Le Dœuff shows what can go wrong in Sartre's crossing of the borders between metaphysics and story line, conceptualisation and imagery, argument and metaphor. Le Dœuff's criticism is not that Sartre is a 'pessimistic' writer who deals too much with desperate situations and feelings. Rather, his writing is ambiguous about one's spirit of resistance and imagination of alternatives, making of our freedom to renegotiate our situation a burden we are doomed to bear. Sartre's philosophy incorporates the oppression it means to deal with, but to recognise what is terrible about life is not in itself oppressive. Le Dœuff says that Beauvoir's book which puts an end to loneliness [by sharing an oppressive situation by describing it well], which teaches people to see, has more importance than all the manifestos in the world' (Le Dœuff 1991: 57).

Le Dœuff modifies Beauvoir's remedy in what she describes as 'operative' philosophy. Like Beauvoir, she describes situations with a feeling and precision that takes the reader 'from one state of thinking to another'. Description, argument, and particularities of circumstance provide a crucial 'distance' from oppression without pretending to be 'above the fray'. She thus shares a good deal with Beauvoir but despite her criticisms of Sartre she, like him, writes in a vein that I call a *rigorous personalism*. Her criticism is that he carelessly mishandles this personal nature of philosophical writing. Nevertheless, Sartre is important to Le Dœuff's ambitions partly on account of his innovations in crossing lines of genre while developing the tradition of ontology and epistemology. The ideal of philosophy to construct its own pure genre has made it hard to see Beauvoir as a philosopher since *she* takes for granted the need to move between the various forms of learned and other informal discourses. It has taken decades to read *The Second Sex* as a work of philosophy, and to accord *The Ethics of Ambiguity* its proper place. It is 'politics', it is 'sociology', or the 'social and literary criticism that helped to create a feminist resurgence'.

Le Dœuff has made her own crossing of genre lines to revitalise philosophy as rigorous and as essentially incomplete. Her first book, *L'imaginaire philosophique* (1980, tr. *The Philosophical Imaginary* 1989a), investigates the conceptual and rhetorical functions of images and of '*l'imagerie*' (the trade in and general business of producing and using a system of images or icons) in classical philosophical writings (Deutscher 2000: 83–93). This is done to strengthen rather than to replace philosophy's age-old commitment to argument for what might be the case. Direct argument is not to be left in the hands of those who use it to silence whoever lives on the margins of articulated power.

Since her work on the 'operative' use of theory and on the nature of the subject as exhibited by Shakespeare and in philosophical discourse (Le Dœuff 1979, 1986, 1986a), Le Dœuff has experimented further (Le Dœuff 1991), writing her research as four 'notebooks' that include semi-fictional autobiographical fragments – '*because no philosophical thought is self-contained ... it proceeds by detour ... [There] is no thinking which does not wander*' (Le Dœuff 1991: xii). The book moves between epistemology and the problems of writing philosophy for itself and in its relation to practical affairs including feminist struggles, which highlight the sense in which the objects of philosophical controversy are independent of thought. This independence requires that '*I postulate what we talk about as an "object"*' *which I throw across to you*' (Le Dœuff 1991: 41). However much Socrates and Meno differ about what virtue is, they have to postulate that it is the same 'one' (internally variable) thing on which each focus. The 'objects' of a feminist discourse will be approachable also by argument and speculation thrown up by discourses outside it. Problems *and* their 'objects' circulate between feminism and philosophy, history, and literature for example. To 'throw an object across to any outside audience', a feminist discourse, like any other, must already throw many of its objects out to its philosophical other selves. Furthermore, feminist studies within sociology and history help to show how the strange language of philosophy can be open to all.

Le Dœuff is moving towards a 'nomadic' thought. In order to practice a kind of universality that permits the throwing back and forth of a common object of discussion, we have to 'travel' by means of an active and informed imagination in order to gain a knowledge of what is 'not exactly us'. Nomadism involves being prepared to 'dwell' in places other than home so that we become 'at home' with being able to live as more than a tourist, elsewhere. Being self-contained and incapable of circulation is one pole of the double risk Le Dœuff sees in all philosophy. Centralism protects the assumption that your place is *the* place, and the desire to write from a neutral position 'above the fray' is part of the cluster of such centralist fallacies. In exposing this ideal of being 'above the fray', she does not simply applaud Hipparchia's choice of the life of philosophy (Le Dœuff 1991: 205–207). Hipparchia's forsaking the loom for the study is a symbol not only of discovery and liberation but is a 'primal scene' intrinsic to the formation of one's identity. The costs of this are considerable, and imperil one's new freedom in philosophy.

Entrance into philosophy is connected with two partially defective ways of being a philosopher. One, typically for a woman, was to find her way into philosophy as the lover or acolyte of some man who functioned for her as a metonym for philosophy itself. The other defective mode, still current, is philosophy as a way of losing oneself. To inflect a brutal neologism from Argentina, in each tendency we find the use of philosophy to 'disappear' oneself. One may 'disappear' oneself by transubstantiation into the form of an idolised thinker, or by reifying a philosophy as exit from an oppressive mode of thought. Philosophy as self-annihilation results in one's practice being hegemonic – constructed by its exclusion of other forms of discourse.

Philosophy as losing yourself is connected also with another tendency of the philosopher, who, as if acting out of rigorous objectivity, adopts the voice of the 'unique speaking subject' and 'speaks as if for the whole world'. It is in these terms that Le Dœuff distinguishes Beauvoir's use of existential philosophy from Sartre's, showing how Beauvoir makes phenomenology bend in unexpected directions, able to hear voices not its own and then to say more in response to them. The possibility of a philosophy which 'moves our thinking from one state to another' might be coupled with a specifically feminine philosophy, but Le Dœuff has profound suspicions about such a genre. A specifically 'feminine' philosophy would not possess the 'universal' accessibility to the objects of a feminist philosophy required by exchange in discourse. Attention to the particularity of argument, anecdote or image opens up the system to observations from outside its own resources, and thus, conceptual systems are co-opted to unexpected ends. What we bring into being when we *do* something in philosophy is a temporary use, a particular inflexion, a bending back on itself, a flexing over and around the objects of pre-existing discourse.

Beauvoir took a phenomenology within which 'no oppression was thinkable' and stretched it beyond its conceptual means so that '*many women found ... reference points for understanding the situation given to all of them, a language to express feelings of unease and the sharing of this unease*' (Le Dœuff 1991: 57). Sartre's phenomenology, in '*[offering] a space for expressing a terror on men's part in relation to women's bodies*' (Le Dœuff 1991: 60), is inflected within Beauvoir's proto-feminist comprehension of the phenomenon. So, for Le Dœuff, the main question is not whether some forms of philosophy are 'more appropriate for women' than others. To find one's way and thus one's voice amongst philosophical genres involves the 'creation' of concepts. This is the 'recreation' by which Deleuze defines philosophy. Theories are not all initially neutral, not equally ready for just any purpose.

It is in these terms that Le Dœuff argues that while *Being and Nothingness* seems to deal with everything, its repetition of specific concepts inhibits interaction with forms of discourse outside the text. This wreaks a 'verbal violence' on every topic with which it deals. This criticism catches an important truth about Sartre's work, but raises difficult questions. After all, any extensive work on a theme provides a way of describing a wide range of phenomena and after a while any systematic work comes to feel oppressive. Le Dœuff's complaints about Sartrean phenomenology must be more than a protest against what had become over-used theory. Whether or not Sartre's passionate abstractions are more prone than other systems of metaphysics to wreaking 'verbal violence', its particular tendency to 'oppression' as much as to 'liberation' arises from particular errors and exaggerations.

Le Dœuff's critique of existentialist philosophy not only exhibits Beauvoir's *tour de force* in using and bending it to create a new genre.

Conducted as part of her own experiments in genre shift, the critique gives new life to the phenomenological tradition, demonstrating how much we can learn by use of our always dubious resources.

* * *

In reading Sartre and Beauvoir I put ideas to work now in order to exhibit them against their own context. The relation of the sexes as reciprocity across ambiguous differences continues to be, in more nuanced terms perhaps, a theme of this new century. And, how to understand one's situation as a 'subjective object' and an 'objective subject' remains a continuing question in philosophy and science no less than in ethics and politics. A careful and creative regard for the work of Beauvoir and Sartre provides room to move. It is not a return to a cell of the past.

What I have written suggests the need to locate the writings of Sartre and Beauvoir in the aftermath of 'post-modernism' and 'deconstruction', but to meet that need would be another work. The reader will soon observe, nevertheless, that I have had a friendly attitude to those trends. I make no particular use of a 'theory' of deconstruction, but gladly acknowledge the influence of its practice on my awareness of the way words slip and slide under the scrutiny of reflection and the pressure of argument. And there is a reflection of Derrida's '*différance*' in my occasional use of '*differs*' to take the direct object. One '*differs*' oneself from another – or one's past self from the present one. One does not simply 'notice' a difference as given apart from involvement in a situation. In the traditional aboriginal culture of this country, for most of its long history, one would 'sing the land', constructing and construing it into recognisable shape as part of the making of shared stories and explorations. I am reminded of this in the way that Sartre's narrator 'nihilates' what is found at hand, 'making nothing of it' as a way of 'making something of it'. And the importance of shared practice in making this possible reminds us of how Sartre, and Beauvoir to a lesser extent, over-emphasise this *making light of* our obdurate world as an *individual* project.

Heidegger tried to institute '*being-in-the-world*' so as to escape the tradition of 'I' and 'my consciousness' as at the centre of it all. In like fashion, Derrida tried to leave behind Husserl's transcendental ego complete with its own objects of consciousness ('noemata') immediately and transparently present to it. So for Derrida, 'there is' this *différance* (Derrida 1982: 1–28) – this differing by deferring and deferring by differing – a play by which there is our precariously significant language, our useful and seemingly pedestrian practices.

Apart from economy, there is another advantage in my having slipped past the relation between phenomenology and the ensuing period of post-structuralist 'deconstruction' and the 'post-modern' change in *le temps* – the weather and the times. The book can be read independently of the controversies about all that, and may thus throw light on them from an unexpected direction.

PART I

GENRE AND GENDER

1
Situating Theory

Theorising from Elsewhere

Cross-dressing Body and Mind

Sartre reinterprets solipsism, dualism and idealism as active forms of consciousness. They express ways of regarding and dealing with people. Philosophers return obsessively to these theories; they express more than a disinterested speculation.

Solipsism is not an idle theory but a powerful moment in consciousness. The solipsist thinks, '*My* existence is what it is *for itself*. My body, history and future may be unreal. Still, *I* exist; *I* am conscious. Other people may be figments of my imagination. Still, *I* exist. *What* thinks and *what* it is to think – this is what we have to investigate and describe. Nietzsche attempts to subvert the Cartesian certainty of oneself as a conscious being. Sartre continues to rely upon it, while exposing the conceit of Descartes' solipsistic enterprise.

Dualism poses as realist commonsense. There is a 'real' mind, and a 'real' body, and a 'real' connection between them. Sartre describes this dualism as 'realism', not to praise it, but to expose its self-conceit. There is nothing realistic about it.

Idealism, often parodied, paraded as the ultimate nonsense professional philosophy creates, is a serious challenge for Sartre. Idealism makes consciousness incomprehensible.[1]

Materialism in its reductive form appears in Sartre's critical analysis of seeing others as objects.[2] (It is a *mode* of perception. Sartre writes that we see others '*at least in the mode of object-ness*'.) The attitude that we can see others *only* 'in the mode of object-ness' is an expression only of bad faith. It is useless, though, to fly back to dualism, idealism or solipsism. The alternative is *nothing. Nothing* separates body and consciousness. To

---

[1] Sartre demonstrates this in 'The Pursuit of Being', *Being and Nothingness.*
[2] In *Schilpp* 1981 Sartre says that identifying thoughts with processes in the brain had been outside his concern, but he might agree with a version of that theory.

be conscious is to 'make nothing of' our being objects. As we make light of necessity, we make a (vanishing) something of ourselves. We create an existence 'for ourselves' in this performance of *nihilation*, to use Sartre's invented word.

In expressing the idea that *I exist purely for myself*, the present author has to use cautionary quotes around 'I'. How is one to express a solipsistic consciousness? Not to use 'I' is to describe, as if impersonally, a *being that exists purely for itself*. The solipsistic outlook excludes the point of view it demands in order to express its truth. (The old joke: *I am so convinced of solipsism that I can't understand how you could deny it*.) The very utterance of 'I' takes for granted what solipsism leaves anonymous. 'I' refers to the one who currently utters it. Without reference to my body and those of others, there is nothing for 'I' to identify. If one could imagine a disembodied stream of consciousness including 'I', the word could retain no function of identification since nothing other than the conscious sentence itself need exist. In that case, the utterance of 'I' would have nothing to *perform*.

Feminist critiques expose something covert in the solipsistic idea that *I am what I am for myself*. The solipsist cannot properly think of *his* or *her* existence as for *him*self or for *her*self. Solipsistic existence must consider itself neutered. To say *she* of the solipsistic *I*, is an 'impertinent' intrusion into metaphysics. No one says 'it' when they themselves are concerned, so 'he' is used, slyly, as if it were a 'mere grammatical convention'. By sleight of word, solipsistic consciousness is commandeered by 'He'. If I break the quiet convention of 'He' then sexuality subverts the solipsistic illusion, just as it mocks theological piety when the conventional *He* of the believer's *God* is challenged by *She*. Solipsism is the conviction that *I* have only to be conscious and all doubts of *my* existence fall away. Autoeroticism is the sexual state encoded by the solipsist's reverie. In autoeroticism, as in solipsism, sexuality becomes ambiguous, enacting being a hermaphrodite. Unlike solipsism's intellectualisation of it, however, the bodily nature of consciousness is manifest. Thus, solipsism's ontology is biased towards masculinity in imagery and preoccupation.

Sexuality in Sartre's Metaphysics

Metaphor, Truth and Sexual Bias

Sartre allows the repressed preoccupation of metaphysics to emerge in metaphor and anecdote. We knew that structures of metaphysical ideas could work as political metaphors. There is a well-forged link between the theory of forms that Plato's Socrates purveys, and his authoritarian visions of the just State. Metaphysics conveys our attitudes to matter and to mind. Berkeley uses anthropomorphic imagery to make ideas in the mind central to reality. He rejects matter as 'stupid' and 'unthinking', as if it were a recalcitrant student. So a critique of sexual bias itself in metaphysics should not particularly outrage those who defend the 'search for truth' in metaphysical structures. Claims of truth must be read through the imaginary system in which they are expressed. If metaphysics relies upon and produces metaphor, its proclivity for sexual metaphor should not surprise us.[3]

Le Dœuff exposes the sexual bias in elements of Sartre's thought. She demonstrates how he makes his 'I' operate as a 'unique speaking subject' even while it assumes the value of masculinity as the 'default' position.[4]

The Sexual Ambiguity of the 'In-Itself' and the 'For-Itself'

Imagery and Abstraction

In considering the sexual significance of the terms and structure of ideas in *Being and Nothingness*, we can proceed to look specifically at the notions of *being-in-itself*, *being-for-itself*, *nothingness* and *consciousness*. Does that language embody a peculiarly 'male' or 'masculine' imagery, or, perhaps, a fusion of a man's point of view with his fantasy of a woman's? Le Dœuff suggests that the casually placed or inadvertent images in a philosophy may be its 'neuralgic point'. So in reading a system of ontology we exercise various degrees of tolerance, probing where we find trouble, but taking care to read and listen carefully to what we elicit. We should not take the notions of *nihilating* and of *nothingness* themselves with a dead literalness, but read them as part of a developing work. We can read from theoretical structure to story and example, and back. Our need is to gain familiarity.

If we look for a 'literal meaning' of Sartre's terms we stop his philosophy in its tracks. To be free is be conscious, he says. To be conscious is to be nothing, he adds. Hence to be free is to be nothing, he concludes. We might mock him: '*So there is no such thing as freedom or*

---

[3] This is not to reduce metaphysics to metaphor. Derrida's 'White Mythology' (Derrida 1982) explains how metaphysics contributes to its own *genre* of metaphor.
[4] See her analysis of the voice of Venus (Le Dœuff 1986a). Also, 'The Sole Speaking Subject' (Le Dœuff 1991: 182–194).

consciousness!'. Freedom is universal, and everywhere it fails to exist. In this terse, ham-fisted *reductio* of Sartre's description of the phenomena of being conscious and being free, the reading takes on a new light. Sartre denies that consciousness is a 'thing', only in order to show the possibility of being conscious. Gilbert Ryle (Ryle 1949) denies that the mind is a thing in order to remind us that we'd better mind out, in philosophy as in life. Likewise our freedom is *not* a thing, to be proudly possessed. Like being conscious, to be free is to 'nihilate' the *in-itself*. That *in-itself* is a 'thing'. Our too swift *reductio ad absurdum* arose from a philosophical refusal to ask, 'What is a *thing*?' Also, *nihilating* takes on mysterious tones when we recite an English translation of a French neologism. *'Néantir'* is 'to void'; to void is to raise up another thing.

Existence In Itself and Being for Oneself

Taken to logical extremes the category of the *in-itself* is meaningless. Only in relation to the creative *for-itself* is there a world of perceivable form and distinction. Like the meaningless atoms for meaning of Plato's *Theaetetus* and Wittgenstein's *Tractatus*, the *in-itself* in itself would be characterless, indescribable. The *in-itself* must differ from the no-thingness that works upon it, thus to turn up the marvel of the *for-itself*. It is by valorising 'negativity' that Sartre describes imagination, creativity, freedom, consciousness and language. To lack these, as does the 'pure positivity' of the *in-itself* prior to any nihilating upon it by a *for-itself*, is thus to lack everything of value. It is to lack the structure of a world we could experience and in which we could live.

When we explain the *for-itself* as the desire not to be a *for-itself* we have to accept, in the one gesture, this *for-itself* and this *in-itself* we desire to become. We fear the threat of the *in-itself*, which itself is held at a vanishing remove ('a thin film of nothingness') by the nihilating activity that *is* the *for-itself*. There are meanings suggested in every expression of these ideas, enough to make those old bones rattle and dance. I recognise how I fear and wish to become no more than a thing that exists 'in itself'. I both fear and wish to live with responsibilities and possibilities, like Ryle's child who desires to ride her bicycle downhill all day long and to come back home. In philosophical adulthood this child desires to live as an *in-itself* that has no responsibility for itself or others. We long for this escape from the anguish of choice and because freedom involves responsibility for consequences we cannot predict.

In another stratagem we take our responsibilities for others to the point of turning ourselves into a pure *being-for-others*, a being that is so totally 'for others' that it *has* no existence for itself. To exist thus, only 'for others', is the stereotype of traditional femininity and of religious devotion. No less than the devotee the religious authority turns himself into pure femininity in relation to an all-powerful all-knowing Lord. There is another side of the bargain.[5] As servants of their husbands and the religious superiors women can renounce their autonomy – their 'being-for-themselves'.

Sartre introduces one's being *'for-others'* through examples of sexual shame. These attitudes prefigure the collapse of one's subjectivity. One's autonomy as *'for-oneself'* dissipates. I may escape – by making an object of the 'Other' – this threat to how I see things. My choice, in mirror image, is to allow myself to be an object for this Other. The metaphysics of the *in-itself* now returns in full force. The attraction and repulsion of the *for-itself* towards the *in-itself* constitute the *for-itself*. The *in-itself* is a construct of and for the *for-itself*. There can be no *for-itself* except as a nihilation of the *in-itself*, yet that *in-itself* can be no ontological foundation for it. The obduracy of the *in-itself* is a symbol of our horror of a pure lack of existence. We will die. We create hopeless stratagems to avoid full consciousness of this. We have the power to choose in the face of the facts of our condition so we identify, spuriously, with this 'transcendence'. We thus can pretend to be some *thing* other than that mere *in-itself*. We differ ourselves from that human body that undoubtedly will die. On the other side of this double gesture we identify, spuriously, with the body and its surrounding conditions. We would wish away our power to make something of all of this, to forestall death in being as if already dead.

Our fascinated horror of the idea that everything should just exist in itself (the *in-itself*) also signifies how we see death as already in life. Alive, we suffer the death of things, people, ventures and ways of life. Things that were part of me die all around me. Qualities die within me that used to be part of others as well as of myself.[6] The metaphysics of the *in-itself* functions as a figurative hole in the sink of an existence that eddies around it and disappears from our view, touch and use. The story begins by *differing* the *in-itself* from the *for-itself*. It ends with the 'revenge of the *in-itself*' upon the *for-itself*. Differing *being-in-itself* from *being-for-itself* promised freedom and consciousness. It delivers frustration and self-deception. Was this *differing* overdone? In its struggle, in its 'nihilating' gestures to make itself free and conscious, this *for-itself* was never a being other than the *in-itself*.

---

[5] 'Bargain' suggests that women in religion are equal negotiators of the contract. Religious institutions form children within their system, with no 'age of consent'.

[6] Hannah Arendt, in *The Life of the Mind*, analyses this continuing 'death in life'.

Are Women to Read this Story Differently?

As Descartes *differed* mind and body, Sartre differed *being-in-itself* from *being-for-itself* to register equally with women and with men. Descartes' *woman* is equal with *man* in having a mind. Sartre's *woman*, as a *being-for-itself*, is equal with *man* in her *being*. Each makes something out of a given body and situation by 'nihilating' aspects of body and of situation. For all that, Sartre lends unequal weight to women and to men as he differs *being-in-itself* and *being-for-itself*. There is a final, rampant identification of the 'feminine' with the *in-itself* as threat to the transcending *for-itself*. His differing of the *for-itself* and the *in-itself* cannot strike women and men with equal force or credibility.

Society, religion and philosophy tend to place women as the incomplete part of the system. Sartre does not 'differ' from this conventional bias. In his existential psychoanalysis, as in Freud's, it is *woman* who takes on the load of the *lack*. The *in-itself* is passive, uncreative – the 'feminine'. The *for-itself* takes on the troubled pathos of existential hero – so strong and yet at the mercy of the feminine. The figure of 'woman' is of an inert figure that must wait for masculine creativity to plug her in to the light. In this phase of the Sartrean dreaming, only thus does the *feminine* gain freedom as quasi-autonomous *being*. The unspoken consequence is that women will be conscious and free only as they transcend this *feminine*.

Some women, who take this story to articulate an existential paradox, find themselves placed as *objects* of a tale they overhear. So women and men may *differ* in receiving it. To introject a fear of oneself as incomplete is to *differ* oneself from someone who, decorously, theorizes a fear of women as a doubt about *woman* or *the feminine*. In Sartre's figure, men fear women as the centre of a vortex. The task of making women complete in body and spirit being impossible, men, defined by it, disappear into the vortex. *To look at* oneself with the stereotypes of another is not *to be looked at* by the constructors and perpetrators of those stereotypes. The body is 'lived'. It has its needs, and its outrage exists even when suppressed, theorized or sublimated. The desire to grasp and to embrace is not the desire merely to be penetrated (Gatens 1996: 13).

Those who are derogated do not have the same motive or ground to take on the attitudes of those who would demean them. Men would share the outlook of Sartre's persona out of a fear of women as threatening their megalomania. As other than those who made them *Other*, women may take an external view of that action. As Sartre depicts the situation, the one who is observed cannot usurp his difference from the observer. Those who can reward and punish – those who control the currency of language – can suppress, distort and appropriate this difference. This is what is made clear in Beauvoir's transmutation of existentialism. Sartre does not refuse women the status of 'beings-for-themselves', and yet he aligns *being-in-itself* with the feminine and *being-for-itself* with the masculine for all that. Women are not beings for themselves *for themselves*. Could *anything* be 'for-itself' *only* for others? That woman should be such a being might be one more of Sartre's 'useless passions'.[7]

'In-Itself' and 'For-Itself' in Reversal

Solid and Fluid

As human a woman is a freedom *for-itself*.[8] Fearing this freedom like anyone else, she fears and desires to slide back towards the *in-itself*. By his metaphors of lack and 'holes' in being, Sartre gives the *in-itself* a feminine connotation. The feminine then exists uneasily between the 'solid' status of the *in-itself* and the fluid creativity of the *for-itself*. This imaginary woman's fear of lapsing into the *in-itself* is more specific than that of *man*. She fears the lack of a *for-itself* to raise her to its status. In this dream she fears the male will not 'come' to complete her being.

There is a parallel reading of this myth: by the bootstrap operation of self-nihilation, a 'he' is already a *for-itself* who has 'made it' from being *in-itself* to being *for-himself*. What *he* fears is the 'revenge' of the *in-itself*. He had left it behind; now it re-attaches itself in the slippery form of the 'ambiguously *for-itself* and *in-itself*' – *le visqueux*.[9] As male, the *for-itself* fears the feminine; she lubricates the slide back into the *in-itself*. The dream reveals the feminine, finally, as *in-itself* without ambiguity. 'She' is nothing but a 'hole' a 'sink in the surface of being' into which he, as a conscious, autonomous being will lose himself. Frantic confusion of love and death.

If a woman accepts the ontology of *in-itself* and *for-itself* she can escape the dilemma it poses. As conscious she is free in a transcendence that can accept, in good faith, that it exists always and only as a function of facticity. She is free to fear she may revert to the *in-itself* and accepts that finally she will die, but she rejects Sartre's *use* of the metaphors of spaces, holes and vacancies. She might accept the association of these with the

---

[7] 'Man loses himself as man in order that God may be born. But ... we lose ourselves in vain. Man is a useless passion' (BN, 615).

[8] I speak within the Sartrean language to test it.

[9] Various clichés: The 'slipperiness' of women and their wiles, the 'slipperiness' of feminist arguments against the impartiality of philosophy, the 'slipperiness' of metaphysics that leads us from the hardness of reality.

female body and feminine nature. In that case she will argue that, as categories essential to the feminine form of the *for-itself*, they have no place in characterising the *in-itself*. Alternatively, she will argue that metaphors of 'lack', 'hole', 'space' do help characterise the ontological inadequacy of the *in-itself* but will refuse to characterise female morphology in those terms.[10] These tactics can work, but she will be aware of the risks, refusing utterly the fusion of any of these pairs.

The metaphysical vision remains uneasy and unstable, but we can at least begin to demystify the chemistry of Sartre's ontology. The 'nothing' that can 'decompress' *being* does not reduce to a static *'hole'* in *being*. What would exist purely 'in-itself' (an unutterable impossibility) would *lack* structure and free possibilities, which would be supplied only by a 'for itself' with *its* 'lack' of fixed stability of being. What can be construed as having some *'lack'* is already more nuanced than either some original unstructured *in-itself*, or a purely originating 'non-being' of a *for-itself*.

Men: Inside or Outside the Reverie?

A man may fear that he shall become a mere *in-itself* by losing himself in 'woman' who, he suspects, has no defence against relapsing into the state of an *in-itself*. At the same time, according to the ontology of *in-itself* and *for-itself*, a man will understand that as a free agent he must already be conscious and free in thus 'losing himself'. As free he can decide that such a fear of loss of his 'being for himself' must be groundless. Suppose he has half-consciously associated the notion of a 'lack' in being with what is female, and has associated the female with the *in-itself*. In that case, his fear of losing himself in the *in-itself* by losing himself in his relationship with a woman is doubly groundless. Since a woman is a conscious free being, he could not, by losing himself in her, lose himself as a *for-itself*.

Such fears of his are triply groundless. The fear that in sexual embrace or in other intimacy he loses his point of view for that of another is paranoia or a fanatical attempt at self-command. What are the limits of what can happen in losing oneself within the life, point of view and body of another? He may change radically from what he was. He may change for the worse, but not inevitably, and, in any case, from whose point of view? He may find himself no longer friend of his earlier self, his old friends or his old philosophies. He may find that his later self is no friend to his new present one. He has no right to think that this is 'loss' in the sense of his having *less*. His 'loss' may enable him to have more, to live differently. In

---

[10] Irigaray's strategy in 'This sex which is not One' (Irigaray 1985b) has its place here. Labia, clitoris, vaginal surfaces 'lack' nothing. They are not the 'absence of the phallus'.

losing his egocentric point of view in favour of one that intimately includes that of another, he has the chance to acquire new texture, colour and atmosphere. There will be new objects, considered as things that exist between himself and another, rather than as simply his own. True, the relationship may fail, or be judged as destructive or abusive of either or both of them. This general risk proves nothing about whether his losing himself into the life of another is the risk of his losing his *for-itself* in favour of an *in-itself*. Living purely as a *for-itself* is more liable to prove destructive and abusive to himself.

Sartre almost recognises this. He observes that in our being and not only in our appearance, we are beings 'for-others'. We are more than a *one-dimensional* ego-point, more than a *two-dimensional* system of intentionalities, more, even, more than three-dimensional conscious bodies in a material world. To gain a sense and knowledge of this ontological thickness we *need* the look of the 'Other'. Sartre achieves this recognition, only to fall away from it. His descriptions come to rest in the sense of threat in being seen by another. This 'Other', who, being at a distance, can discern what you cannot observe for yourself. Sartre exaggerates the 'distance' of another, in his metaphysics of the 'Other'. Also he overlooks another side of this situation of one's being observed. Even as another's observation of me threatens to displace my ego-centred vision, their regard can create a sense of ontological security.[11]

Within Sartre's abstract ontology, women and men are, equally, conscious free beings. Only late in the piece do the *for-itself* and *in-itself* become gendered – the *in-itself* as feminine (marshy) ground, and the *for-itself* as masculine creative transcendence. In imagery and in anecdote however, this difference is engendered from the outset. It is, of course, the division of *being-for-itself* and *being-for-others*, achieved in the centre of the work, that permits reference to sexual relations. Long before that, however, Sartre's image of conscious being is of '*nothingness ... coiled in the heart of being – like a worm*' (BN, 21). As already within the apple of Eve's knowing eye, this same 'worm', symbolic masculinity that raises *being-in-itself* to the status of *being-for-itself*, is what is rotten at the core of existence. Eden's serpent that offered the apple of knowledge (carnal or otherwise) had the dignity to approach Eve openly; he had to beguile. Sartre's 'worm' is immanent, a mere infestation.

Sartre's image is revealing. If masculinity is inscribed within consciousness, the destructive part of the trick lies not in overt masculinity

---

[11] Le Dœuff reads More's *Utopia* as symbolising the desire for tranquility, and responds: 'Social life can ... steal my inner tranquillity; but it can also provide me with something better than tranquillity' (Le Dœuff 1989: 27).

(Eve's serpent) but in the little phallus that feeds within knowledge as a union of thought and being. The 'worm' spoils, mindlessly, the apple of pure existence; it is not the intelligent serpent that boldly proposed to Eve that she choose the knowledge rather than obey the patriarch. It is the (absolute) 'in-itself' *in itself* that is accorded the highest value. This *in itself* is a 'plenum', a 'fullness of existence' complete in itself, the foundation upon which the *for-itself* can raise itself.[12] The condition of the *in-itself* is figured as the most desirable. Sartre describes us as hankering after it. We dread our null status as a shiftless *for-itself*. It is only a burden, binding us forever to negotiate a future at which we cannot arrive.

The 'Femininity' of the 'For-Itself'

If femininity is symbolised in the *in-itself*, can it remain a threat to the *for-itself*? The absolute positivity of the *in-itself* is 'dense' or 'full' only in being undifferentiated. Admitting no negativity the *in-itself* allows no differentiation. We cannot characterise it.[13] This 'original', primeval *being-in-itself* is not merely unintelligent. We cannot entertain the very idea of it as a source of existence in itself.[14]

We do understand the *in-itself* because we read the category in contrast with the *for-itself* whose activities found the domesticated world, the patter of little feet – these innumerable 'in-themselves'. This self-creator of form out of formlessness is a god that moves over chaos, bringing order, light, animal life, man-Adam and finally, as a clinamen, woman. The association with theology might overwhelm us. We might fail to see how the imagery reverses, re-dresses, cross-dresses. As *being-for-itself* arose by 'making nothing of' *being-in-itself*, we can regard ourselves, male and female, as equal co-authors. We can read the (masculine) *for-itself* as purely positive – thus lacking creativity – and the (feminine) *in-itself* as purely negative – the source of freedom and consciousness.

There ceases to be a god-creator as external force. Out of Eve's non-conscious body, the *in-itself*, Adam-god creates himself as intelligent and knowing being. Lack now lies at the heart of the masculine principal [sic]. As nothingness *Adam*'s creative spirit gains what was feminine sexuality in Sartre's reverie. Lack, space, a cavity, a hole in being.

---

[12] Berkeley (Berkeley 1972: 98) speaks of unthinking matter as 'inert' and 'stupid'.

[13] Sartre's metaphysics recalls Socrates' dream of reality in Plato's *Theaetetus* – and the logical 'atoms' of Wittgenstein's *Tractatus* (Wittgenstein 1922). Also, Derrida's play of *différance* which precedes all recognizable differences (Derrida 1982).

[14] Derrida (eg. Derrida 1982: 157–205) deconstructs the idea of an original source, and a pure presence to found speech and truth. *Being and Nothingness* sets out with an essay to bridge the gap between pure metaphysics and phenomenological ontology.

But what is a hole? We must handle '*hole*' with 'tweezers' (Le Dœuff 1991: 81). Is the mouth a hole? If the nose 'protrudes' does the mouth 'gape open'?[15] (On protrusion: Do only some noses 'obtrude'? Is *a protuberant nose* a pleonasm?) If the mouth is decently closed, is it a simple *cavity*? There's a pretty picture of nothingness! I drop a post into the *cavity* of the post-hole and ram earth around it. I lay the body in a shallow *cavity* in the earth. A *dental cavity*. 'I need that like I need a hole in the head!'. 'Let your ear-hole take this earful!'.[16]

What threatened the free consciousness of the *for-itself* now appears essential to it. In this imaginary system, woman arises within man's body to complete it as a conscious intelligence. As symbol of plenitude his body signifies a positivity that is inert; it lacks that 'spark' of nothingness essential to his being *for himself*. What the masculine requires of the feminine is the despised cavity that signifies the possibility of existing at a distance from oneself. If the 'positive' is also a sign of value, then it is the negative that is the 'positive'. It is 'he' whom 'feminine negativity' frees and makes conscious.

Sartre's metaphysics oscillates. The sexual load rolls back and forth, from feminine port to masculine starboard. The system is a precarious perch for feminism (Le Dœuff 1991: 57–60) even though it does contain the resources to explain the 'Otherness' by which women form a 'second sex'. Even after the reversal of polarity by which 'lack' becomes the material condition of woman's free space, it is this 'worm coiled up in the heart of her being' that provides her creative 'negativity'. According to that stage in the phantasmagoria of metaphysical sex, of sexual metaphysics, it is as if Sartre has said that woman is, yes, free and conscious for herself, but only because liberated by an inner masculine principle.

The growth of the *in-itself* as a 'feminine' threat to a venturesome *for-itself* was not nipped in the bud. Now it comes to flower, smelling to one like a ripe peach (Ricks 1976: 139–142), and putrescent to another (Le Dœuff 1991: 83–88). If the feminine is the threat of death to the masculine, the fear of the *in-itself* is merely the fear of loss of ego in sexual intimacy. The categories of

Being and *nothingness*

reduce to

life or love and *death or hatred.*

---

[15] On the notion of 'gaping open', see Sartre (BN, 613).

[16] This indented section is my own interpolation, of course.

The 'operative' or 'enabling' contradiction of the system disguises this.[17] We must also make the reverse reading. Nothingness is intrinsic to the being of life or love. In itself, *being* cannot be distinguished from death.

Towards the end of *Being and Nothingness* the initial feminine metaphors of space, coital images of filmed surfaces, become 'holes' waiting to be 'plugged'. 'Megalomaniac' ravings (Le Dœuff 1991: 87), written by one who knows there is no escaping exteriority by a transcending consciousness.[18] Nevertheless, Sartre also tells simple stories that convey the moment of being shocked by someone's regard, and by your own freedom. You realise you are free and conscious. You see others as spirited conscious beings, centres of their own worlds. Together with his abstract characterisations of *l'être* (*what it is to be*), the other recalls you to yourself as an exteriority, even as you are an interiority. Sartre brings this thought into the home of intimacy. What we are for others is essential to what we are for ourselves. In its very interiority consciousness is an observable exteriority.

My exteriority is not directly accessible to myself; my interiority is not directly accessible to others. There is a dimension of my interiority that is accessible only to others; it eludes my power to define or to command it. Sartre brings this intimate exteriority into the foreground (the fairground?) of philosophy but does not see how this exteriority expands my sense of self and of others. Sartre's theory excuses the desire to escape this exteriority, since it is a struggle we are doomed to enact.[19] Sartre senses, as intrinsically threatening, the view another takes of him. Is this merely the fear of an absurdity coming true? Is it not the more bracing fear of what women would say, to all and sundry, were they present with men in public life in equal numbers and power?

---

[17] See P. Deutscher's *Yielding Gender* (Deutscher 1997: 103–110, 134–140, 157–168).

[18] Sartre did not succeed in fully rejecting Husserl's transcendental ego – not only in 1937, in *La Transcendence de l'Ego* (Sartre 1957). Even more, in 1943, in *L'Être et le Néant* (see particularly BN, 233–252), his adaptation of Hegel's 'for-itself' relies on Husserl's insight that it is not Descartes's 'soul' as a 'spiritual thing', but the sheer framing or bracketing of our material condition that marks our difference from unthinking matter.

[19] My thought here recalls Husserl's subtle treatment of the problem of the 'other' in *Cartesian Meditations*. Part V (Husserl 1970a).

2
Doing Lunch

Woman has ovaries, a uterus: these peculiarities imprison her in her subjectivity, circumscribe her within the limits of her nature. It is often said that she thinks with her glands. Man superbly ignores the fact that his anatomy also includes glands such as the testicles, and that they secrete hormones (SS, 15).

A woman knows very well the intentions which the man who is speaking to her cherishes ... She does not want to realise the urgency ... He says to her 'I find you so attractive' ... She disarms this of its sexual background ... The desire cruel and naked would humiliate ... her. To satisfy her ... desire must address her personality ... her full freedom. At the same time ... this desire must address her body as object (BN, 55).

The Second Sex

Women and Men: Differences Without Essence

Beauvoir is aware from the outset of the risk of raising up the very mystification of '*woman*' that she means to dispel.[1] The risk arises from making a special issue of the 'question of woman'. Using satire to diminish the risk, she evokes the oppressive airheads who raise the spectre of the possible disappearance of 'woman' ('Even in Russia, women are still *women*') and then proceed to declaim that anatomy and physiology makes women what they are.

For Beauvoir, the sciences establish our 'characteristics' as interactions between the organism and the environment. She rejects, nevertheless, the claims typical of some successful women that *women* are nothing but humans by a different name. She locates a position between such a *nominalism* and any *essential femininity*. Some differences may

---

[1] Sartre's story of a couple 'doing lunch' has been attributed to Beauvoir's observations, but, in any case, her view of how a woman is liable to be perceived differs from Sartre's – for her, *woman* is made to play a special role in mediating *man*'s problem of bad faith.

be destined to disappear, but still they are real, says Beauvoir. Clusters of characteristics vary from individual to individual, but one need only

> go for a walk with one's eyes open to demonstrate that humanity is divided into two classes of individuals whose clothes, faces, bodies, smiles, gaits, interests and occupations are manifestly different (SS, 14–15).

'*What is a woman?*' in that case, asks Beauvoir. The very existence of the question is questionable, for there is no comparable question '*What is a man?*' The term 'man' (*l'homme*) is co-opted to represent humanity in general – either of the sexes. And it signifies just one of the sexes. By this double use, 'man' becomes the dominant term, the definer of issues, the 'positive' term against which 'woman' is a negation or lack. It is then women's '*peculiarities*' that mark her off, that '*imprison her in the subjective*'. Men do differ from women, and women from men, Beauvoir agrees. The bias is that women are described in their peculiarities of *differing from men*. If *humanity* rather than *man* were the neutral term, and *men* and *women* each equally distinct forms of that humanity, then the *peculiarities* of men would be remarked upon in the same vein, with equally counterpoised weight:

> [Whereas] woman has ovaries [etc. which] circumscribe her in her nature [man] superbly ignores the fact that his anatomy also includes glands ... He thinks of his body as a direct and normal connection with the world, which he believes he apprehends objectively (SS, 15).

Beauvoir couples this trick of using man as both the predominant term and as the neutral one that stands in for both, with the tradition of 'man' as the 'one who knows'. If knowledge is objective it is unbiased and therefore not the possession of women as such. Knowledge is a human concern. But since 'man' signifies humanity generally, knowledge is the concern of *man*. '*So yes*' it is said, charitably, '*of course women have knowledge – just so long as they don't let those "peculiarities" that mark them out from general humanity get in the way*'.

Scratching Beauvoir's observation uncovers the origins of contemporary debates. How are 'women are placed in relation to the tradition of knowledge'? Do women know 'in a different way' and are they to be read 'in their difference'? Can women achieve the ideals of objectivity and scientific precision that marks out 'man's knowledge'? Beauvoir slips between the options of *nominalism* and *essentialism* regarding the differences between women and men. Her terms avoid the mystique of 'a special women's way of knowing', but do not require that women suppress their individuality in miming styles established by men. '*Man superbly ignores the fact that he too has glands*', as Beauvoir puts it, caustically. Her line of criticism would have us ask whether, in being 'man', men must suppress their masculinity in order to have knowledge. Macho bravado excludes understanding. That would be a 'peculiarity' to be dismantled if they ('we') are to gain knowledge and understanding. Men, like women, women, like men, are sexual beings who draw upon the ways they 'hold bodily sway in the world' (Husserl 1970b). To renounce that 'holding sway' is to renounce realism, élan and success.

This co-option of 'humanity' by man so that women 'differ' from it in their 'peculiarities' is the construction of women as *Other*, argues Beauvoir. There is a long history of this distortion and marginalisation. For Aristotle, the female nature is 'defective'. For Thomas of Aquinas, similarly, woman is an 'imperfect man'. (Beauvoir's contemporary, Bendu, still writes that the '*body of a woman lacks significance in itself*'.) But Beauvoir has no wish to set up a new 'feminine mystique' – any group can be set up as an 'Other'. A human being becomes a *foreigner* just in virtue of being 'not of my own country'. '*One's own country*' operates as the predominant term, and as the touchstone of 'normality'. Beauvoir's observation applies to contemporary debates about cultural relativism. With this tawdry apparatus in place, the complacent national then questions – with all due 'tolerance' – the defining peculiarities of the 'foreigner'. 'Liberals' uncomfortable with this process are in a dilemma. Do they deny national differences? This would be unreal, and also inhuman, as if one were blind to rich diversity. And yet, to make an issue of national differences sets in motion the racist, the nationalist, apparatus of inquiry into the 'peculiarities' of others. At best the others will 'learn Western values', gradually become fit for 'democracy' and 'scientific culture'.

To avoid such cultural centralism, others are tempted by exoticism. They will extol 'Eastern' religion, or 'Eastern' ways of knowing, though '*being west of ...*' could never have defined a *kind* of democracy or science. This obscures the fact that any speaker is of some particular country or culture and might be viewed from elsewhere according to those peculiarities. In this lack of imagination, '*the native abroad is shocked to find he is a foreigner*' (SS, 17).

The Momentum of a Prejudice

Why haven't women disputed this male sovereignty – not only on some occasion or in extremity but continuously, as everyday normality? Beauvoir observes that women are not a minority who might thus identify themselves as delimited and threatened. Neither do they form a separate collective like a trade union. They are present in equal numbers with men and yet dispersed in society. They are (*'they become'*) women in virtue of the operation of culture upon their biological difference. Unlike oppressed minorities or classes, they cannot find the source of their oppression in some historical event.

Women don't regularly say 'we', observes Beauvoir. When men say 'we' no one is surprised that what they are speaking of, predominantly, is 'we men'. If, generously, they include women, or refer to women separately so as not to forget them, that is, as it were, a generous, optional, extra. She alerts us to Claude Mauriac's remarks about the place of women in discussing intellectual matters. Mauriac says, '*We* listen on a tone of polite indifference (to what women say)'. If he had said, 'When a woman speaks, we *men and women* listen on a tone of polite indifference', he would have given the game away. He had men in mind in order to say 'we', and yet speaks as if to make a general point.

Beauvoir searches further into the assumption of masculine dominance. The system has been challenged from time to time since antiquity. Evidently, it has considerable resilience. Men need women, and Beauvoir inquires why this has given women only the power to exploit their role as Other. It is scarcely surprising that women hesitate to renounce this role as 'Other' in case they lose any (conditional) powers and privileges it provides. One can explain why the system is liable to continue, but how did it begin? Beauvoir suggests there is no general explanation. The further she investigates the phenomena, the more she doubts any one theory as adequate. There is the myth of a seizure of power on account of women's vulnerability in childbearing. There are economic analyses of the advantage to capitalism of women as an unpaid labour force. Some, like Nietzsche, invoke a 'will to power' – people use whatever power that they find available. Each of these ideas has some truth and force while none of them, alone or together, constitute a full explanation.

Beauvoir's phenomenology animates explanation by description. Oppression between the sexes works within the minutiae of life, and her explanations follow suit. She does not think it trivial to point out how men derogate women outright, or else remove them from contention by '*benevolent condescension*'. The conservative hoax that 'men and women are equal in their difference' involves a conception of 'difference' formed in subjugating women. Beauvoir's strategy is neither to deny difference nor to make a thing of it. She is a pioneer in exposing how difference between the sexes is constructed, and how that constructed 'difference' is exploited. Though one is not 'born a woman', biological difference is relevant.

Unlike Sartre in *Being and Nothingness*, Beauvoir describes situations within the frame of power and economy. She demonstrates how men profit from women being in a position of 'Other-ness' (*alterity*) and are not motivated to change things. Some men gain little material benefit from complicity and yet '*it is a cure for their sense of inferiority*', she observes. Beauvoir is interested in the subtle details of quiet oppression, not only in oppression by violence. Many men now '*postulate women as their equals ... [I]n the concrete events of conjugal life she stands there before him as a free being*'. In the day to day there appears to be '*freedom and respect for the dignity of the wife. He can therefore feel that social subordination between the sexes no longer exists, and that ... in spite of differences, woman is an equal*'. While serendipity lasts he speaks of 'equality', but just so long as it costs nothing:

> [W]hen he is in conflict with her, the situation is reversed: his theme will be the existing inequality, and he will even take it as his justification for denying abstract equality (SS, 26).

Objectivity, Freedom and Transcendence

Beauvoir has summed up the 'ancient quarrel between the sexes'. Now she poses, with some irony, questions about knowledge, human nature, and sexual difference. '*Who is to judge this quarrel?*' When people quarrel they argue badly, she points out, and each is an interested party. Yet, as she remarks dryly, an angel – sexless – '*would be poorly qualified to speak*'. Beauvoir toys with the idea that '*we [today's women] can afford the luxury of impartiality*' (SS, 27),[2] but has to recognise that it is '*impossible to approach any human problem with a mind free from bias*' (SS, 28). This 'bias' is a virtue, however – a commitment to candour in open enquiry: '*Every objective description, so called, implies an ethical background*'. Concerning objectivity, her tone shifts back and forth productively. She claims a new impartiality; she concedes a (regrettable) 'bias'. Then she appropriates a considered 'bias' as a basis for serious enquiry. This biased basis would replace nostalgia for a world where knowledge and judgement were 'neutral' and 'impartial'. She has already exposed the fraudulence of a 'neutrality' so easily claimed by men. If neutrality is the disguised self-interest of men, or the uninvolved incomprehension of 'angels', one might

---

[2] Le Dœuff questions her 'we'. Who are 'we' who have 'won out'? (Le Dœuff 1991: 125).

approach a (new) objectivity in accepting one's values within a critical subjectivity.

The search for a new kind of objectivity connects with a suspicion of the rhetoric of happiness. Beauvoir declares that she is *'interested in the fortunes of the individual as defined not in terms of happiness but ... of liberty'* (SS, 29). This does not entail that liberty is more important than happiness. Her *'interest'* arises because of the threat of stagnation that arises from women's role as an 'Other'. In this situation, to place happiness first is to compromise liberty. The dubious *rhetoric* of 'happiness' represents it as a compromised acceptance of comfort – *'happiness is one's private interest'*, *'women of the harem [may be] happier than women voters'*, *'the housekeeper [may be] happier than the working-woman'*. The problem is that *'it is none to clear just what ... "happy" really means and still less what true values it may mask'* (SS, 28).

Her language exaggerates the tension between liberty and happiness, for we do question the 'happiness' of someone who has lost their liberty – of mind, or movement, of feeling. These dangers of 'degradation' and 'stagnation' predominate as the Introduction concludes. One might agree with Beauvoir that those deprived of their liberty will be 'pronounced happy' by those who oppress them. But are those deprived of their liberty happy? That someone must accept their situation says nothing of how they feel about it. Dull acceptance is only the avoidance of further misery. Perhaps they have lost sight of happiness. Beauvoir might have grasped the rhetoric of happiness for herself. Since objectivity requires partiality – a moral decision in the use of terms – she could have rejected dull capitulation as happiness. Beauvoir expresses her own violent unhappiness at the prospect of a life in which she gave up her right to think and feel for herself. So, rhetorically, her choice is for *freedom*, which is to emphasise, rightly, that one has to take one's chances about happiness. And yet, for all that, it seems to me, the hope for happiness may still remain paramount.

Le Dœuff points out that Beauvoir never argues for freedom on the basis of a promise of happiness (Le Dœuff 1991: 112–113). Beauvoir's appeal to freedom as paramount places happiness within her 'ethical background' of choice. One must live freely and hope for happiness. One does not demand it as a justification for freedom. And yet, happiness remains an issue in and between the lines of *The Second Sex*, as it does not in Sartre's *Being and Nothingness*. Against this ethical background of hers, someone should be unhappy because deprived of liberty. In particular, a sense of sexual freedom, while not guaranteeing pleasure or happiness, is a necessary condition of both.[3] The possibility of a species of 'free happiness' haunts Beauvoir's caustic critique of the rewards for women of living life as the 'Other'.

So the value of happiness does appear between the lines but Beauvoir distorts the image of a free life by rejecting happiness as a distinct criterion. Freedom appears within the scenario of a hero's life. The writer's brief use of '*we*' for an '*us*' who were to be understood as, predominantly, women gives way to a standardised '*he*' again: '*Every subject plays his part ... through exploits or projects that serve as a mode of transcendence*' (SS, 28). The very 'he' that Beauvoir deconstructed at the outset now infects *her* prose. Why would *he* (and *she*) *desire* to live like that? For Beauvoir at this point, not for happiness, fame, nor love, nor recognition: '*There is no justification for present existence other than its expansion into an indefinitely open future*' (SS, 28–29). But is it enough that one's existence expands into an open future? I need be no more than reckless to live like that. Like Sartre, Beauvoir has in mind our *projects*. These structure one's future even though one cannot be sure of success. And '*project*', as against '*adventurism*', reveals *happiness* as ready to share the stage. Without the power and will to undergo the risk of choice, we cannot be *happy*. At best, we then avoid excess of pain by chemical measures. Happiness has its own value; the value of liberty consists, in part, in helping us achieve it. To value liberty alone is to value Alexander's unfeeling ruthlessness equally with the life of generous reciprocity that Beauvoir signals as her ideal. To argue for one's preferences at this point is not to lose one's objectivity. Beauvoir is alert to the cowardice disguised in common appeals to objectivity. If, as she says, '*every objective description ... implies an ethical background*' then one must determine and defend one's conceptions of happiness, no less than those of freedom.

*   *   *

'*[L]ike any human being*', claims Beauvoir, '*woman is a free and autonomous being*', and yet she is compelled to *act* as if fixed by her biology as a *woman*, as an 'Other'. Le Dœuff (Le Dœuff 1991: 55–60, 88–99) questions the existentialist ontology involved in Beauvoir's description of this situation as of '*a transcendence*[4] *fall[ing] back into immanence, stagnation*' and would like to impute this to Sartre's influence.

---

[3] 'Sexual freedom' as choice of one's partner could be monogamous.
[4] The freedom that every human being is capable of, just in being conscious, is described as a *transcendence*.

Whatever the facts about that, Beauvoir's repugnance about a 'fall into immanence' is itself a loss of freedom of mind and of feeling.

Dreams, Fears, Idols

As she commences Part III of *The Second Sex*, Beauvoir tells a more socially and sexually specific story about the 'bad faith' of women who disappoint the expectations men have in virtue of their fantasies:

> [M]en have always kept in their hand the concrete powers ... they have thought it best to keep a woman in a state of dependence ... and thus she is then established as the 'Other' (SS, 171).

It is not only that '*this arrangement serves ... economic interests*'. This arrangement also has '*ontological and moral pretensions*'. Only '*friendship and generosity*' allow us to recognise each other '*in a reciprocal manner*' as subject and as object. Here she attempts a synthesis of the value of freedom and of generous feeling that Sartre found impossible to include in the theory of *Being and Nothingness*. The language remains that of the existential hero, however: '*Freedom and generosity*' are man's highest achievements, and to achieve them '*we have to outdo ourselves at every moment*'. I have to 'renounce' simply *being* what I am, and 'renounce' the aim of establishing myself through possessions – whether material or intellectual (SS, 172).

So Beauvoir's account resonates with that of Sartre's 'bad faith', but she describes the existential situation in different terms. Sartre would never speak of some '*trouble of the spirit*' as the price of learning generosity. Her words are '*trouble*', '*disturbance*' and '*disquiet*', rather than Sartre's '*terror*' and '*anguish*'. She makes her own diagnosis of the fear of freedom from observations of *man*'s principal means of dealing with it. Her account more easily explains that someone who acts in 'bad faith' is capable of recognising herself as a free consciousness. She writes of a *man* who dreams of gaining '*quiet in disquiet*', an '*opaque plenitude endowed with consciousness*'. This dream involves a '*woman*' who takes the mythic role of '*mediator between conscious life and what exists simply in itself*' (SS, 172). Beauvoir raises up this phenomenology from common sayings, religious beliefs, political demands and her observations of life. Within her story, women, with men, are freely conscious but have different difficulties in 'escaping immanence'. Critics have attacked Beauvoir's representation of a woman's body as a 'snare' for she who inhabits it:

The feminine sex organ is mysterious even to the woman herself, concealed, mucous and humid; it bleeds each month, it is often sullied with body fluids, it has a secret and perilous life of its own. Woman does not recognise herself in it, and this explains in large part why she does not recognise its desires as hers (SS, 407).

Such critics mistake her descriptions of living in a certain kind of world for a recommendation to do so. It is not the business of phenomenology to lay down how things ought to be observed or felt. Nevertheless, to describe is not to say *'That's how it is so it's no use protesting!'*, either. A critique emerges from such descriptions, in what I would call an 'operative phenomenology'.[5] Sartre's phenomenology seems to cement things in as they are, while Beauvoir's works away from within the world as one finds it, eroding not only the 'facts' and generally received wisdom, but also one's intimate awareness of these things.

Beauvoir thus makes a foray into a virtual 'enemy territory' that has been established within her own body. This reveals that women and men are not placed equally in dealing either with their existence *'in itself'* or their existence as it is *'for themselves'*. To say that man's sex is like a 'neat finger' while that of a woman is a 'swamp' is to write on the edge of satire. Beauvoir thus summons up a vision the reader can recognise and then challenge. She has reminded us of male anxieties about his 'neat' organ as subject to erection or detumescence. In his nocturnal emissions he too is 'damp'. A foreign territory inhabits his body too, she might have said. The mythical 'phallus' that has to rise to its social demands comes to occupy the site of his, inconstant, tissue.

The prevalence of myths and the ready-made terms in which biology and anatomy appear to illustrate their validity supply 'man' with 'woman' – a mediator between what exists *'in itself'* and what exists *'for itself'*. This 'woman' has to play a double role. 'She' offers him the magic of a being that, free and conscious, recognises 'him' in his freedom. At the same time she is 'built to be docile'. She may question what he says but then 'it is her nature' to be convinced by him:

> [W]oman opposes man not with the hostile silence of nature, nor the hard requirement of reciprocity. She is conscious, and yet he can 'possess' her in the flesh (SS, 172).

If he can 'possess' her though she is free and conscious, then there is an *'escape from the dialectic of "master and slave" that has its source in the*

---

[5] I acknowledge Le Dœuff's notion of an 'operative philosophy' (Le Dœuff 1979).

reciprocity between free beings' (SS, 172). We shall have to see where Sartre stands in relation to any such 'escape'. Both he and Beauvoir are impressed by Hegel's problem that the one who is object of another's consciousness is thus dominated, losing their freedom, and depriving the dominant observer of the recognition he needs from this 'Other'. In terms of recognition the 'master' emerges as the weaker of the two. Beauvoir slips the figure of 'woman' within this conundrum. Woman is the 'inessential Other' who does not dominate *man* by *her* look. She acts as his 'absolute Other', vindicating his vision of himself without the risk of a reciprocated regard (SS, 173).

Beauvoir places religious myths within this frame. Eve is created from Adam to 'give him a companion' – a conscious being who is naturally submissive. If to be conscious is to be free, as Sartre maintains, a contradiction arises here. Actual *women* enacting an impossible role at great cost are needed to dispel its appearance.[6]

These myths are still at work, says Beauvoir (in 1952). '*Women have no religion or poetry of their own: they still dream through the dreams of men*' (SS, 174).[7] These are the myths that half a century of renewed achievement has eroded, but Beauvoir's observation that '*the myth ... thrives on contradiction*' still holds good. Woman is at once 'Eve and Virgin'. If she moves beyond the role of homemaker, nurturer and support to her husband, a 'backlash' to her claims to equal reciprocity recasts her as 'evil'. She 'exploits' her combined powers of intelligence, new social status, and sexuality. Beauvoir is prescient about ever-new inflexions of *woman* as man's '*other*': as 'Other', she is evil because she lacks the 'good' of rational wise, law-giving *man*, but as a negative condition she is necessary to the good, and so is good after all. There is no stable concept of *woman*, Beauvoir concludes.

As part of this contradictory system, '*man seeks in woman, the Other as Nature and as fellow being, all at once*' (SS, 175). From the anxiety of this contradiction arises, on the other side of an adulation that demotes women, paranoia: '*She is the weaker who triumphs over him*' (SS, 175). Paranoia grows in messed up logic like that exhibited in the tradition of the male as the one who is truly creative.[8] He is the generator – life is imagined as already fully preformed in his 'seed'. Needing 'mother earth' in which to 'plant his seed', he reacts against the 'carnal' state that disproves – though

---

[6] Totalitarianism, Beauvoir remarks, where everyone has a functional role, involves a cult of women as reduced to '*Kinde, kuche, kirke*' – a new mystique of essentially passive consciousness.

[7] In Part IV we shall examine Irigaray's call for a 'feminine divine' as a genre.

[8] Sartre's involvement with this myth is analysed in the preceding chapter.

it enables – his power. The male child born into this culture cannot come to accept his mother's body as it is both 'for him' and 'for herself' as sexual (SS, 179). Within such a fantasy it is *man*'s curse to be conceived and born. As free by *contrast* with what exists '*in itself*' – *woman* – man is 'frightened of this Night'. And yet, from this 'night', this 'moist earth', comes new life (SS, 183).

Needing *woman* to mediate his self-recognition, but in dread of her power as *maternal*, man desires *woman* as a means to 'riotousness'. By this 'riotousness' he is released from the strictures of 'reason' that constrain his 'true', 'free' nature. If *man* signifies reason, control, and transcendence of what exists '*in itself*', then *man* is afflicted with the desire for release from this rational formation. He desires a place that permits him to experience an 'excess' to the boundaries of the self. Beauvoir quotes Bataille's vision of 'our' longing to repossess a 'lost', 'tragic', 'blinding wonder'.[9] *Man* finds this 'wonder' 'only in bed', sustaining his fantasy of woman as 'Other'. This unique role for *woman* does women no good. They do not match the fantasy, and men do not live up to the demands of the phallus.

Not that Beauvoir would demystify sexuality into banality. When neither sex co-opts the free consciousness of the other, sexual reciprocity casts them in uncharted waters. In reciprocity each exists 'for the other' and 'for themselves'. Beauvoir will question the symbol of *woman* as muse who inspires (a-muses) the creative Master painter, poet, inventor, scientist (SS, 214). Apart from the injustice of the role, there is incoherence in it. To *be* muse, she possesses a mysterious intelligence and feeling from which the 'Master' artist can be supplied. Intelligence, as a power, is something other than 'docile'.

Within this half-dreamed existence of inspiration by unintelligent intelligence, the man, inspired to become rich in money, art or invention, is vulnerable. To whom shall he give his 'wealth'? An appearance of generosity is bogus since the gift functions only to prove his power (SS, 214).[10] So there is little for women in *man*'s finding himself in the 'mystery' of her flesh; he makes a mystery of her to confer value upon himself. He cannot associate '*Mother*' and '*Wife*' and recognise the 'alchemy of life' that nourishes him. Thus, by the 'feminine mystique', he separates '*wife*' as everyday fact from '*lover*' as what enchants his world.

By the same argument the Wife is 'dangerous prey' too. If he does take pleasure in her, this 'arouses fecundity' and he loses the charm of a free consciousness that could also be *possessed*. His sexual organ as signifying

---

[9] Luce Irigaray's renovation of wonder is examined in Part IV.

[10] She cites Citizen Kane who proves his wife's value by *making* her an opera star.

transcendence and power is threatened by the involuntary character of its 'erection', and its detumescence signifies to him his loss of power rather than his having given and received pleasure. Simply being sexed threatens his fantasy of 'possessing' another free consciousness. In 'sowing' his seed he exercises a power that is then no longer his. He renounces it in its announcement. If he avoids intercourse as if to preserve himself, he is subject to the 'uncontrolled weakness' of nocturnal emissions (SS, 194).

Beauvoir thus locates the appeal of a dualism of body and mind in an impossible dualism of *sex* and *brain*. In order that mind can seem to control body in its sexuality he must regain control in sexuality by using it as appropriation. 'Branding' a woman as his, the 'weakness' in his sexual system is lodged in something that is 'his' and yet 'not him' (SS, 196). This is a vision of *woman* as inevitably a betrayer. If she enables him to 'master' his body, there is her 'treason' again – *'the man masters flesh by becoming flesh, and is drawn into immanence'*. It is the self-defeat of the coloniser who proves his power by dominating a culture to which he attributes his weakness. ('The white man's burden'!) In making their bodies conform to his will, they touch him. Fearing 'going native', he violently rejects what he had appropriated. Beauvoir remarks that this 'being overtaken by those one dominate' is *magic*, where power emanates from the passive figure – 'colonised' woman appears exotic, mysterious (SS, 197).

Since he cannot possess what he *loves* in such a twisted fashion, *man* may try to *become* this thing he cannot possess. But he has to incorporate bodily difference within his own identity. He will reject it not only as 'not him', but now as not even a 'proper' part of woman. Within this sick narrative, the vulva becomes an 'unclean wound' (SS, 200). He has to 'clean up' this figure which was to have 'saved' him from the body – his own and woman's – that challenged him as a 'controlling mind'. Irigaray will later write that the Christian religion presents *woman* as if her sex was to be 'sewn up' (Irigaray 1985a: 188, 1985b: 30). The cult of maternity – 'mother of God' – displaces a woman's erotic life for herself. Christianity has the *Mother* kneel before the *Son* (SS, 203).

Eroticism cannot exist within the imposed ideals of marriage, argues Beauvoir. Erotic life is at odds with what would attempt to guarantee its 'proper place' (SS, 219). If we look at the institution of marriage in the light of the preceding analysis of *man's* fears of *woman* as threatening his image of self-controlling reason, then we can regard the aim of marriage as to immunise a man against his wife (SS, 220). Man wants power over woman, not just to get what he wants for himself, but so as to prove his power over himself. The 'good husband' wants to *give* to the woman he possesses, but finds her *taking for herself*.[11]

Man is still caught in the self-contradictions he had projected onto *woman*. To mediate (his) nature she must be a free being, but as free she is formidable, like the Nature he wants her to mediate. So erupts *'woman the devourer'*. He has offered her his materiality, his 'phallus', to enable her to become an existence *for itself*, but someone who already exists *for herself* takes this symbol. His 'gift runs out of his control and the 'safe' womb becomes to him a 'pulp of humours', a 'dark contractible gulf'. We can observe this system of fantasy condensed in the contemporary rhetoric of the 'right to life' movement. The man's seed was to have been given 'a safe place', and neutralised *woman's* own desire. But women have 'transcended' this material condition by their own 'free choice'. The bumper stickers announce:

THE WOMB: THE MOST DANGEROUS PLACE IN AMERICA.

(Karpin 1992)

A system of thought and social conduct that originates in contradictions and subsists only by projecting onto everything it touches is not idle. *'Men find "everything" in women because they impress these contradictions on them'* (SS, 224). Finding everything and thus nothing in women, they do anything to maintain the system of confusion. Why not maintain such a one:

A wonderful servant capable of dazzling him – and not too expensive [!] (SS, 224).

Beauvoir traces another twist in this spinning contradiction of man as 'reason' and as free to be unreason. *'Men want to "lose themselves" too'* (SS, 225). The dualism of 'sex and brain' that is expressed in the metaphysicians' dualism of body and mind requires *man* to maintain an artificial structure at high cost. The related, endemic, contradiction is man's desire to be done with the very system that preserves his image of control. Beauvoir quotes Henry Miller, who thinks *'that in going to bed with a prostitute he sounds the depths of life and of death and the cosmos'* (SS, 226). He thinks, not that he is making tawdry contact with someone who needs to make some money, but that he is engaged in a magnificent dissolution of *'a hypocritical world'*. Miller's fantasy is that, *'in contact*

---

[11] Sartre's café scene appears differently in this light. A man 'gives' a woman his advances only to find her *taking*. She 'transcends them', so he sees her as a 'tease'.

with a pariah at the edge of society – the "fille perdue" – he escapes the conventions that alienate us from *'life and death and the cosmos'* (SS, 226).

This fantasy is one more of *man*'s projections upon *woman*: *'She is servant and companion but he expects her to be audience and critic and to confirm his sense of being'* (SS, 229). Men too, pay a price for *man*'s exploitation of contradictions about *'woman'*. Amongst all this she always, in some hidden crevice at least, lives for herself. In this, *'she opposes him with her indifference, even with mocking laughter'* (SS, 229).

Sartre's 'Bad Faith'

'Conscious', 'Distant from Ourselves', 'In Bad Faith'

For Sartre as for Beauvoir, consciousness is the cluster of ways in which we 'exist' our body. 'To exist the body' is a 'neologism' in English, as *'exister le corps'* was Sartre's in French. He used a direct object after *'exister'* to avoid suggesting a 'mind' that *used* the body. One might say 'we *body* ourselves'. We 'exist' the body musically when we sing – we 'body ourselves musically'. The one who gives orders 'exists their body' authoritatively. The one who obeys 'exists' theirs, obediently. As a *'being-for-itself'* we establish a 'distance' between what we have been, making room for free action now. We also establish a 'distance' between ourselves and anyone or anything that is 'not-ourselves'. We perceive clouds, trees, rainbows, streams, rocks and buildings. These exist 'for us' *in themselves*, but not *'for themselves'*. As conscious creatures capable of choice we exist in this mode of *being-for-itself*. I, in *'being for myself'*, establish this freedom by *'distancing'* myself from *myself* and from what exists *'in itself'*. Thus is created the imaginary space of consciousness. To have being *'for-itself'* is to create distance – between oneself and an object, oneself and others, and between oneself and oneself. This last 'distancing' brings with it the possibility of bad faith. Though 'lucid' consciousness tends to expose this murky machinery, we *are* the very parts that we set at a distance. In self-imposed obscurity, we can deny the very consciousness that we are.

In a clear and open state of consciousness, Sartre explains, we are aware of being free in our choices, but to realise this freedom is to suffer anguish – vertigo (BN, 29–33). To escape this dizziness, we soften the light upon our situation. We put our situation to the fore, deluding ourselves that we 'have to do' this or that. But there is paradox in this flight:

> In a word, I flee in order not to know, but I can not avoid knowing that I am

fleeing, and [so] the flight from anguish is only a mode of becoming conscious of anguish (BN, 43).

This flight succeeds in bad faith, which is unstable. We are in bad faith about a state of mind precisely when in that state of mind. How is this possible?

> What then are we to say that consciousness must be, in the instantaneity of the pre-reflective cogito – if the human being is to be capable of bad faith? (BN, 43).

This 'pre-reflective' awareness that Sartre writes of is the natural state of consciousness. To smell a rose is to be conscious of the perfume, not of *smelling* it. The fact *that* we smell something – our awareness of how we are conscious – is available only peripherally. And yet, in bad faith, this immediate 'directedness' towards objects can become divided against itself. Sartre states that *'consciousness is a being whose being is put in question in so far as it implies a being other than itself* (BN, 47).[12] To be conscious of something involves a (pre-reflective) awareness of something tangential to it. To perceive something is itself a state of consciousness, and involves a (pre-reflective) awareness of some 'negativity' in oneself. Sartre says that a

> [h]uman being is not only the being by whom negatités are disclosed in the world ... Consciousness is a being the nature of which is to be conscious of the nothingness of its being (BN, 47).

As a human being, that is, *'one can take negative attitudes with respect to himself'* (BN, 47). Sartre has declared, famously, that *'nothingness lies coiled like a worm – in the heart of being'* (BN, 21). Now it appears that bad faith lies 'like a worm' in the heart of our consciousness of what there is. In explaining how humans are capable of this (paradoxical) bad faith, Sartre calls upon his concept of a *negatité* – an absence such as *Pierre's not being in the café*. Sartre elaborates:

> My consciousness is not restricted to envisioning such a negatité. [It operates to] constitute itself in its own flesh as the nihilation of a possibility which another human being projects as its possibility (BN, 47).

This sentence is designed to jolt the reader. Descartes took consciousness as immaterial but Sartre sets out from consciousness as present in bodily gesture and expression. Thus, *'consciousness constitutes itself in its own*

---

[12] He inflects Heidegger's 'Man is a being for whom his being is in question'.

flesh'. In so doing it can *'nihilate other people's possibilities'*; it can 'make nothing of' what they do – those feelings and actions others 'project' because their consciousness, too, is *'constituted in its own flesh'*. Someone wants me to do something. I say 'no'. My *'nihilation'* of their wish is present in the 'set' of my body – in its disposition. If I submit like a 'slave' it is not merely to the *word* 'no':

> [I]t is as a Not that the slave first apprehends the master ... Others [have] made the Not a part of their very subjectivity (BN, 47).

The slave sees the master as *embodying* that 'Not'. Otherwise the word would lack force. There are various forms of negativising behaviour. Sartre mentions irony where, in the same act as I claim something, I annihilate it. This playful undercutting of what I say as I say it, is a lucid model for what I do when, in bad faith, I deceive *myself*. To understand bad faith is to understand what I do in directing *'consciousness against itself'*. In describing bad faith as deceiving oneself, Sartre compares it with lying. In bad faith with respect to someone else, I can keep a clear head in deceiving them (BN, 48–49). But how can I lie to myself? If I am to deceive myself,

> I must know in my capacity as deceiver the truth which is hidden from me in my capacity as the one deceived ... [I]f I deliberately and cynically attempt to lie to myself, I fail completely in this undertaking ... [T]he lie falls back and collapses beneath my look ... Our embarrassment then appears extreme, since we can neither reject nor comprehend bad faith (BN, 49).

An anecdote then puts this language to work. Sartre writes as if making notes in a café, interpreting the interaction between a couple sitting at a table near him, using these metaphysical terms of *being-in-itself* and *being-for-itself* and *bad faith*.[13] For the woman who does not wish to deal with her lunch companion's moves on her,

> the man appears sincere and respectful as the table is round or square, as the wall is blue or grey. The qualities thus attached ... are in this way fixed in a permanence like that of things (BN, 55).

Sartre describes bad faith as deeming conscious feelings and actions to have qualities *'fixed in a permanence like that of things'*. He is alluding to a tradition, ancient and modern, of 'qualities' as 'inhering' in 'substances'.

---

[13] Whether or not Beauvoir told him the tale, they discussed the book at every stage.

Qualities that Inhere in Things

Descartes and then Locke set a tendency for modern philosophy in posing the question 'Do colour, shape, and temperature "inhere in" the objects that are seen to be coloured, shaped, warm?' Are they 'objective' qualities? Sartre's phenomenology finds new meaning in this question. To treat a quality as '*objectively in*' something is to take no responsibility for its being as it is – no obligation to respond positively or negatively to it. This is to 'make an object' of it.

Sartre's way of describing what it is to treat a 'quality' as 'inhering' in something[14] has contributed to our current idiom of '*treating someone as sexual object*'. In Sartre and Beauvoir's language this is to treat someone as 'pure immanence' rather than as a 'transcendence'. At the same time, one is equally in bad faith in treating someone as a '*pure* transcendence' – as if they were something *other than* the visible, tangible being that 'exists the body'. Both attitudes deny the reality of the person concerned. We are subjects, not objects, and, as sexual subjects, neither objects nor neutered spirits (Deutscher 1983: 21–27). In thinking of how we relate to people as if 'things', we deceive ourselves that how we relate is 'not really us'. That is, one objectifies not only other people, but also one's conscious feelings and actions as if one were enacting a social convention that is not one's own business. One lives at a 'distance' from oneself.

The detachment by which we consider our own styles of consciousness can heighten sensibility. Or destroy it, letting us fancy that though we deal with people, really we live in a void of undetermined choice: '*Things, other people ... they are thus and so. What I make of them and do in relation to them is something else altogether*'.[15] We 'make a thing' of the body, or of the expressions, actions, and bodily dispositions we observe. We 'make a thing' of our own feelings and thoughts. In the bad faith of 'immanence' we identify with 'facticity' – what we are observed to be and do. To identify with one's *transcendence* involves a mis-identification of this 'facticity', too. Both forms of bad faith exploit one's transcendence. In identifying with one's facticity one would escape reproach through the thought that '*after all, that simply is what I am*'. In identifying with one's transcendence, one escapes reproach in the thought that '*after all, I am something essentially beyond these acts and feelings of mine*'.

The story of bad faith may be told in terms of '*being-for-itself*' and '*being-in-itself*'. In bad faith, '*being-for-itself*' would be only a form of '*being-in-itself*'. Sartre observes a waiter as 'acting too much' the waiter.

---

[14] And in a different way, Beauvoir's, as we shall see.
[15] This leads us to the work of the next chapter.

This *actor-in-waiting* poses as being only his function, as if nothing more could be asked of him. He makes of himself 'nothing more' than is consumed within his role. Someone who lived by taking other people's goods might, too, convert his actions into a kind of a 'thing' – a *being-in-itself* called a 'thief'. *'That's what I am!'*. He might dramatise it:

> I am a thief. That's why I have acted as I have and why I will continue to do so. I am no more to be blamed than the clouds for being blown along.

He would describe his life neutrally – '*I live by taking other people's goods without their permission*'. Then, exploiting the fact that it would be 'bad faith' to think of himself as a thing, he denies he *is* a thief. He pretends that as *being for himself* he does *not* have being '*in itself*'. In the other form of Sartrean language, he enacts '*pure transcendence*'.

Because in being conscious one exists *for oneself*, inner complexities arise. In the one moment, in irony, say, we can set up and demolish a way of being ourselves. It is in bad faith that we *obscure* this duality of purpose – unlike irony and play, we hide self-disengagement from ourselves even as we engage in it. If we were to keep these manoeuvres in mind the 'project' would be impossible – it is absurd to lie outright to oneself – '*the lie falls back and collapses beneath my look*'. Imagine the absurdity of his attempt:

> I know what I will do now. I'll convince myself I'm feeling fine though I'm feeling bad; I'll persuade myself I like that person though I can't stand them.

We may reflect upon having fooled ourselves in the past or ponder that we might do so later, and we can observe others 'taking themselves in'. But we cannot observe taking ourselves in.

In the Café: Privacy in Public

Waiting on Customers: *Waiting for Propositions*

Sartre's waiter, from another tale, haunts this café, framing a man who, playing at being a 'man of the world', is 'trifled with' by the woman who enacts his interest, and hers, as asexual. Can she deceive herself without checking on her stratagem? Can he close himself off from himself (and from her?) without being aware of it? Here are the vital elements in Sartre's tale of a woman acting in 'bad faith' (distilled from BN, 55–56):

She agrees to go out with this man 'for the first time'.

She knows the man's intentions 'very well'.

She does not want to admit she knows what he wants. It would humiliate her.

She 'disarms compliments of their sexual meaning'.

The man is 'sincere and respectful as the table is round and the sky is blue'.

She is 'aware' of his desire but would not be charmed by mere respect.

His desire must be addressed to her personality, her freedom.

Faced with this tension, she obfuscates, refusing to recognise his desire.

She transforms his 'desire' into 'admiration', 'respect' and 'esteem'.

The man takes her hand, creating a dilemma for the woman.

To leaves it there is to be involved.

To withdraw it is to 'break the unstable harmony'.

She leaves her hand there without noticing she has done that.

She 'draws her companion up to lofty regions of sentimental speculation'.

The 'divorce of body and soul' is complete.

The hand rests, neither consenting nor resisting in the hands of her companion.

Various things may strike us. At lunch 'for the first time', they do not know each other much. This affects what each can expect of the other's understanding of the situation, and what the author should attribute to them. So how can the woman be said to know the man's intentions 'very well'? Has he said so? Does she see so plainly that he is interested? How can the narrating onlooker interpret her behaviour? As to him – we are not told if *he* is disguising anything, or what tones he adopts, or what expression – but as to her, only that *she* does not want to 'admit anything to herself'. She finds herself in a new situation. In this public restaurant, she has to permit some ambiguity in his words and actions so as not to define his desire – and her own – in advance. But why *would* an open proposition be 'humiliating' to her, as we are assured? Why doesn't she ask what he wants? Why doesn't he make himself clear?

A second stage. He 'pays her compliments'. How is she to respond? She might be pleased even if she doesn't want to get involved – why must she be 'horrified' at arousing overt desire? And if it's all snake oil, she *may*, in good faith, treat the sexual manoeuvres cynically, as the empty objects they are. For then the 'sincere' and 'respectful' utterances *do* have the banality of '*the table is round*' or '*the sky is blue*'.

She would be 'unsatisfied with a purely intellectual interest' and yet the story leaves her feelings in obscurity. If she is indeed a '*coquette*', experienced in flirtation, she does not need to deceive *herself* to play a game with him. Or, if inexperienced and unable to fathom his intentions, she is not *deceiving* herself either. If we read the story in its author's terms, she *refuses* to name the man's desire, but bad faith remains an obscure diagnosis unless he has conveyed his interest and asked about *hers*. The author says that it is *her* desire that she will not name, but the question of 'bad faith' hangs on the reason why.

When he takes her hand, this certainly does 'create a dilemma' if she doesn't know what he wants and hadn't defined her own wishes. She does not to want to disturb the '*troubled and unstable harmony that gives the hour its charm*'. This memorable phrase leaves undecided which of them is in bad faith, and the 'hour' is not so 'charming'. The narrative conveys what Sartre later describes as '*engluement*' – a 'sticky' situation. We slide over these questions of *whose* feelings and *whose* lack of candour gums up reciprocity, for *we* are being seduced by a desire for metaphysics. We want to hear how, in bad faith, her *experience is as of dualism*. To consider in more detail what she was doing by not withdrawing her hand was too much for us. It was enough that she '*[drew] her companion up to the most lofty regions of sentimental speculation [and that] the "divorce of body and soul" [was] complete*'. The story is a fetching allegory for dualism.

Social Attitudes and the Appearance of Metaphysics

Clogged feelings and unshared intentions place 'her' in a bind and yet she is held responsible for the bad faith, discolouring this myth of the origin of a dualism of body and mind, and yet the mood that Sartre conveys, brilliantly calls attention to the oppression that generates the dualism. He achieves mental detachment by placing behaviour within metaphysical categories, and this conveys the oppressiveness of codified behaviour. Sartre shocks us, for instance, with the assertion of self-contradictory form – '*I am not what I am*' and '*I am what I am not*'. The form of abstract absurdity forces the reader to take stock. If I am what I am, then I can be criticised for it, but, if I feel and do things in bad faith, no reproach can touch me. I have deluded myself that 'what I really am is my transcendence'. And so, phenomenology meets metaphysics. The metaphysics of my mind, conscious of itself, as distinct from my bodily behaviour turns out to be an existential performance of self-abdication.

Metaphysics, from Plato's *Republic* to *The Second Sex* and *Being and Nothingness*, generates social criticism. Categories are made to apply universally and carry writers beyond what they had intended to reveal. They invite the reader to rewrite the tale from another point of view. So an existentialism inhospitable to women becomes an effective structure for Beauvoir's proto-feminism (Le Dœuff 1991: 55–64). Such philosophical practice, releasing a new freedom of thought, may be a snare, too. An air of metaphysical inevitability attaches to cultural practices. The narrator's assumption of the woman's inner life makes her motives and feelings inaudible, and her companion's lack of candour exacerbates her vulnerability to his impersonal desires. He disguises them as sociability, and her inevitably mannered responses are then trivialised as those of a 'coquette'. It is her male companion's subjectivity that Sartre leaves out of the picture.[16] Speaking of bad faith in the terms of 'transcendence' and immanence', the woman first treats the man as if he were a 'transcendence' of himself. Then, when he makes a pass, she 'transcends' her own bodily actions. Leaving her hand clasped by the man, she ascends into a realm of 'pure intellectuality'.[17] Where Beauvoir appeals to transcendence as a desirable exercise of freedom, invoking bad faith as the refusal of it, Sartre sees bad faith as inevitable in our transcendence of situation and feelings.

Looking Back at Sartre's Stories

Contemporary Enlightenment

Can an author who overhears a couple in a café, so freely interpret their behaviour? Le Dœuff points out that only the woman's (alleged) subjectivity is subject to judgement. The man's intentions and understanding of what he does and how she responds are presented only by implication (Le Dœuff 1991: 62–64). As if innocently, Sartre observes what she is doing, but the sketch of the man is a faceless outline. We know him only as through her eyes. As adopting the status of 'omniscient author' Sartre could have told us about the man, too. Silence about his feelings and his not 'naming' them rests upon a cliché that 'we all know' what the man desires.

---

[16] The man whom Sartre later describes as in bad faith, is homosexual – 'not quite a man'.

[17] 'Pure intellectuality' recalls Sartre's image of my slipping free leaving the Other with nothing but my 'tattered rags'.

Later, Sartre attends to the metaphysics of sexual desire. His story speaks of a need to make consciousness 'rise to the surface' of the other's body. The satisfaction of desire is to fill a haunting sense of vacancy, to possess the one loved within his world while yet remaining free. These themes are already at work as the sub-text of 'doing lunch'. By denying the man her 'mind' – what she thinks and feels of him, herself, and the situation – the woman can foil his attempt to produce the illusory magic of possession. Even if he 'possessed' her body, she would have foiled the effort of sexual desire to overcome dualism. In denying him her 'mind' she has denied his need to make her consciousness 'rise to the surface' of her 'body'. Whatever he does to that, *she* is 'not there'. This is acute, and should be read in tandem with Beauvoir's analysis of *man*'s desire for possession. But Sartre does not continue to probe the origin of the dualistic illusion; he does not allow the consciousness of his male protagonist to 'rise to the surface'.

The story is Sartre's philosophical fiction. We can criticise its terms and assumptions but cannot postulate a hidden, more instructive reality in a fictional story beyond what its narrator recounts. We can imagine a Sartre for ourselves, though. As authors ourselves we can imagine him as we please. He's here, saying:

> All right already. It was 1943 not 2002 when I told the tale. It wasn't sophisticated Sydney you know. A woman or a man, acting as I observed them, might have been acting not in bad faith, or in some different form of it. As you say, the woman might have been unsure about what she wanted. I did indicate that they scarcely knew each other. She wouldn't have known what relationship was implied in the situation, or what options she had. What he wanted in being sexually manipulative, if that's what it was – what he wanted out of sex with her if that was the 'obvious intention' I saw – is an unanswered question – no doubt for him, as for me the note-taker.
>
> Yes, had she said frankly, 'authentically', 'candidly', 'in all good faith' what she felt then she might have set up an embarrassing conversation – a false intimacy – with someone she hardly knew. She may genuinely have had no desire for this – or reason to risk it. In saying to him, openly, that 'she was not sure how far she wanted things to go', she would have stepped upon a plane of uncalled-for, unsustainable intimacy. That she meant it doesn't mean she could have expressed it – in that situation – in good faith. Yes, only if he himself approached her in good faith, only if he showed what he felt could she be more open with him. He risked nothing about himself so she couldn't, in good faith, take all the risks upon herself.

Our time-travelling Sartre goes on ruminating:

Yes, I see. But if you reject my story because of its bias, you miss looking at something important. Can't you, man or woman, gay or straight, recall doing the sort of thing I imputed to the woman? Suppose the *woman* took the *man*'s hand. What does he think? Perhaps that she is just friendly, perhaps sympathetic about how she imagined he felt; perhaps it is a sexual advance. Or perhaps it is her way of testing the waters – to see if she really does 'know the man's intentions'.

Anyway, I would no longer write, complacently, 'We all know what happens next'. I don't know 'what happens next' when she takes his hand. He might be delighted, or confused – maybe angry, thinking he is being pitied for having been inadequate in his approach. He might respond warmly. He might find out what she wanted, or take things further in the direction he had envisaged. He might be bold or he might bluff. In any of these moves there might be a good deal of pretence, too. And, yes, he might lapse into bad faith. I feel closer now to what he is doing. His 'bad faith' is his inadequacy to deal with these chancy and self-revealing options. I imagine he hadn't decided himself just what he'd wanted, so when she takes his hand he jumps to the conclusion that this is a 'move' on him. Finding that he's the one the 'hard word' is being laid on, he feels a lack of control – he's on unfamiliar ground. He is too macho to admit himself that he's passing up pleasure – or even love – so pathetically.

So, yes. It is he who 'leaves his hand there as if it were a thing, resting inert between the woman's hands'. He pretends to himself that 'he'd never meant anything'. 'We were only doing lunch' he murmurs to himself in irritation. Woodenly, he says to her that he 'thinks he might have made an appointment for a work-out at the gym'. He tells himself – 'lunch had almost made me forget'.

* * *

Retelling these stories it is not a matter of 'being fair to both sides', as if now an author or reader can 'see all sides at once'. In her introduction to *The Second Sex* Beauvoir asked '*just how are we to propound [the question] at all*', given that '*[m]an is at once judge and party to the case, but so is woman*'. Recognising the inescapable fact of bias, she suggests that '*[w]hat we need is an angel*'. But she adds, mordantly, '*Still, the angel would be poorly qualified to speak*'[!] (SS, 27).[18]

I wrote earlier that this 'bias is not a fault but a virtue of candour and of commitment'. In advance of the next half century of thought about these issues, Beauvoir articulated clearly that '*every objective description, so*

---

[18] An 'angel' as an a-sexual being, of course.

called, implies an ethical background' (SS, 28). For, imagine that Sartre's couple had in fact been involved in the process of beginning to form a couple. The awkwardness, the hesitation about one's response takes on a quite different moral flavour – of sensitivity and care rather than of what had appeared as 'bad faith'. And 'bad faith' itself, while sometimes contemptible, may be so transparent that it elicits sympathy, as nothing more serious than being ridiculous – a failed ploy to avoid appearing socially naked, or a tactic of self-preservation when one lacks the wit or courage to assume a better style.

Dualism as Representing Conscious Life

Sartre's account of bad faith begins to expose how dualism can make its appeal to common sense. Bad faith gives an aura of solid 'realism' to the distinction of mind and body. The tricky arguments of idealists and materialists attempt in vain to dislodge it. In bad faith I exploit the fact of my 'transcendence' of what I have been. Aware of these things, I am motivated to form new desires and plans. To deny this power is to regard myself as a 'victim of fate', but to accept this 'transcendence' should not *negate* my 'facticity'. However much I fancy I 'learn from the past', those past acts remain. They formed my character and personality, and that, in turn, inflected their style. In consequence I have a predisposition and a temperament that any realistic plan I make for my shiny future must take into account.

   To recognise my transcendence engenders self-deceit, for I identify with my power to create future possibilities and thus would escape blame – and lose the chance of praise – for what I have been. Sartre remarks satirically upon the state of mind in which we exploit our 'transcendence': '*no reproach can touch me, since what I really am is my transcendence [my power always to renew myself]*' (BN, 57). My accusers go to seize me, to hold me to account for my bad feelings and lack of perceptiveness. But *I* am no mere bundle of such dusty facts! A metaphysical slime coats my soul. What another observes is fixed but I leave them holding that 'ragged cloak'. With a chuckle, *I* slip free.

PART II

'A THIN FILM
OF NOTHINGNESS'

3
Bound to be Free

And in fact you have begun at the end. It is there, invisible and present, and it is the end which gives these few words the pomp and value of a beginning (Sartre 1965: 62).

The Call to Freedom as Ignoble

So have we come to the end of our affair with freedom – no longer 'free' to respond to the appeal of the very word? *'Appeal'* is part of the problem. *'Freedom!'* was always a call, forcing us into self-definition when we refused to respond, or when it spurred us into some muster of feeling.

In speech these days, in parliament, on talk-back radio, the call has all the nobility, the 'ring' of a gun lobby's rant for the right of every woman child and (infantalised) man to 'bear arms' – anything from cute 'personal' handguns to battlefield automatic weaponry. As one attempts to set down these fantasies of freedom that run free from inspection, words betray 'them' – those others who dream to shoot, and 'us' who'd bring them down with words. *'Bear arms!'* Hard to resist going dada or deconstructo – *bare arms* hanging out of a macho's sleeveless shirt, the *arms* of a *bear* – a grizzly ready to swipe the hunter.

But as we recover the decorum of discursive reason, as they used to call it, that *'bear arms'* reveal(s) that *'Freedom!'* always occluded the business of any call – to impose new loads upon the hearer, even while the appellor[1] slipped free of them. In a thoughtful moment it will seem that the weapons of 'true' freedom must float before us, not to be borne but to bear us – aloft or at least into a bullish economy.

Oh yes. *'Freedom entails responsibility'* – inscribed on any desk calendar and we've heard all that goes with it before and enough already. Part of the operative contradiction of the right's rights. The newly rediscovered right to beat one's child. (*He* was as free to *have* it borne as she was *not* free to have it aborted.) The adult has already stowed away the

---
[1] 'Appellant' is modern, but restricted to a legal context. I prefer the archaic usage.

child's access to the weaponry afforded by the general('s) right to arms against an aggressor, unnamed but not unknown. The bullies blown away in the schoolyard.

The left falls in step, swinging right. Seduced by freedom as a call to arms. But I did not set out to write a diatribe on shooting freedom. I will defer this by way of the cool theme of 'metaphysical' freedom – one's power within the field of causes that compose the site of what one does. (Note, I did not write 'the site of *action*' – as if freedom in deploying causes must appear in the fine guise of *action*, *'agency'* and *'autonomy'*.)

Suppose we leave this reified freedom, look to freeing, and take up *nothing* as a verb. *To free* is to *noth*. To *noth* in one way is to *someth* in another. And vice versa. If *freedom* is *nothing* then, certainly there is no such thing as freedom.[2] There is no such thing as consciousness and still we are conscious. To be conscious is indeed to be free – it is to 'make nothing of' what one is and what surrounds one, so as to 'make something of it'.

Now the weight of waves of impending words is overwhelming. We must look to some textual craft – the work of reading and interpretation become as *nothing* on the instant. We make nothing of it, that is, we are free to do it, and we become conscious of the textual needs and powers. Consider the very year of 1968 around the 'events of May' in Paris and the rising ride of opposition to the U.S. involvement in the war in Viet Nam. Jacques Derrida in America was then settling a Sartre, not of *nothing-ing*, but of a reified consciousness, freedom and *man* ... settling all that into clay, ready to bake it for consumption in the remaining decades of the century. That Sartre's *being-for-oneself* and *being-for-others* were an *absence of being* could not be perceived through the thickets of a text that proclaimed a 'lucid consciousness'. If 'being is conscious (of)[3] itself' must this not be a 'metaphysics of presence'?

In connection with the standbys of metaphysical humanism, the repetition of *'liberté'*, *'conscience'* and *'homme'* carried the day ahead of Sartre's repeated *'nihilation'*, *'négatité'*, *'evanescence'*. Even the 'impossibility' of *man* as something that *is what it is not, and is not what it is* could not surface for Derrida, but now we are free to make a lighter reading of *'consciousness is a nothingness'*. To be conscious is 'to make nothing of' something about *being* – 'to make light of' how things are. Sartre's climber, conscious of a rocky crag, makes nothing of its obduracy to a road

[2] As in *'Freedom is for the birds'*; *'Freedom's when you've nothing left to lose'*.

[3] Bracketing the 'of' is a device Sartre introduces in the opening pages of *Being and Nothingness* to indicate that he is not alluding to some object *to which* consciousness is related. Thus, the consciousness (of) sadness *is* the consciousness, sadness. This 'of' has its counterparts in contexts like 'The City of Paris', which means, simply, 'The City, Paris'.

builder and in her desire to be on high, makes something of its leverage. *'To be conscious is to make nothing of something (or other)'* also makes light of *nihilation* itself. If we make nothing of *nihilation* itself it won't settle into a process behind the scenes. As if thus we might have understood how we experience the world that appears to us in all its guises.[4]

The adventures of these textual devices of Sartre's map those of Derrida's *différance, trace, supplément* and *relève*. Nevertheless, I would resist the inclination to use the parallels between *nihilation* and *différance* as a legitimation of Sartre after the event (Howells 1988: 194–201). To attempt that would produce inspissated scholarship – lead weights in Sartre's and in Derrida's boots. At the same time, tacitly to be conscious of these reverberations is to be free in the face of them, that is, to *nihilate* those very similarities. One's consciousness of 'them' will be left 'unthetic' – we make no 'them' of it, for our consciousness is nothing in the face of its objects. As understood in such a 'post-Sartre-ist' post-modernism, consciousness works as a catalyst – something that remains free of the substance of the reaction, enabling it to proceed at a lower temperature and at a more rapid rate. Derrida's own writing of the sixties and seventies, too, is now almost a matter of (living) history like the innovations by Sartre in 1943. We cannot make Sartre contemporary by 'doing a Derrida' upon him, or by making a Derrida of him. We take our own responsibility now, establish our own freedom in relation to each of them equally.

Freedom regains nobility in appealing to empathy with *oppressed peoples*. A government suppresses specific freedoms – to speak in public on political issues, to negotiate with others for a fair wages, to travel freely. The struggle to regain these freedoms – to do such things without humiliation or loss of one's rights – recovers for *freedom* its ring of a fine calling. *Freedom entails responsibility* sounds a call to those with power – not a threat of further burdens laid upon those already deprived. Freedom's *responsibility* then falls upon those in authority to grant, protect and foster *freedoms* for all citizens – and for visitors and those seeking asylum from *oppressive* authorities.

Being Determined and Being Free

'Hard', 'Soft' and 'Determined'

Sartre's *liberté* does not fit into the categories of solution to the 'problem of *freedom*' within which *'Everything is caused'* goes by the title of

---

[4] This reading expedites the critique of Sartre by Xavier Monastero (Silverman 1980).

determinism. '*Soft*' determinists hold that all events and states (including intentional actions) have their causes, and that nevertheless we are *free* in what we do. For '*hard*' determinists, since everything has its causes, we cannot be *free*. These titles are confused; each identifies *determinism* simply *as* the existence of causes for everything that happens or remains constant ('events' or 'states'). For both, if everything has its causes, everything is *determined*. Their difference is not of a 'hardness' or a 'softness' in their *determinism*, but whether, if everything (including intentional actions) is *determined*, we are still free.

No meaning beyond '*having causes*' is attached to *being determined*. The idea that 'Our actions are *determined* in that there are *causes* of what we do' nudges us to conclude that if there are causes of what we do, we are not free. Too late, the '*soft*' determinist takes issue, with a '*problem of freedom*' defined by '*determinism*'. One has to *dis*-lodge the idea that, in taking events as caused, a scientific view therefore regards them as *determined*. Otherwise it is axiomatic that 'nothing else could have been done'.

Thus, *soft determinists* appear in the guise of apologists, unable to rid their language of the tone of vainly striving against the odds. They are like those religious apologists who strain to show that '*although there is undeniable evil in the world for which we are not responsible, there may yet be an all powerful all knowing beneficent Being*'. It is an uphill task; the challengers waver between the heroic and the quixotic. The aura of foolhardiness persists even though the conclusion they would *safeguard* (a significant word) is 'common-sense' – that we are free and responsible.

As a first approximation, Sartre's attack on *determinism* as an attitude of bad faith resists the inference from *determinism* to a *lack of freedom* by means of a *moral* analysis. He neither refutes determinism *nor* shows it as consistent with our being free. He exposes the determinist's pretence of not possessing the very consciousness in which they choose one philosophical view over another.[5] It is the *determinist* whom Sartre charges with 'bad faith', not the one who says that there are *causes*. What emerges is that the language of *determinism* as describing a situation of cause and effect expresses a certain attitude on this causal situation. One might add a point in the style of J.L. Austin – those who have posed the problem as the relation of *one's being determined* and *one's being free* have been insensitive to the inflections of *determined* within various syntactical constructions.

---

[5] In a recent T.V. series on brain and consciousness headed by Susan Greenfield, John Searle jeered at those who believe in 'determinism' and preclude freedom. 'Every choice they make from a restaurant menu belies their view', he chortled.

To *be determined* in what one does is to take the utmost responsibility for it – to have exercised freedom to the full. '*I am quite determined to do this!*' I declare, rebutting any suggestion that I shall act compulsively, idly, in blind conformity, or on any other 'automatic pilot'. I tell you how and why I *am determined*, thus laying hold of the motives and considerations in what I have undertaken, making them my own business. I have *being for myself*, in Sartrean terms. I 'make nothing of' these factors which, as external *things in themselves*, would '*determine*' me in what I do. I suggested that, as a doctrine, 'determinism' ignores syntax. That everything has a cause implies that whatever I do is caused by some factors. But this does not imply that since everything has a cause, what I do is *determined* by them for me. And certainly it does not imply that since everything has a cause, I am *determined* to act – *determined* not to let life pass me by.

* * *

Do *causes* determine changes and continuances so that I misperceive some of them as 'my being *quite determined* to do (whatever)' rather than 'my being *determined by forces outside my control or ken* to do (whatever)'? We cannot prise apart these two inflections of '*I am determined*'. Despite our '*determinist*' leanings or fears, the passive form of '*being determined* in what I do' flips over into one's '*complete determination* to do it'. Not being able to prise apart these forms is our new form of Sartre's 'To be free is to '*nihilate*' – to '*no-thing*'. This speculation makes sense of Sartre's language of 'being conscious of', and thus 'metaphysically free of' causes. (A *nothing-ness* 'slips in' between past and present, present and future, decision and action.) One clears up the difference between *my being caused to do something by factors (outside my choice)* and *there being causes of my choosing and acting*. And then, instead of deciding whether *determinism* excludes freedom, we distinguish between accepting causes and declaring a '*determinism*'. The idiom of *determined*, ignored in the 'determinist' debate, allows that causes *make* us free. ('*Because of that, I am quite determined to do this.*') Equally, the idiom has it that by these same causes we are made *unfree*. ('*The causes determined me to do what I did.*') The difference between ' *hard*' and '*soft*' determinism vanishes.

Thus, an unflattering spotlight falls upon the word '*determinism*'. There are causes for the onset and persistence of my reasons and feelings and for these coming into play when I do something or when, more dramatically, I '*take action*'. But to say that these factors *determine* my reasons, feelings and motives adds nothing to saying the factors are causes of them. Nevertheless, the *determinist* language stacks the cards in the play of discussion of freedom. The figure that poses as a stern icon of science – *being absolutely determined by a full and complete set of causes* – is set against pathetic heroic *man*. In the face of 'overwhelming forces' this *man* must battle in vain.

Various philosophers have argued[6] that Sartre's position is close to '*soft*' determinism in its acceptance of causes and its insistence upon radical freedom, but it is much more precise to say that he challenges the link between the recognition of *causes* and the language of any *determinism*. '*Soft*' determinists insist, correctly, on the difference between '*This is fated*' and '*This is caused*'. This difference between *fatalism* and *determinism* closes over when pleading ceases, however, for the worlds of the '*soft*' and of the '*hard*' determinist are identical. In the Sartrean mode, '*nothing* lies between them'. In challenging the vision of *determinism*, Sartre can accept the causes of what we do as delineating the field of freedom. Naturally, there are, in turn, causes of this process of gaining freedom by recognising the field of causes. But the process continues. In recognising the causes of being able to recognise some factors and not others, we gain some freedom over that. There need be no process of freeing without its causes, nor any field of causes closed to the critical attitude that is our freedom in respect of them. There are three traditional models of how causes relate to freedom:

> Freedom is an epiphenomenon – a surface effect of causal processes.
>
> Freedom is a function of the whole field of causal processes that constitute illusion.
>
> Freedom is a 'counter-cause' from outside the field by which we withstand our inheritance, conditioning, habits and desires.

Sartre rejects the first as a delusive image of causal factors as '*bringing about*' what '*I*' do, for he rejects the ego as initiator. It is an evanescent *object* of consciousness. He asks, not about this 'I', but what it is to be conscious. Unlike Hume, he can welcome not being able to find the self. He rejects the second option ('libertarianism') as lacking credibility, since we do continue to uncover causes of all phenomena. Libertarianism, if resting on our 'sense of freedom', is an exercise in bad faith. I divorce my 'real' self from the world of influences, desires and habits, as if there were a *separate* 'I will' that can disclaim all of that. What Sartre says is closest

---

[6] For example, Morris 1976, McCulloch 1994 and Wider 1997.

to the third option. I *am* the complex web of causal processes that constitute me. 'I' am not in the grip of them for they are not external to me.

But how am I free, if I *am* this web of processes? If it is in bad faith that I regard my own emotions, habits and prejudices as if there were foreign to me, to combat with my free will, then freedom is exercised in the way I live out what I am. There is indeed no such 'thing' as freedom. This is what makes it possible for us to deceive ourselves, to overlook that we are constantly engaged in freeing ourselves from an attitude of submission to these causes. Freeing arises in 'making nothing of' these causes, as the situation demands.

Coping with Causes

Thus there exists freedom in the style with which we meet a situation, in the way we deal with what impinges, with how we confront habits and tendencies, though we cannot remove ourselves from the field of causes that stages every choice and event. Mostly, we construe these causes *subsequent* to the event, and this limits our control. Nevertheless, we can see in advance how someone will react with amusement rather than aggression to a certain kind of insult; or with understanding rather than rule-enforcement to a child's fractious behaviour. That we can predict what people do evidences, not their *lack* of responsibility as '*merely determined*', but that they were wholehearted. A person with mental strength, intelligence and good humour is reliable; he or she *bears with* remarks and behaviour that drive others to angry authoritarianism.

In the anglophone tradition there are persuasive exponents of a position like this, but the differences are important (Hume 1967: 399-407, Dennett 1984). In the position I am developing from Beauvoir and Sartre, it is not the '*soft*' determinist's picture that is compatible with freedom, since to be free is not to accept *determinism* as compatible with freedom, but to handle causes in certain ways. Reasons differ from causes, but as a kind of cause that is handled freely. Reasons are causes that I have 'nihilated'. I evaluate them as relevant to what I would achieve, and the causes of this evaluation themselves appear as already construed by a free consciousness. It is the attitude of *determinism*, not the existence of *causes*, that Sartre and Beauvoir challenge. In construing causes as *determining* me, I *abdicate.*

Responsibility requires not only that we appreciate what causes prevail but that this appreciation makes a difference to what we do. We develop mental balance, so to appreciate the causes that bear upon us, and we turn these to our advantage. This *power* has its place in the field of play of factors that influence and modify outcomes, but to lay claim to this does not mean: '*everything I do is, at bottom, merely caused*'. Freedom gives pride of place to the language of cause and effect *qua* power of thought or sense of humour. This is to accept, in turn, the causes for this partial freeing of oneself from causes, many of which will be unknown, but this does not threaten our freedom to choose opinions – about the issue of causes and freedom itself. We develop a freedom in respect of those hitherto unknown causes of freeing, too. Learning something of brain function, we modify the level of seratonin, decrease our intake of alcohol. And with less obvious chemistry, we have always known to take a deep breath, to stop and think. So, in the everyday we 'free ourselves from the causes' that would confine us to paths of over-determined conduct and feeling.

Like some causes that bind us, the causes of freeing oneself operate in the field of desires, fears and perception. We cultivate pride in some of our habits, skills and commitments, and enhance their effectiveness. Nevertheless, we must simply 'live in the light of them' for the most part, if we are not to fall into a regress of critical reflections. We understand the causes of how we free ourselves from causes by taking for granted our freedom in other respects.

Those with a theoretical eye for causes as the 'default' language of explanation will emphasise, as if against the language of freedom, how our 'free' control over causes must have its causes, known or unknown. But the autonomy of the language of causation does not authorise an attempt at hegemony. Neither '*caused*' nor '*free*' goes by default. We may reasonably assume, with Sartre, that causes operate in every field and in every case *and* that they may always involve our freedom. Our tissue of thought and resolve has been formed by previously chosen lines of action, thought and feeling, and our having taken issue with (or caved in to) the pressures to conform. Husserl calls these effects of habitually reinforced thought and choice, *sedimentation* (Husserl 1970b).

Interpreting Sartre's 'Absolute' Freedom

After the first wave of commentators[7] in the sixties and early seventies, LaCapra (1978), following Derrida, produced a new style of critique of *Being and Nothingness*. For LaCapra, '*part of [the book's] greatness*' consists in '*forms of internal self-questioning*', and he describes it as a creative form of writing that '*center[s] analytic and dialectical movement and [has] a decentering supplementary movement*'. He claims that the

---

[7] Including Warnock 1965, Manser 1966, Naess 1969, Lafarge 1970, Richter 1970, Grene 1971, Natanson 1972. Danto 1975, George 1976, Morris 1976 and Caws 1979.

weakness of Sartre's work is that '*the centering movement dominate[s] and the decentering movement [is] submerged*' (LaCapra 1978: 122). In this 'centering' movement Sartre insists on saying what consciousness *is*, what 'man' *is*, and proclaims a 'radical freedom' in which each man is absolutely responsible for his life. In this LaCapra follows Derrida (Derrida 1968) in diagnosing Sartre's text as a return to dualism. *Being-in-itself* and *being-for-itself* are counted as 'two realms of being'. '*Being-for-myself*' (to coin a phrase) is an 'immediate self-presence', a 'translucency of consciousness', and an 'invulnerability to doubt'. The being of something *in itself* is a 'pure positivity' that is incomprehensible in itself. The world I deal with is this *in itself* as it is *for me*.

Sartre's phrase 'two realms of being' occurs provisionally, early in the text. Shortly, it turns out that *being-for-oneself* (to coin a phrase) is not a being in addition to *being-in-itself*. It is a *lack* of being. So far as *being* is concerned there is only *being*, in itself. Sartre's *le néant* is not a *being*, but an absence, a *lack* of being, and in this *lack* we are conscious and free. LaCapra sees this as a sub-theme, overtaken by the 'positive', 'centering' tendency of the text. This 'sub-theme' appears to me in the foreground, as it does to Christina Howells, writing ten years after LaCapra. The question whether Sartre set up this division of *being-in-itself* and *being-for-itself*, of non-conscious and conscious, of unfree and free, runs in parallel with some other problems. Is Sartre's recognition of freedom and consciousness as always already in situation of language, culture and prior choices, also a 'sub-theme'? An 'absolute and radical freedom' that does not deny causality and has no sympathy with libertarianism seems to be deconstructive of metaphysics rather than traditionally 'positive and centering'. LaCapra declares that

[t]his tension between a notion of freedom as pure and total and a notion of freedom as always already situated is basic to the hesitations, equivocations, and paradoxes of Sartre's text (LaCapra 1978: 127–128).

But there is more to the genius and to the limitation of Sartre's 'freeing as no-thing'. The absoluteness of this freedom is its *faintness*. (Not that there is anything wrong with that, as Seinfeld liked to say.) I am free no matter what my situation because my freedom *is* the non-identity of consciousness with situation – that of which it is conscious. As such, (absolute) freedom has no purchase on the situation, being a perfect lubricant – the 'thin film' that 'slips in' between the past and the present, the motive and the intention, the intention and the act. This slippage is the guarantor of the 'purity' of freedom. And though this 'absolute' freeing has no power over a situation, *I* am effectual in the world. I have control over various parts of my psycho/physical life. As 'doer' I am responsible.

It is refreshing that in Sartre, as in Beauvoir, there is no neo-libertarian grand talk of '*Agent as incontestable author of his actions*'. Recent and contemporary 'action' theorists, intent upon importing moral seriousness into metaphysical analysis, speak of freedom with an over-emphasis that betrays anxiety. We should probe the jumpy nerve. My actions *are* contested as being my own if someone has prevented me thinking for myself. Furthermore, simple *doing*, if considered as *being author of my acts*, makes fiction of what was promoted as *real*.

But LaCapra reads this 'pure and total' freedom of Sartre's as like that grandiloquence just described – describes it as '*an empty spontaneity that approximates blind will, and allows only for a "leap" into commitment*' (LaCapra 1978: 122). Now, there *is* a 'blindness' in the freedom we have in being conscious, and Sartre's writing effectively calls attention to it. Consciousness is of its object, freedom arises in that consciousness, but only *after* the event is one conscious *of* the nature of the choice. Within the event of the act there was only (peripheral) awareness (of) one's choice. Though deliberate planning is possible, this 'what I plan' cannot coincide with 'what I do'. I may 'do as I had decided', but as formed by circum-stances and unforeseen eventualities, what I do is a reality of which the plan was a bare sketch. I took upon myself a concrete quality in what I did that I could never have previsioned. This 'spontaneity' in careful action is accentuated by deliberation, which separates itself off as prior to what I do.

LaCapra praises Sartre for the tensions he encompasses within the language of freedom, while upbraiding him for not '*undertak[ing] a sustained "deconstructive" reading of that tradition [of Western metaphysics]*' (LaCapra 1978: 128). He calls Sartre's statement of freedom a total '*appropriation*' of the metaphysical tradition, played off against minor '*decentering movements of contestation*'. In fact, Sartre describes freedom as situated and involved in a world structured by language, culture and death – outside the control of the one who was declared 'absolutely free'.[8] Sartre may not '*control that movement*' but he details situations and 'coefficients of adversity' and enables the reader to do so.

Sartre's story *is* more credible than his hyperbolic pronouncements, then, but serious questions remain. Does his differing of *being-for-itself* from *being-in-itself* permit that, in *freedom*, we gain purchase upon the world? '*Nothing but consciousness can bear upon consciousness*', he says, and consciousness as freedom must work upon being 'in itself'. Certainly,

---

[8] This constitutes the whole Fourth Part of *Being and Nothingness.* And Beauvoir devotes parts of Volume I and a great deal of Volume II of *The Second Sex* to the issue.

prior to the *Critique of Dialectical Reason*, Sartre placed freedom in a social context, but we shall have to see whether this is consistent with the categories of the first three parts of *Being and Nothingness*.

Xavier Monastero has begun to show how Sartre can combine his '*being-in-itself*' with '*being-for-itself*', so that his '*freeing as no-thing*' can be placed within situation and adversity. Monastero emphasises that we regard, as our very self, the body as it is 'in itself':

> The torrential river carries us ... and we go downstream with the other things ... [O]ur struggle with the river may come to an end, if we are knocked unconscious ... So we are not merely *in* the world; we are *of* the world ... Had Sartre realised his being as a body-thing, he could have sent his for-itself to sleep (Silverman 1980: 56–57).

This graphic narrative underrates Sartre's own emphasis that '*at least one of the modalities of the Other's presence to me is objectness*'.[9] Nevertheless, that he uses '*the for-itself*' as a grammatical subject makes it appear as a *self*, separate from the *in-itself*. If, for Sartre, the 'ego' or 'self' is a constantly changing *object* of consciousness,[10] then the conscious *for-itself* is no more what *I* am than is the body when considered as merely *in-itself*. *I* am not anything at all. To put this in Ryle's manner, 'I' is neither a name nor a description, but a token-reflexive. A by-product of the French infinitive, the definite article ('*the* in-itself' and '*the* for-itself') reifies *being-in-itself* and *being-for-itself*. '*L'être-pour-soi*', abbreviated to '*Le pour-soi*', becomes '*the for-itself*' rather than '*to be for itself*' or (as syntax demands) '*being-for-itself*'. This reification is uncalled for. '*Being-for-itself*' should rather be read as a mode like '*being sad*'.

That is how we may read Sartre's declarations that consciousness and freedom are *nothing*. So when Monastero describes the unconscious body as the same thing as what has *being-for-itself*, he is closer to Sartre than his tone implies. He writes that '*this allows us to see that the kind of freedom Sartre attributes to us in* Being and Nothingness *has little do with our reality*' (Silverman 1980: 62). Yes. Sartre's freedom and consciousness have *nothing* to do with our *reality*, if that is being *in itself*. Being *for itself* is not another 'reality', but an absence, an *activity* of 'nihilation' – not that life's difficulties lack 'facticity'.[11]

In dealing with the puzzling nature of Sartre's 'absolute' freedom, David Detmer (Detmer 1986: 57–70) rightly resists explaining omnipresent

---

[9] 'Objectité' – having the status of object, sometimes translated as 'objectity'.

[10] As he argued in *The Transcendence of the Ego*, prior to *Being and Nothingness*.

[11] Sartre's Chapter IV deals with differing 'in itself' from 'for itself', and bridging them.

freedom as a power to *think* as one likes, rather than the (incredible) power to *do* or to *be* what we choose. This distinction of 'thinking' and 'doing' was merely the scholastic strategy, '*when in contradiction, make a distinction*'. This use of it would save Sartre's credibility only by making his view banal. It does not explain that the freedom Sartre is interested in connects with social, political and economic choice. The freedom these 'moderate' critics offer as a palliative is a placebo, a daydream of freedom. And, in any case, there *is* no omnipresent 'freedom' to *think* what we like. Oppression can stall the power to think as we please, as it can stall anything.

Detmer also rightly dismisses another common palliative – that Sartre's absolute and omnipresent freedom is our power to form whatever *intentions* we please. A freedom to form unrealistic intentions, untested against any possibility of carrying them out, does not have the value or the omnipresence that Sartre would attribute to freedom. It smells of self-indulgence, foolishness and irresponsibility. Furthermore, it is *not* always and everywhere available to us. Time for prior deliberation is a rare luxury, and the phenomenology is inaccurate in any case. A freedom intrinsic to being conscious is not found in the continual formation of intentions.

Detmer maintains that Sartre's 'absolute omnipresent' freedom is distinguished from *practical* freedom, as *ontological*. This does not limit freedom to the power to *think* what we like, or to form whatever *intention* we like. If it exists, it has its place in everyday business, pertaining to anything we think, feel, intend or do, and does not mean that 'if we but try', we can do whatever we set out to. But what is this 'ontological' freedom, and how does it connect with our practical powers of choice?

We must recall, and take more seriously Sartre's idea that one is free simply in being conscious, and 'freely' conscious in *nihilating* what has being 'in itself'. This is what warrants Detmer in calling our (absolute) freedom 'ontological'. To *nihilate* is to 'make nothing of' a given situation. This is what it is to be conscious of it. There is only a semantic difference between the mode of being that is at once our *being conscious* and our *being free*. '*Conscious of*' points towards objects of perception, feeling or sensation, whereas '*free to*' prefigures *doing* this, and *thinking* or *feeling* that.[12] Detmer also reminds us how Sartre 'absolute' freedom *requires* its 'coefficients of adversity' to create the stage on which it plays out its part. It is this fact that connects freedom with practicalities – social, political and economic realities.

---

[12] This 'consciousness' is pre-reflective – that (of) which we are conscious.

Living Bodily in Time

A Narrator's Megalomania

Sartre presents us with an exciting image of us as living in time – displaced from our past as it slips from our grasp by the nothingness of what separates it from our present. That slippage, that displacement, occurs at the same rate as our movement ahead. This image presents us as free – from the past. A freedom we may desire intensely. In the same stroke, it seems, we can accumulate no capital from the investments we have made already in our deeds, emotions, connections with others, nor responsibility to ourselves as a continuing life. We may be left more exhausted than inspired by the promise of the next day as so 'new' that it is too fresh to be helped by yesterday.

Le Dœuff makes a powerful critique of Sartre's *relève* of absolute freedom, maintaining that the 'absurd passion' to be God, a *for-itself* as *in-itself*, saves the day for Sartre's demand for continual self-renewal:

> [T]he megalomania had to be endowed with a weakness and the For-itself's achievements be undone, so that Sartre could say that 'man-in-the-world' can only make himself 'a failed God' ... [I]t is necessary that ... a counter-figure should undo the work of integration and persistently compromise the For-itself in order to ensure that ... the For-itself's projects of conquest can continue indefinitely (Le Dœuff 1991: 87).

Le Dœuff elaborates. Sartre's narrator alternates between paranoia at woman's power as an indecipherable 'other', and triumph at her as a *being* that collapses into the *in-itself*. The (masculine) *for-itself* finds its 'sugary death' in the (feminine) *in-itself* – a bizarre, but not a gratuitous image:

> An encounter with death ... was necessary to guarantee the ... For-itself's identity, this being ... necessary for the perpetual repetition of its destiny. Every morning 'man' ... a For-itself starting from scratch ... must ... differentiate himself from woman-decay who is assimilated to a thing. He works in a god-like way, trying to integrate the In-itself by means of free action and knowledge. But every evening his work is undone, the In-itself takes its revenge and everything has to be started over again ... Moreover, anything which could not be given a theoretical foundation, but is necessary to make the system hold together ... is provided by sexism (Le Dœuff 1991: 87).

This acute (a cute) analysis exposes not only a philosophical motive, but also the logical dynamics of the system. Placing contradiction within the desire of 'man', theory is spared responsibility for its inconsistency. Le Dœuff insists that the theoretical outlook is *someone*'s, some *body*'s. We might add that if is not that of the youngish Frenchman M. Jean-Paul Sartre, then it is the (imaginary) body of the *narrative voice*. Jean-Paul must take responsibility for this authorial imaginary body that is immediately responsible for the body in the text, as for the body of the text. The narrative voice is responsible for discontinuities and awkwardness in the textual body, even as admiration accrues for its moments of levity and grace. Sartre does not ignore the constraining situation of action, but he does seem unaware of the constraints and biases of the authorial body. His authorial imaginary body is specifically masculine when it suits, then gender neutral, universalist, when that facilitates the story.[13]

Persisting Motivations

> Between the conception
> And the creation
> Between the emotion and the response
> Falls the shadow.   (T.S. Eliot, *The Hollow Men*)

What is the relevance of prior knowledge, decision, motive and habit, if a 'film of nothing' slips between them and the moment when we do something? If this 'film' puts out of play everything that has occurred up to the moment of action, shall we not be in terror at being out of control? Sartre sees us, rather, as in anguish at having to do one thing rather than another. Certainly, choice is made in a field that can impede or impel, but factors do not, intrinsically, impede or aid us. Their value changes as we reconstrue motivation. Sartre's famous rocky crag is an obstacle to a pathway, a challenge to a climber – or an inspiration to Cézanne. However I construe my motivation, I deal with a 'coefficient of adversity'. Climbers contend with the precipitousness that challenged them. Cézanne renders, in paint, within the bare frame of stretched canvas, the massive materiality of a mountain.

In the same way, there would be no chosen formation of temperament and character without a field of choice that includes one's irascibility, learned skills, and state of nerves. Mountains change their signs, depending upon how we deploy them. We can expect no less of our habits, liabilities and proclivities.[14] For instance, an irascibility that threatens a friendship

---

[13] Jean-Paul's record is only par for the course. To challenge it even now evokes cries of SUBJECTIVISM! PERSONALISM! RELATIVISM! POST-MODERNISM! DECONSTRUCTION!

[14] There is a seepage of terms from Ryle's *The Concept of Mind* here.

may be productive (in the short run) in business affairs. Plato's Socrates would say to his beloved Charmides that it must be 'tempered' by what is needed. One's 'nature' is not simply an impediment or an advantage. Like a mountain, a web of tendencies and skills is specified by reference to what we do, in what style. And, 'nihilated' into figure and ground, personal tendencies and skills, like mountains, form into 'given' objects that we confront and use. I cannot thus give myself a temperament, character or mood any more than I can give myself a situation or a mountain. This 'absolute' freedom that exists simply in my being conscious of these things haunts the stage, as utterly *faint*.

Sartre rightly points out that '*I resolved all this yesterday*' always permits '*What shall I do now?*' New facts may change the issue, or I may reassess the alignments and priorities of what I had worked out. This slippage does not make prior deliberation and resolution irrelevant – causally or morally – to what I proceed to do. We go over all the pros and cons of buying a house – its space, location and 'feel' – the repairs needed and the commitment. We decide on our maximum bid for tomorrow's auction. Yes, we tell ourselves, as we grow anxious about a decision, *we can always decide not to bid, to stop short. We are still free agents!*

This is true, but the sense of a consequent irrelevancy in prior deliberation is self-deceptive. To have given so much attention to the property, committing thought, time and imagination is to have set up a motivated momentum. It takes the force of mental effort, or unexpected events, to dissipate what is set in motion. If it's unwise to buy, it's better not to have looked so hard. On the other hand, the feeling '*we could always rearrange our priorities*' expresses, even as it smokescreens, a lack of commitment to the process of deliberation itself. The experienced car salesman picks the 'tyre-kicker' who plays at buying a 'motor'.

In the main, Sartre is right. To have deliberated and resolved to do something does not force me to do it when the time comes. I close on the deal – or just walk away from it. It is a free undertaking, so that when what I choose turns out to have its unexpected problems, I shouldn't pretend '*I was forced into it because I had already decided, had already told others I would*'. The social ceremonies associated with momentous choices such as marriages, and house or automobile purchases, are constructed to make it harder for 'purchase anxiety' to annul deliberated resolution. To walk out of the ceremony in front of the people one has prevailed upon to attend is embarrassing and difficult. Society can assume that only upon the emergence of very strong feelings will someone double back at the last moment. Does causation simply determine these formations of motivation and resolution, then? The question is misguided. Just as mountains, whether climbed, quarried, or painted, exist beyond the control of thought and imagination, the causes we deal with in thought, decision and action work in a field that one continues to construe even as one is affected.

The interplay of freedom as 'absolute' and as absolute in being subject to a situation is reflected in the interplay between freedom as burdensome and as liberating. Sartre's ground-rules seem to have instituted freedom as an inevitable and constant burden:

> [T]he meaning held for me by this desire, this fear, these objective considerations of the world ... must be decided by me alone. I determine them precisely and only by the very act by which I project myself towards my ends (BN, 450).

Sartre begins to resolve that old theme in a new direction, however:

> The recovery of former motives is not distinct from the project by which I assign new ends to myself and discover a supporting cause in the world. Past motives, past causes, present motives and causes, future ends, all are organised in an indissoluble unity by the upsurge of a freedom beyond causes, motives, ends (BN, 450).

And in a number of subsequent passages Sartre recognises *liberation* as a phenomenon beyond the weight of the freedom to which we are condemned. He writes of '*marvelous instants*':

> The instant at which Gide's Philoctetes casts off his hate, the instant when Raskolknikoff decides to give himself up – when the prior project collapses in the light of a new project which rises on the ruins ... in which humiliation, anguish, joy and hope are delicately blended, in which we let go in order to grasp and grasp in order to let go (BN, 476).

Sartre's emphasis on the burden and anxiety of freedom requires the reaction of such a flourish of optimism. This counter-image of thrilling creativity is prompted by the continuous theme of freedom as a 'nihilation' within otherwise stifling being. And yet Sartre likes to minimise these more creative moments – as when he evoked so well how 'we' arise as a subject. He states that these 'marvelous' instants make his view of the '*inefficacy of voluntary decision less offensive*' (BN, 476). Motive, cause and occasion of an act gain their significance in the action they promote. But Sartre still proceeds to infer that prior deliberation is a sham because it does not directly cause what I do. (Sartre, 'les jeux sont faits': Wittgenstein, 'a wheel that turns no wheels'.) This resembles a parallel mistake made by Gilbert Ryle who rightly debunks the 'will' as a special or unique inner cause, but wrongly infers its causal irrelevance to our 'inner' as to our 'public' life.[15] Prior deliberation stands amongst the factors that inflect or moderate or intensify what we do. There *is* an existential gulf between deliberating and taking action. This does not, however, negate the effect, whether faint or striking, of that deliberation whose effect is observable on the pattern of inner life. Deliberation modifies feelings and intentions – and thus the form and style – of what we do. This change is partial, unstable, evanescent, and real.

Demoralised

'Back to the rough ground' (Wittgenstein).

The 'nothingness' of freedom generates the Sartrean hyperbole: *Freedom is absolute and unlimited. We are always and everywhere free. Nothing can limit our freedom. The prisoner is as free as his warder.* And yet, far from denying social impediments, poverty, sickness and oppression, Sartre emphasises that these set us to act. His metaphor of a 'film' that frees cause from effect, past event or action from present is instructive. The source and viability of this 'nihilating' is the business of the next chapter – the question here is what liberation from our situation it can achieve.

We have to place equal weight on both words of Sartre's subtitle to *Being and Nothingness* – a 'phenomenological ontology'. Sartre is at once continuing within ontology – speaking of what there is and how we can thus understand phenomena – and insisting on the primacy of phenomenology – on being *as it appears*. This 'ontological freedom' must be already *domestic* – not a 'barely intelligible somewhat' that lies behind experience, but decipherable within experience at every moment. We therefore stay close to 'ordinary language' in assessing this 'ontological' freedom, even as we recognise that this omnipresent freedom, real and detectable, is not one's power simply to change things as one would desire.

But can we accept an attribution of absolute freedom to all conscious intelligent beings? The language of 'freedom' as simply the other side of 'consciousness' cannot make a *theme* of oppression (Le Dœuff 1991, 55– 74). Sartre would admit the fact of oppression as the enforced pain of some choices, but this might not be enough for the victim of oppression who is conscious of having lost, not merely this or that specific freedom, but their power of choice. In Sartre's terms, and at times in Beauvoir's, the victim is

---

[15] For more on these issues see Arendt 1971. Also, Husserl's contemporaries, Reinach, Lipps and Stein produced important work on motives and causes (Sawicki 1997: 9–43).

deemed existentially *guilty* – of 'bad faith' (Beauvoir 1972: 21, 288). Despite the emphasis on 'situation' in the fourth Part of *Being and Nothingness*, freedom is a challenge for victim and oppressor alike.

It is demoralisation that threatens the elemental freedom that Sartre identifies, and here, Beauvoir has shifted the treatment of freedom in order to recognise oppression. A demoralised victim of oppression loses a sense of freedom of choice, feeling they have no mind of their own, no place, no *premises* for action. Only someone acting in solidarity with the demoralised might reinspire in the victim the voice of the universal but 'faint freedom' that *it is I who thus respond to my oppressor*. This is not a standing fact to be pronounced from the heights of metaphysics; the need for solidarity with the oppressed must be grafted on to Sartre's existential ontology. The persistent consciousness of outrage at oppression that Beauvoir displays is part of that very work of solidarity that *achieve*s rather than *decrees* a universal free consciousness.

A perpetual conflict exists – political, conceptual and empathic – between freedom as part of the very existence of any conscious intelligent being, and as something that may be hammered out of someone who is still consciously doing something. There is, for instance, a controversy in Australia on an issue called 'mandatory sentencing'. Every attempt even to state the problem exhibits 'bias' to those who desire a particular solution. A government of a 'Territory', in response to some popular opinion, has enacted laws that impose a mandatory prison sentence for any repeated offence, whether for major crime or for petty theft. No discretionary powers are allowed to a magistrate or judge. The legislation is aimed particularly at those – predominantly aboriginal and frequently very young – convicted of repeated minor theft or similar infringements upon private property. In a case that made front-page news, a fourteen-year-old aboriginal boy, convicted of stealing a packet of biscuits and given a six-month prison term in a town hundreds of kilometres from any relative who might have visited him, committed suicide.

One may wish to have nothing to do with such an ugly and conceptually messy piece of domestic politics. It is easier to keep to the purity of Sartre's 'being' and 'nothing', or analytical philosophy's 'determinism' and 'free-will'. And, if one does swing into social controversy, how much easier it is to flourish clichés than to engage in the unnerving business of deconstructing them. You know the phrases – 'democratic freedom to enact what the people want' as against 'freedom of the judiciary from parliamentary interference'; 'uncontrolled juveniles who have to be taught the value of property', as against 'impoverished and alienated victims of white invasion' and so on. We can make some use here of Sartre's exposure of the ambiguities in attributing absolute freedom of choice to all conscious intelligent beings, and recognising that this freedom is bound within a situation of friction and obstruction without which it would not even exist.

Apprised of this ambiguity, we are then more ready to articulate how the seizure of the language of freedom by the powerful has the power of its unassailable contradiction in enforcing an image of *being free* upon those with least power. We can then trace the detail in the use of *'free'* in populist self-proclamations. A majority of voters in a district *will* be 'free of the local trouble-makers'. They *will* be 'free to elect whoever we please to enact whatever laws please us'. They *will* be 'free to tell those soft-minded do-gooders,[16] what sentences they must announce, regardless of the offence'. It is at once bizarre and natural that this 'seizure' in the name of freedom' *enforces* complicance on those who do not have the power to lay hold of freedom themselves.

In this connection, commentators on Sartre's *Nausea* have observed how the speech of the (reactionary) Autodidact is a virtual parody of the language of absolute freedom employed in *Being and Nothingness* (Howells 1988: 65-67, LaCapra 1978: 107, 114). *'It's always up to us to make something of our life'*, *'You've always got a choice'*, and so on. The voice of 'radical freedom' and the voice of 'right wing ruthlessness' have the same lexicon. This tells us something. It is in tone – as aware of the power status of speaker and hearer – that they differ. That tone reflects the actual or imagined status of the speaker. When Le Dœuff reads in Sartre's system, *'It is therefore senseless to think of complaining since nothing foreign has decided what we feel, what we live, or what we are'*,[17] she hears something more. She hears the voice of men who have *'from time immemorial alienated, beaten and deprived [women] of political, sexual and social rights and legal identity'* (Le Dœuff 1989: 100). An oppressive voice that blames the victim.

However, one can detect, in Sartre's insistence on an implicit 'choice' in all of one's conscious life, a different tone of voice that is in sympathy with the oppressed. To hear this, it is best to start from Kafka, a writer admired by Sartre and Beauvoir. In Kafka's stories it is the powerful who deny their own freedom. *The Trial* and *The Castle* exhibit the bureaucrat, who holds power over Kafka's disempowered narrator, as affecting powerlessness – as if a puppet of his role. The language of *Being and Nothingness* enables one to see (and say) that one who has *'being-for-themselves'* (to coin

---

[16] Those, that is, who are imagined to constitute and influence the judiciary.

[17] Le Dœuff cites this from *Being and Nothingness* (Le Dœuff 1991: 60).

a phrase) is free to stretch what their position allows. One can take an initiative – bring a problem forcefully to the attention of a superior, risk one's position when an urgent injustice demands it. Here, the language of an absolute freedom, however slight its power, cuts into the hypocrisy, indifference or cruelty that is so 'properly dressed' in position and law.

If the call of 'absolute freedom' is not to condemn Kafka's disempowered narrator, it must sacrifice part of its conceptual investment. Still aware of impinging events, someone may have temporarily lost their freedom in what they do, feel and think. One may be dominated by another's will, paralysed in thought and feeling by the unbreakable silence of enforced conventions, or demoralised by shame and threat. And yet we need not forget the *appeal* of Sartre's metaphysical proclamation that in every situation every conscious one of us is free. None of us can choose our situation of choice, yet the recall of this absolute freedom, faint as it is, is of the utmost value to life.

On a radio program, women who had become pregnant in their adolescence now recall what they had experienced as their total lack of freedom in 'giving up', as it was described to them, their babies for adoption. They describe their state of mind when in the hands of their parents, priests and nuns. Their thinking occurred in such terms as '*I had no option but to part with my baby*', '*All I could think of was to do what my family expected*' or else an absence of terms – '*I was in a fog about everything*'. Now, in a spirit of relative power and comprehension, some having now reunited with their lost children, they wonder about the nature of the paralysis of thought, feeling and will that had, apparently, so totally possessed them. They ask just the kind of questions one might find in *Being and Nothingness*.[18] '*I was told that I should not see or touch my child*', said one, '*but what actually prevented me from just getting out of bed and going to the crèche in the hospital and holding my child?*' One of the women ponders, '*The baby was my own. Why didn't I just take it and walk out of hospital?*' Another speaks of the '*censure of silence*' that seemed impossible to break through. It was not even said, by her parents, that it would be impossible to face the neighbours if she appeared in the street, unmarried, with her baby. Everything conspired to produce the effect that if only she kept silent too, and they kept silent about the necessity of silence, everything in the home and the street would simply go on as usual. Nothing would ever have happened.

---

[18] Immediacy of feeling within abstractions is bizarre, but provokes thought. This is Sartre's strategy in creating movement between story, image and argument.

In what these women recall, the reader of *Nausea* will recognise Roquentin's feeling of disconnection from words, the disconnection of those words from things, and his disconnection from events and people. In subsequent writings (BN, 338), Sartre explains that this reference to 'nausea' is not a *metaphor* of disgust, but is nausea at the obdurate fact of our existence. *Anguish* became legendary as the Sartrean[19] emotion that reveals to us that inescapable freedom implicit in being conscious of anything, but at this later stage what comes to the fore is an equal *factual* necessity in the awareness of the existence of the body in its conscious freedom. It was in *anguish* that we felt more *intensely* – as inescapable – the freedom that arises in *voiding* the body of its mere factuality. But nausea is no less intimate and consuming than anguish though it operates (in fact and as literary figure)[20] at the level of sensation rather than emotion. So the strange atmosphere of *Nausea* and of *Being and Nothingness* is made more comprehensible by such stories as those women tell, of disconnection. Disconnection operates both as cause and as effect of loss of affect. With that loss goes loss of the sense of choice, and with that, the loss of choice itself.

---

[19] Beauvoir's writing is more inflected: '*[H]e does not like difficulty; he is afraid of danger. He aspires in contradictory fashion both to life and to repose*' (SS, 172).
[20] To say that *nausea* operates as literary or philosophical *figure* jars with Sartre's denial that it is a *metaphor* for disgust. But *nausea* has become a powerful figure despite himself.

4

A Void

A Void in Perception

'Le Néant' and 'Les Petits Riens'

Le néant – void, emptiness, nothing – is to be found in a myriad of *négatités* – *les petits riens*,[1] and these *négatités* are found by scrutiny, or a casual glance. Sartre expresses, with the skill of someone who understands the sources of such an error, the feeling that what is positive presents all that has to be said about a situation:

> [T]he café by itself with its patrons, its tables, its booths, its mirrors, its light, its smoky atmosphere, and the sounds of voices, rattling saucers and footsteps which fill it – the café is a fullness of being (BN, 9).

What *is* there but positivity? Negativity is what there *is not*. Telling the story of the presence, (that 'fullness') of positivity produces its own deconstruction. The image of presence provokes our perception of the other side of the story. A specific 'nothingness', someone's absence, is given to the senses. I can be correct or mistaken about whether someone is *not* in a room. I can see them or tell from their voice that they *have* arrived, or look and see that they have not, or hear that their voice is absent from a buzz of conversation. Perceptual skills are involved in determining such absences:

> When I enter this café to search for Pierre ... each element ... a person, a table ... attempts ... to lift itself upon the ground constituted by the totality of the other objects, only to fall back ... into the undifferentiation of this ground (BN, 9).

Sartre's figurative description summons up the questioning eye that scans the room, a schoolmaster inquiring whether a certain student is present. 'Pierre Jourdain?' he asks of each, who 'attempts to isolate himself', to lift himself from his anonymity amongst the 'totality of the others', only to

---

[1] The source of the phrase is the title of some clarinet music by Mozart.

'fall back once more into this ground' as he mutters 'No sir!'. The other figures are present as a mass, constituted by each 'not being Jourdain':

> Thus the original nihilation of the figures which appear and are swallowed up ... is the necessary condition for the appearance of the principle [sic][2] figure ... of Pierre (BN, 10).

That was the scanning stage,

> but now Pierre is not here ... In fact Pierre is absent from the whole café; his absence fixes the café in its evanescence; the café slips into the background; it pursues its nihilation. Only ... it presents the figure everywhere to me (BN, 10).

The narrative, oiling the wheel with *'evanescence'* and *'nihilation'*, gathers momentum:

> This figure ... is Pierre raising himself as a nothingness on the ground of the nihilation of the café. [W]hat is offered to intuition[3] is a flickering of nothingness ... of the ground ... and the figure ... slips ... to the surface of the ground (BN, 10).

The narrative summons the metaphysics. The eye flicks across the room to check for Pierre, so 'nothingness flickers!' Pierre's absence involves every – and yet no particular human sized – volume of the room – *'Pierre is absent from the whole café'*. The use of 'nothingness' as a subject that 'flickers' is given currency by the activity of the senses. The flick of the eye, the inquiring touch. *'It is an objective fact at present that I have discovered this absence'*. Yes, and yet this 'fact' invokes the ghostly: *'Pierre absent haunts this café and the setting in which I am looking for him'* (BN, 10). Subjective objectivity. Objective subjectivity.

How we 'Cause' these Voids

We who observe these absences are not innocent bystanders:

> [T]o be exact, I expected to see Pierre, and my expectation has caused the absence of Pierre to happen as a real event concerning this café (BN, 10).

My expectation *'causes'* this absence? This has to read with intelligence. What is 'caused' is that *Pierre is in the café* amounts to an 'absence', a

---

[2] A slip in the translation – evidently 'principal' is intended.
[3] Sartre's 'intuition' here is Kant's 'direct sensory awareness of something'.

'real event'. Sartre points out that for most names, it is 'no event' that the person was not there:

> [J]udgements which I make subsequently to amuse myself, such as 'Wellington is not in the café' ... have a purely abstract meaning ... without real ... foundation ... they never establish a real relation between the café and Wellington (BN, 10).

Sartre sets up the scene to show negative judgements as founded in experience, but produces the reverse effect:

> We believed for a moment that the negation could arise from the comparison instituted between the result anticipated and the result obtained (BN, 11).

Sartre has brandished the rhetoric of *objective fact*, which contributes to his logical embarrassment: The *café ... with its patrons, tables, booths, mirrors, light, smoky atmosphere* loses its hold. Pierre has not come; the narrator must leave. We overhear the curse: *I expected to find 1500 francs – there are 1300!*[4] Ontologists, too, must pay for what they drink while waiting, and the hard-nosed Sartre now pays his logical debts, too. When we contemplate an absence we have in mind how the world is, not only that we use 'ne ... pas', he says. The hope (or fear) that made us scan the café elicited absence as a fact, obdurate, like presence.

Although the *absence* involved a tension between the narrator's expecting Pierre in the café and his perceiving only others there, it is a further *perceptual* judgement (*'that Pierre is absent'*) that reveals how things are. Context as well as expectation makes a difference. Mittérand was not there either, but unless he was liable to frequent Paris cafés he was not *absent*, any more than was the Duke of Wellington. Stated in 1943, *'Hitler is not in the café'* is marginal between an empty thought and a perceived reality – 'here, briefly, life can be normal'. The pomp of the dictator means he excludes himself.

Sartre argues that because most true negative sentences can be stated only facetiously,

> non-being does not come to things by negative judgement; it is the negative judgement, on the contrary, which is conditioned and supported by non-being (BN, 11).

---

[4] The mood descended earlier, too, from talk of 'being' to counting cigarettes.

But how is negativity 'objective' if negative statements can be taken seriously only in limited contextual conditions? An argument ensues. That the narrator *has* 1300 francs and *expected* to find 1500 does not amount to the negative fact that he has *lost* some, or does *not have enough* money. It is not correct to place negation 'in the mind' as a *'form of sorting out and separation'*. This would *'remove ... negativity from the negation'* – that something was *not* present would add nothing to what *is* present.

Sartre apprehends a wish to 'make nothing of' negativity itself. We might come to confine it to the empty thoughts which may be *'suddenly released by [our] affirmative judgements'*. To sit in a café (m)uttering *'Ned Kelly is not here'* or *'The café is not made of margarine'* is to have let loose that irruption of negative sentences of which Sartre has warned.[5] Sartre has let loose a productive thought, though. The emptiness of most true negations is mirrored in the emptiness of most true affirmations. As I sit in the café saying, *'The expresso machine is on the counter top'*, *'At the café they serve coffee'*, *'At each table there are chairs'* I lose, equally, all sense of language having any purchase on the world. As Sartre remarks, almost inadvertently, it is the emptiness of statements uttered with no contextual or perceptual point that disturbs the sense of their 'grip on reality'. Truth becomes a triviality with no leverage.

How close to the wind of subjectivity must Sartre sail, to rescue negativity's objectivity? Truth as *just lying there, waiting to be stated* is not enough. All true negative statements, 'formal' and 'real' would be objective, but *'negation is a refusal of existence ... by which a being ... is thrown back to nothingness'*. This force of intervention is our observing absence, loss and death. If there were only positivity there would be nothing 'poisonous' about strychnine. Someone would imbibe it, go into spasms, chemical processes would occur in their muscles and nervous systems. Then (to 'disrupt the wall of positivity') bacteria *decompose* the body. The need for this 'disruption' taints negativity with 'subjectivity', but looking for objectivity in positivity leads to paradox. *Being-in-itself* can be described only in context, so only *being-in-itself* 'in itself' – pure being – would be purely positive. This *Being* cannot be judged, perceived or theorised. *Being itself* thus stands still, still stands – an unspeakable silence as the condition of the noise of inquiry. As Sartre pronounces,

Being is. Being is in-itself. Being is what it is (BN, xlii).

---

[5] 'Philosophy is what happens when language goes on a holiday', says Wittgenstein.

Freedom and Vertigo

How Causes Slip Away

Le néant had slipped in to the café without the perceiver's striving – a disturbance of *a full world of things and events* rather than its *source*. Sartre described a real moment in experience. Then vertigo, induced by *le néant*, lodged *nausea* in philosophy's gullet. Still, the existential imbalance could right itself. If there is vertiginous *nothing* to keep us on the path above the abyss then, equally, there is *nothing* to make us plunge headlong. Freedom appears as something by which we can lever upon our actions and emotions, on the fulcrum of causality. This freedom emerges as something we might take up, lay aside, or leave to *bind*[6] in dis-use.

But freedom was to be something no conscious being could lose. Consciousness *is* nihilation – freeing past from present, me from you, one aspect of emotion from another. And yet, freedom appears equally as a precious power to be guarded, always liable to be diminished or lost. This contradiction produces alternating images of freedom as intolerable, and as a relief from suffocation. If we leap forward to the Fourth Part of *Being and Nothingness*, we find Sartre considering the obstacles to action, analysing what oppressed workers lacked. As conscious, they must have

> the permanent possibility of effecting a rupture with [their] own past ... so as to confer on it the meaning it has, in terms of the project it does not have (BN, 436).

Suffering does not alone explain the 'rupture with the past' we call revolt:

> [M]an immersed in the historical situation does not succeed in conceiving of the failures and lacks in [the] ... economy ... [H]e apprehends it in its plenitude of being (BN, 434).

Sartre connects not the 'harshness of conditions' but the perception of *absence* – of what *should* be present – with the gaining of freedom. This is an achievement of imagination. Only then do we

> conceive of a different state of affairs; a new light falls on our troubles and our suffering and ... we decide that these are unbearable (BN, 435).

Only by this imagination do we *'effect a rupture with [our] own past'*. To appeal to pre-existing *motives* already presumes the possibility of revolt.

---

[6] The lubricated surfaces of machinery left in the weather 'bind' to each other.

We form motives out of sufferings and skills when the image of what is *not*, 'effects a rupture' between past and present.

Now, Sartre had described, hundreds of pages earlier, how in being conscious we strive, frenetically, to reconvert feeling into the stable form of the '*in-itself*'. So how could the workers have failed to make the 'rupture' between past and present? The break between fact and possibility achieved within suffering is itself a work of consciousness. Sartre's text becomes uneasy, and historical examples pretend to ease the tension:

> [F]ollowing a riot, the workers at Croix-Rousse do not know what to do with their victory; they return home bewildered, and the regular army has no trouble in overcoming them (BN, 435).

Well, a worker might '*lack education and reflection*', and this could explain why he does not know what to do. No doubt, for such a one,

> [h]is suffering is the pure affective tenor of his non-positional consciousness [that] ... he does not contemplate (BN, 435).

But this suggests that freedom lies in *reflective* consciousness. Is the 'refusal of freedom in bad faith' just one's failure to reflect, then? As Sartre's theory develops and faces our situation, its tensions become acute. For all that a motive is not a blindly operating cause, a worker's suffering may be a motive even before he contemplates it, since conditions are *suffered*. This suffering speaks of the work of consciousness, of a 'rupture' with facticity. Nothingness has already slipped in between fact and response since feeling is a nihilation. Sartre's workers already constitute themselves *as suffering*. They escape realising this only by another 'wrenching' nihilation – *bad faith*. In being conscious they cannot be innocent. But here, at this late stage, Sartre issues a metaphysical pardon. For the workers, '*suffering and being are one and the same*'. In this, Sartre evinces class-consciousness – nostalgia for the 'unquestioning life of the peasant'. In being placed outside the cycle of bad faith he derogates the workers. Will their consciousness have to be raised by an 'avant-garde'?

Critics complain that Sartre has not dealt with the economic and political setting of action, and, nearly two decades later, Sartre was to construct his *Critique of Dialectical Reason* to deal with this. Yet, even here, to sheet home this theoretical 'lack' to the 'bad faith of the author' would miss something more interesting – an '*operative contradiction*' in his metaphysics. If consciousness is a 'nihilation of being', the suffering cannot exist as undifferentiated. Lack of education may leave suffering's motive unformed, but for uninformed workers no less than guilty-as-hell employers, 'nothingness lies coiled in the heart of being', and identification with one's situation is a frenzy of bad faith.

If feelings are to take form as specific motivations, anyone needs specific information, a precisely formed imagination. But to suffer, to have feelings, is already to have *some* motives. Those feelings are described with respect to the motives they form, and are already a form of freedom. If one feels fear there is freedom:

> I have put all my freedom into my fear and I have chosen myself as fearful in this circumstance. Under other circumstances I shall have put all my freedom into courage ... All my modes of being manifest freedom equally (BN, 445).

I have 'chosen myself' in taking responsibility for what it turns out I have done – not for 'announcing choices'. To 'choose myself' in what I do is to be like the athlete who, when the gun is fired that silences qualms and wild hopes, instantly takes up the very pace s/he can sustain.

An Ontology of Voids

Sartre concludes this phase with a strange question: '*Where does nothingness come from?*' Naïve? Profound? The question generates a further search into being, value and freedom. '*Being*'? Like Heidegger's *being*, Sartre's is not an abstract 'universal'. He takes Hegel's warning:[7]

> Pure Being is pure abstraction and consequently absolute negation, which taken in its immediate moment, is also non-being (BN, 13).

It is the gesture towards *being itself* which provoked us to bay at the moon. If *nothingness* is itself '*complete emptiness, absence of determinations and of content*', ponders Sartre, '*are pure being and pure nothingness then the same thing?*'. Hegel thinks that '*this difference cannot be named; it is only pure opinion*' (BN, 13), and Sartre joins with Heidegger in claiming that phenomenology should distinguish *being* and *nothingness*. But, then, does *nothingness* derive from being, are they reciprocally dependent, or is *being* founded on *nothingness*? Sartre rejects the last:

> Being and non-being [are] on the same plane [but] we must be careful never to posit nothingness as an original abyss from which being arose (BN, 15).

---

[7] Sartre is like Wittgenstein in criticising 'sensations' as 'private': Each asks, in effect, 'What is the difference between nothing, and something about which nothing can be said?'

Nothingness 'always supposes a preliminary specification of being'. *'Touch nothing'* ... means, *'nothing of that collection'* (BN, 15). What of *being* and *nothingness* in cosmology? *'Can't we ask ourselves "what was there" before a world existed, and ... reply "Nothing"?'* (BN, 16). The world may not always have existed, but this establishes no priority for a 'nothingness' before 'something'. That the world did not always exist is founded upon our involvement within its existence.[8] Thus metaphysics comes home to roost in narrative and imagery. Haven't we heard something like this, three hundred years before the 1943 of *Being and Nothingness*?

> What then am I? A conscious being [res cogitans]. What is that? A being that doubts, understands, asserts, denies, is willing, is unwilling; further, that has sense and imagination (Descartes 1954: 70).[9]

This Descartes doubts everything. He would place everything within the realm of *nothingness* rather than *being*, but is thrown back onto *being*, something required in order that the world *be* 'doubted' ('bracketed', as Husserl will write), treated *as if* it had no being. What of the status of the *being* which is summoned up? It must be, it seems, none of the beings already 'doubted'. Nor can it be the *nothingness* that would belong to everything if his doubts happened to be right on the mark after all. And 'the rest is history' – downhill all the way. Descartes raised up the *soul* as another substance and gave it nothing but headaches. That his argument for the distinction is a formal fallacy has not lessened the fascination of its site of operation. We have had Leibniz's in-communicating monads, Hegel's *Geist* and Husserl's *transcendental ego*, that does everything ever asked of Descartes' 'substantial self' without having to *be* anything.[10] We have suffered the last five decades of this last century in Ptolemaic epicycles of effort, trying to show that everything to be said of the self as a 'thinking doubting being' is *fully* stated within the language of the 'physical'.[11] Desperate problems, desperate measures. What are Sartre's?

---

[8] Unprovoked denials speak of suppressed possibilities. Hebraic and Australian Aboriginal creation myths, for instance, pose the problem as how order was brought of chaos. Matter is there in order that creation be possible.

[9] Hair stands up on the back of my neck when I recall how it is the *negativity* that Descartes finds in his being from which he derives a God within himself.

[10] An old proof of the non-existence of God: If God is that being no greater than which can be conceived, then God does not exist. An all-powerful being that did not need to exist would be greater than one that depended upon it.

[11] To have any bite, that last term has to stand for 'physics'.

Laying Hold of Motivations

The Nothingness of Undifferentiated Being

Sartre inflects Heidegger's '*Dasein is ontically distinguished by the fact that in its being (it) is concerned about its very being*', writing, '*The being by which nothingness arrives in the world must nihilate nothingness in its being*' (BN, 23). Thus he elaborates on scanning for Pierre, whose '*absence requires a negative moment by which consciousness constitutes itself as negation*' (BN, 27). From such gentle beginnings fierce consequences flow:

> Insofar as I use negatités to isolate and determine existents ... the succession of my 'states of consciousness' is a perpetual separation of effect from cause (BN, 27).

Sartre offers an image of deriving that metaphysics of causal separation:

> [I]nasmuch as my present state would be a prolongation of my prior state, every opening by which negation could slip through would be ... blocked (BN, 27).

This is to think of cause and effect as operating in the (illegible) realm of pure positivity, as if 'one thing caused another' within being itself! Since the picture of 'one thing' and then 'another' is intrinsic to 'cause' and 'effect', cause and effect involve differentiation, and differentiation *already* involves negativity.[12] This (ontological) negativity is the other side of the *nihilating* function. Conceptually, causality cannot be prior to it. This suggests a line of argument against Sartre's image of 'nihilation' as the creative (and destructive) rupture between cause and effect.

Like the everyday nothingness we encounter as *les petits riens*, cause and effect too arise only on the ground of (prior) nihilation. The world of cause and effect is 'always already' built in as the arena of the freedom implied by nihilation. To find causality incompatible with freedom would be absurd. The physical and social arena of football (or of painting) that is created by our joint and repeated choices to kick a ball to someone (or to put paint to canvas for exhibition) cannot be incompatible with the activities that set in train their (now) more highly structured motions.

How does the 'ontological dimension' impute this 'separation of cause from effect' to negativity? Sartre had said at the outset that '*every question ... posits the possibility of a negative reply*' so that '*an Existent can always be revealed as a nothing*'. That is, something can turn out to be other than

---

[12] Negativity is no threat to the status of causality if it too is 'ontological'.

it appeared. This '*possibility of a negative reply*' means that '*we realise a nihilating withdrawal in relation to the given*' (BN, 23).

Suppose there is a waterspout, its fall suspended in mid-air 'given' in a sculpture garden.[13] I make what Sartre calls a 'nihilating withdrawal'. You know. '*What is going on here? Solid? Liquid? Is it real?*'. Sartre would say that what is given '*fluctuate[s] between being and nothingness*' (BN, 23). Yes, the 'given' – the water falling, hanging in mid-air – 'fluctuates between being' ('*yes, its really happening!*') and 'nothingness' ('*no, its a thin film of water over a perspex mould, collected behind the lower ridge, and pumped back*').

That *trompe-l'oeil* is not purely 'nothing' – no thing could be just *nothing*. Sartre rightly rejects *nothingness* as such along with *being* as such. (His '*petits riens*' are not petty, though, since no set of positive propositions amounts to the statement of an absence.) But how exactly does the 'nihilating' function of the *for-itself*, in questioning anything as given to us in perception, achieve a slippage between cause and effect?

In Slips the Void

The slip is engineered by what dwells in an '*exquisite region of Being*':

> It is essential therefore that the questioner have the permanent possibility of dissociating himself from the causal series which constitutes being, and which can produce only being (BN, 23).

Sartre forestalls the reply that a cause/effect series is a total determinant of every event in every aspect, prior to any interpretation:

> If we admitted that the question is determined in the questioner by universal determinism then that the question arises would become ... inconceivable (BN, 23).[14]

Interpretation establishes distance between effects as positive events and as free acts of raising questions – and this is not to deny causality. In the Fourth Part of *Being and Nothingness* Sartre rejects any (neo-medieval) 'libertarian' self whose freedom consists in '*there exist[ing] no [full] prior cause*' for one's decision. Sartre claims that '*there is no action without a cause, and that the most insignificant gesture refers to causes and*

---

[13] I 'bracket' what is 'given', as Husserl would suggest.
[14] I have abbreviated and adjusted the standard translation here.

motives'.[15] Sartre argues that since *'every action must be intentional, each action in hav(ing) an end ... is referred to a cause'* (BN, 436).

Sartre refers to the *tediousness* of the debate between the libertarians and the determinists. Each is hooked into the 'blindingly obvious'.[16] The libertarian *knows* he must be right, since we *are* free. If everything were caused there would be nothing to choose. The determinist knows he *must* be right, since he sees the causes and constraints of a choice of which each 'I' *appears* as free author. Sartre explains the *tedium* of the debate as its bad faith. Each has internalised the other's position; it is part of each, even while each is engaged in denunciation of the 'other'. *Each already is their opponent*. Like the prosecution whose imagination contains that of the defence, with a hitch of the gown libertarian becomes determinist (or vice versa). Motivation and its role with respect to 'causality' and 'nihilation' was in the air from the start:

> If we think of prior consciousness as a motivation, we see that nothing has slipped in between that state and the present state (BN, 27).

And there is no 'indeterminacy', if considered as an absence of causation:

> There is no weakening of the motivating force of the prior consciousness. What separates prior from subsequent is exactly nothing (BN, 27).

This *separation by nothing* will recur throughout *Being and Nothingness*, being explained in the description of conscious freedom. Here Sartre invokes Husserl's 'bracketing' operation:

> [T]he prior consciousness is there and ... contains a relation of interpretation with the present consciousness but ... is put out of the game, out of circuit, between parentheses, as in [Husserl's] phenomenological epoché' (BN, 27).

Cause and effect appear on the ground of (free) nihilation.[17] Hence, to recognise cause and effect is already to have accepted freedom. The gesture that made the knot appear now loosens it. My nihilating of a positive situation raised up the positivity of 'effect following upon cause'. I 'caused' there to be causes, as I 'caused' Pierre to be *absent* from the café. The 'nihilation' essential to the existence of causality as a phenomenon is this 'film' that is enough to separate my present state from my past.

---

[15] Like Hume and R.E. Hobart, Sartre differs freedom from lack of causality.

[16] Benjamin's 'ideology' *is* Marx's 'blindingly obvious' – the 'natural facts'.

[17] This does not imply the 'ideality' of cause and effect. Absence, too, appears on the ground of nihilation but is real, and subject to perceptual judgement.

This filmy separation is like Husserl's 'bracketing out' of the everyday objects of perception that leaves them in place, just as they were, but under scrutiny (Husserl 1970a). *He* stands to one side so as not to disturb what we would inspect while *Sartre* lets a film slip between impulse and act. What we glimpsed slips from the way we were looking at it. The past, real and obdurate, scintillates with what we are now to make of it. This oily iridescence of concept and phenomena is enough for freedom. A freedom as faint as it is absolute. 'Freedom', since I can grasp actions and states of mind as my own. 'Faint', because I am guaranteed no power to make things go differently from that moment. 'Absolute', because there is no moment of conscious existence in which I can declare myself free of it.

As I lay out how freedom is to be 'thought' along with cause and effect, this is not to demonstrate his story as adequate to some grand task of RESOLVING THE TRADITIONAL PROBLEM OF FREEWILL AND DETERMINISM. I do not aim '*to have squeezed the universe into a ball/ To roll it towards some overwhelming question/ To say ... I shall tell you all*' (T.S. Eliot). My use of 'faint freedom' derives from the evanescence of Sartre's phenomena of being free and conscious. What is vital to us disappears as it appears. Sartre's image is of a 'film' that allows our phases to be perfectly adjacent yet disconnected, whose dimension is an asymptotic limit, a singularity, a shadow, momentous as it tends towards the insubstantial. An Husserlian pair of brackets that leave assertions, syntax and meanings untouched. And 'brackets' remind me of 'claws' and thus again of Eliot – a modernist contemporary in process of deconstructing dreams of freedom:

> I should have been a pair of ragged claws
> Scuttling across the floors of silent seas.

Perfect freedom, in perfect inefficacy.

Falling into Anguish

Anguish as the Impotence of Freedom

This delicious power that slips between one moment and another becomes a source of anguished impotence. The film that would let us do something, loosens our grip on what we had decided, what our motives had been, what we will do next. This slippage between immediate past and existential present gives us anguish – worse than fear:

A situation provokes fear if there is a possibility of my life being changed from without; my being provokes anguish to the extent that I distrust myself and my reactions to that situation (BN, 29).

The distinction of fear and anguish is a challenge to Sartre's metaphysics. As it hits me, as from some cause, fear is beyond my power of nihilation. I hear terrible news; the blood drains from my face, I can scarcely breathe, my mind and feelings are numb. But then I 'recover myself' – in anguish, unless I am caught up by force of circumstance. Shall I 'make nothing' of the news – *these things happen; death comes to all.* Shall I make a nothing of my own life henceforth – *everything is finished now. I wish I were dead.* Anguish is directed at what is *beyond recall or redress; what cannot be predicted but must be anticipated, what we prefer to predict but must effect.*

In ancient as in modern times, the philosopher feels that disaster will arise from taking a wrong turning. Socrates wants people to escape from evil by defining the good. In his search for certainty Descartes cries out, '*I am bewildered, as though I had suddenly fallen into a deep sea, and could neither plant my foot on the bottom nor swim up to the top*' (Descartes 1956, 66); Husserl's sense of mortal danger in philosophising is no less intense:

It seems so easy, following Descartes, to lay hold of the pure Ego and his *cogitationes*. And yet it is as though we were on the brink of a precipice, where advancing calmly and surely is a matter of philosophical life and death (Husserl 1970a: 23).

Sartre's image of the solitary climber is not only an example of existential vertigo, therefore, but a figure in philosophy's process of creating theory. It begins with ordinary fear:

I am on a narrow path – without a guard-rail – which goes along a precipice. The precipice ... represents a danger of death ... I can slip on a stone ... the crumbling earth ... can give way ... I am passive in relation to these possibilities; they come to me from without, insofar as I am also an object ... subject to gravitation (BN, 30).

Sartre contrasts fear of accidents – 'external causes' – from the anguish of realising it is up to me to be reckless or careful. So it is up to me whether the precipice is a danger or an opportunity. The tale takes on its own life, however, not doing its author's bidding. A scene of causes and effects laid out like a panorama disconnects us from an established world, feeding our anguish at an ever-present and vanishing freedom. Certainly, disconnection can arise when fear rather than anguish is at work. In imagination I separate what I am doing from what might happen. I am climbing firmly and surely, but '*there is no guard-rail [nihilation already!], the path might crumble*'. (Nihilation again.) Fear slides into anguish as ('nihilating') imagination works its way into this 'precipice' narrative: '*I am given to myself as passive in relation to these possibilities*'. I begin to screw myself up over these hazards.[18] The imagination of indefinitely many risks is not the attitude of the experienced climber who *checks specifically* on the soundness of the rock into which s/he drives a piton. Anguish is provoked by an open set of dangerous possibilities, but fear arises in connection with my situation, and can be geared into dealing with it: '*fear appears ... I push away the threatening situation with all my strength*' (BN, 30).

Sartre is writing a double text. 'Pushing with all my strength' is a response to an event, but he describes the onset of this 'pushing' as the end point, not of the crumbling earth or jittery pebble, but of the thoughtful reflection they prompt. If I have imagined only possible dangers, my fear will be no more than reflective. It verges on anguish. Guided by fear, I will pay attention to loose stones and keep from the edge. This is not the *reflex* of '*pushing with all my strength*' that brought me out of anguish into operative life-preserving action. Sartre does not yet recognise the impact of experience upon reflective consciousness, and this infects the metaphysics that succeeds his story of the climber.[19] Not only in bad faith but also in the heat of the moment, on its spur, we freely escape freedom's anguish.

The edge of the path *did* crumble; my foot *skidded* towards the abyss; a pebble *became* a ball bearing under my boot. I was a falling body. Undecidability of choice vanished. I pushed with all my strength to gain a support. '*With all my strength.*' It takes *all* of it. There is none left for anguish, imagination, or even fear. I am solid again, free of anxiety and haunting thoughts of identity. ('Am I really a climber, or disguising a suicidal bent?') I was launched by fear of death into the desire to live:

> [M]y possibilities are substituted for transcendent possibilities where human action has no place.[20] And because these conducts are my possibilities, they do not appear to me as determined by foreign causes (BN, 30).

The action whose vigour dispels anguish, however, is the very source of the reflection that disturbs and leads me back into anguish: *Nothing determines me to save my life rather than to risk it – or to end it.* That 'nothing' slips into the text like the *film* between my thought, feeling, motivation and

---

[18] In anguish, I vainly 'wring my hands over' what has happened.

[19] In 'The Existence of Others' he evokes a visceral shift in consciousness.

[20] 'Possibility' suggests what I might *imagine*. Sartre's 'possibility' is what is open to me.

actions up to this moment, and my thought, feeling, motivation and action right now. In that 'nothing' slips in, I am disengaged from the *non-inauthentic* action in which I was taken up. Sartre argues, persuasively, that, *as a project*, authenticity is itself bad faith, but this does not leave us with only *in-authenticity*. I have no *project* of authenticity when taken up in a situation. My involvement is '*not-inauthentic*' – I need not be hiding myself in commitments.

Sartre restores the priority of reflective bad faith by attention to my subsequent pondering upon these actions later. Pondering is a pool where a stream loses momentum, a metonym for all philosophical reflection. Then, in my sullen anguish, 'nothing' compels me to maintain those resolved motives I had formed:

> Anguish is my consciousness of being my own future ... [I]f nothing compels me to save my life, nothing prevents me from precipitating myself into the abyss (BN, 32).

The Truth of Involvement

When events catch up with me I fight for my life or the life of another. Later I can reflect that I might have acted in self-deception – the mentality of '*I have to do this!*' Yet I am no less prone to deception when thinking, later, '*nothing compels me now to follow what I resolved in that emergency*'. Sartre raises up active involvement to solve the metaphysics of a paralysed will, but has to record how reflection provoked by that very involvement corrodes that new confidence. In disparaging engagement, he appeals to his metaphysics of consciousness along with the undesirability of a 'bourgeois' life that imposes itself upon us. And yet, Sartre *does* evoke the truth of an involved world:

> Now at each instant we are thrust into the world and engaged there. This means that we act before we realise what is possible for us (BN, 37).

True, when I am disengaged a different truth threatens, but involvement has permanent consequences for Sartre's thought. If we *are* 'engaged there' at each instant, then we are 'engaged' in our reflective, as in our 'active', moments. When Sartre thinks that in reflection we can see the bad faith of our acceptance of value, of social obligation, he is like Husserl in thinking he could bracket *all* objects of 'natural attitudes'. We can remain unaware of much of the character of what we are involved in doing. But equally, we are unaware of much of the character of what we do in detached reflection.

As with involvement, only in retrospect do we appreciate the silliness or the insight of our reflections.

> The alarm that rings in the morning refers to the possibility of my going to work, which is what lies before me. But to apprehend the summons of the alarm as a summons is to get up. The very act of getting up is reassuring, for it eludes the question 'Is work [what lies before me]?' (BN, 37–38).

Announcing what I have to do, the alarm awakens me to 'possibility' – what I might do. 'Possibility' continues to irritate the surface of the text. (I have modified the standard translation, above, from '*Is work my possibility?*' to '*Is work what lies before me?*'.) In this context, 'possibility' is too vague. The question is what lies to hand for me. '*Of the various things open to me, this is my choice*' would also soothe the textual surface. Questions arise, however, about the extent of such 'possibilities', such 'openings'. Sartrean 'possibilities' involve my making light of aspects of what exists in itself. In the café this nihilation was of the people and things that were not Pierre. Without that, his *absence* would have been an empty negation. So not everything I could think of doing are my 'possibilities', even if they are within my power. I can think, '*I might be sky-diving*', or '*I might be telling our Prime Minister a few home truths*', or '*I might take up a new profession*', but thoughts of such actions are empty. I have not made them 'open to me'. Promptly, if more thoughtfully, I get up in response to the alarm. I have not even negated these fancies to raise them as 'my possibilities'. They never attained that status. Sartrean 'possibilities' are no less than factors that structure my immediate future as I get out of bed – or stay in it. On some mornings there *is* only one possibility – to get up. Nothing else is open to me. All other 'possibilities' are empty thoughts of what I 'might do'.

Involvement

Consumed by Involvement

Amongst my options, I may choose involvement rather than continuing to think, in anguish, '*I and I alone am responsible for the meanings I find*'. As Sartre argues, an involving activity is a '*consciousness of [some] being*', which implies that I have pre-reflective consciousness (of) the activity by which I escape anguish,[21] but not (of) every aspect of it. To write about the philosophy of consciousness may itself be an evasion of choice.

Sartre could reply that were we detached from the option (the 'possibility') in which we have become involved, we would perceive in anguish that 'nothing' made us choose it. But he would have to presume that to be involved in an activity is to be conscious (of) *every aspect* of it, and thus conscious (of) my involvement as my way of evading anguish. This presumption provokes uneasiness about every aspect of existence. Either I am disengaged – in anguish about having to choose though 'nothing' determines me – or I am engaged and uneasily half aware (of) what anguish would result from reflecting on what I am doing.

Sartre's metaphysics strikes a chord in a thoughtful reader. His way is paved with many a good truth. We do escape anguish by 'burying ourselves' – in work, politics, writing, or social life. We do have some pre-reflective awareness of what we are doing in involving ourselves. For I am intelligent and imaginative rather than fanatical in what I do, just to the extent that I see what my involvement means. What I am *not doing* when I do something is central to this other meaning.[22] There is a 'negativity' in any action – what I 'make nothing of' is the key to placing value on what I choose. By such arts we maintain value in life. I *should* be 'ready' to be aware of what I am *not-doing* when I persist in a line of action, in order to maintain an active imagination of *what I might have been doing*. I imagine other 'negativities' and make them an intrinsic part of what I am involved in doing. I consider *how other people do this differently*, and I wonder, '*Should I have done it that way?*'

It is by means of his metaphysics that Sartre articulates the shock of realising that I have buried my choices in obligation, fate, or duty. After the shock, whether in pleasure at feeling free or in panic at my options, I realise that my projects and commitments, together with my brief impulsive acts, stem from choices – choices maintained by negotiation. Recklessly, I may break out of a stifled sense of freedom, only to live in anguish, having merely enacted fantasy.[23] Even one's efforts at a 'mature' freedom that is responsible to the needs of others, degenerate into a consciousness as of being 'put upon'. And yet, better moments of feeling are equally real. We realise in pleasurable relief that what we 'have to' do is a condition of achieving what we have chosen. To love someone may commence in an onset of feelings, but then we choose what to make of them, for in the

---

[21] Sartre does not claim that I really *know* I am evading my responsibility. He distinguishes pre-reflective consciousness (of) something, from *knowledge* of it.

[22] Ryle investigated these possibilities *via* the notion of 'negative' actions (Ryle 1966).

[23] Beauvoir values freedom for itself, hoping for but not promising happiness.

ensuing momentum we are moved to recognise the desires and needs of others – and different desires and needs of our own. Responding to this is not rightly felt as an imposed 'burden'. We gain a feeling for a social reality, for physiological reality and for vulnerability to accident and attack. Sometimes this generates enough love to sustain the consequent responsibility. Hatred also sustains commitment, but only as blind to new facts. Dislike capitulates to hatred, as affection capitulates to sentimentality.[24]

That the human, as a being, 'nihilates' its way into freedom out of being 'in-itself' does not *entail* its anguish at the fact. The 'film of nothingness' between a prior decision and the moment of carrying it out does not *contain* anguish. If we 'use our memory' (Wittgenstein) in doing philosophy, we are more likely to be relieved when we recall that we 'choose our lives'. We may be caught in wonderment at the fact. The shock of recognition liberates us, if briefly, from a thick-witted consciousness of our doings – from the block-headedness of bad faith that thumps out what we do as '*the only possible thing!*' and cries out against anything else as '*unthinkable!*'

Letting Go

We can allow influences to operate upon us, and this is a particular freedom. I am free when I let things happen, allow myself to fall, or fling myself down:

> There is a certain type of flight before facticity, a flight which consists precisely in abandoning oneself to this facticity, that is ... in trustingly reassuming it and loving it in order to try to recover it (BN, 456).

This freedom, one archetype of liberty, is expressed in abandon:

> To abandon oneself to hunger, to thirst, to let oneself fall back upon a ... bed with sensual pleasure, to relax ... to let oneself be drunk in by one's own body, not now beneath the eyes of another ... but in the original solitude of the For-itself (BN, 456).

There is a paradox in self-abandonment. One allows oneself to *be* one's fatigue or sensuous pleasure but in allowing this, one exists as more than the fatigue, hunger or pleasure. Even relaxation is charged with tones of

---

[24] I admit that such ethically workaday social realism can look out of place within Sartrean metaphysics. I trust it is not like the low-cost moralising (Atheist! Immoralist! Pessimist! Negativist!) that greeted the publication of *Being and Nothingness*.

attempting the metaphysically impossible! This being *'for-itself-as-in-itself'* that had been a project of force, we now try to achieve by ease:

> [N]one of these forms of behaviour can ever be confined to itself ... [I]n another person they irritate or attract. Their condition is an initial project of the recovery of the body ... an attempt at a solution of the absolute [of the In-itself-for-itself] (BN, 456).

Yet, for all the 'impossibility' of the project, in this 'abandonment to facticity' we recover a freedom that extends beyond letting things happen. In writing about letting go, Sartre represents us as able to enjoy a freedom we can lose and recover – the power of a freedom beyond anguish and burden.[25] He dramatises the freedom by which we break with obsessive activity within which freedom seemed unrelenting in its demands. Freedom was a millstone, when it was buoyancy we needed.

I have argued that, as no more than a consciousness (of) nihilation of what *is* in itself, metaphysical liberty is *faint* freedom. Such freedom is not the power to change ourselves, let alone our circumstances. Sartre recognises this when he says that though an inferiority complex is 'a *chosen* self-destructive state' we are not able to opt out of it. In living it out I have made some nihilation of what *is* in itself, but

> I can be 'freed' from my 'inferiority complex' only by a radical modif-ication of my project which could in no way find its causes and its motives in the prior project, not even in the suffering and shame which I experience, [which] are designed ... to realise my project of inferiority (BN, 475).

To challenge my bad faith in being involved in a project of inferiority does not give me the power to depart. Bad faith becomes habitual – an entrenched way of doing things, and becomes part of my facticity – a function of 'transcendence' and of what exists in itself. And even the first act in a pattern of bad faith is already a *fall* that I can criticise only after the event. Sartre's reiteration of the attitude that 'only I am responsible' for what I am and do does not mean that I had a power to do otherwise. That I am responsible means, rather, that I should not evade what I have done. That is the strength of Sartre's language, but its rhetoric glosses over my need for others to break up the impasse, since in self-deception I have lost the frankness that forestalls bad faith – lost some of the power that comes with a sense of freedom.

---

[25] Absolute freedom haunts everyday freedom.

We are free in Sartre's primordial sense even when we have lost a *feeling* of freedom, but this feeling is what gives us confidence to lay hold of what is open to us, to keep a grasp on strategies of freedom. To lose a sense of freedom is to lose free play of imagination, and with that goes style and spirit. We then make choices by default and fulfil responsibility in apathy. So freedom is a burden, suicide seems the solution and reason must remind us that for a moment we have to break out of apathy. We might as well use the moment to break out into life.

We are not always free if sometimes we are caught in a pattern of bad faith from which we can exit only with the help of people with skill and good will. Not every sense of obligation and necessity is in bad faith, since there are actions we *have* to take, to break out of a cycle of bad faith. To escape bad faith involves regaining a sense of freedom, so there is an obligation to freedom, to take the steps necessary to take hold of it. Without this free hand on our freedom, Sartre's other face of consciousness does emerge as a burden borne in anguish. And yet, as we have seen, Sartre does recognise *liberation* as a phenomenon beyond the weight of the freedom to which we are condemned. He writes of those points in time we have mentioned when '*the prior project collapses ... in the light of a new project*' and '*we let go in order to grasp and grasp in order to let go*' (BN, 476).

If metaphysical freedom is the work of nihilating consciousness in construing figure and ground, then it is at the heart of our imagination of possibilities, and this requires us to combat compulsions and obsessions. Metaphysical freedom demands the *project* of liberation, and that is the work of a book like Beauvoir's *The Second Sex*. Sartre reminds us that moments of liberation ('*the most moving image of our freedom*') are only among '*its many manifestations*' (BN, 476). However, the moments we realise in anguish are also '*only amongst freedom's many manifestations*'. Vertigo is Sartre's 'blazon' (Le Dœuff 1989: 14), but liberation disrupts the image of freedom as a 'wrenching' that is experienced *only* in anguish.

What Sartre then says about 'freedom' as one's 'fundamental project' completes a spiralling loop that returns to place freedom as an impossible project of consciousness at the centre:

> The free project ... is my being. [A]mbition, the passion to be loved [and the] inferiority complex ... must be understood in terms of a primary project which ... can no longer be interpreted in terms of any other and which is total (BN, 479–480).

This project to make the *for-itself* an *in-itself* would repair the rent in *being*, and confer stability on human nature. We began to investigate the fantasies of sexuality and of sexual difference that emerge when Sartre looks for an earthly symbol of this '*in-itself*' in the '*feminine*', in '*woman*'.[26] The next chapter pursues this idea that if *woman* were considered with regard to her own reality 'she' would not pose the surreal threat Sartre describes.

A Void in Consciousness

A Void in Reflection

In portraying involvement as avoiding the anguish of our freedom, Sartre plays on the truth that our activities, worthy in themselves, are sometimes ways of avoiding responsibility and surrogates for reflection. But involvement as such is not an evasion of reflection, since reflective understanding is its own kind of involvement. The truth is, then, that one involvement may be an avoidance of another. This is to mock the existentialist rhetoric that pits corrosive reflection against active involvement, and reminds us of those who never come to terms with what their parents wanted, living as glazed-eyed engineer rather than sparking accountant.

This 'involvement as evasion' connects with the perception of absence. The insignificance of the infinitely many people who are 'not present' when Pierre fails to show up in Sartre's café requires the narrator's silence about them. To mention an 'empty thought' of absence starts up that absence into possible significance. To place *Wellington* as not in the café is to place the *café* firmly in the century after him – the café in a Paris now free of British domination. Because of the omnipresent thought (for Paris in 1943) of Hitler's domination, to allude to *his* absence from the café, for instance, sets up a new comparison of absent figures, each, for different reasons, not-expected-to-be-in-the-café. The only *utterly* empty 'absences' from the café are the ones the narrator would never *utter* – the absence I observed earlier as from my 'elsewhere' – the absence of Ned Kelly from the narrator's Paris café of 1943.

This present text emanates from Australia and *for us*, Ned Kelly *is* absent from Sartre's café. His absence marks the cultural distance that we cross so often in reading philosophy that we overlook the identity-sapping journey. *Text-lag*. When *I* now write that Ned Kelly is not in Sartre's café I make his absence present there, which then calls out for an essay on contemporary Australian, other anglophone, and recent European philosophy.

---

[26] 'Situating Theory', this work.

There are *absent lives*, vacancies within each reader's smoky café, each a 'fullness of being' with its *booths, its light, the sounds of voices, rattling saucers and footsteps*. Infinitely many figures remain 'empty abstract thoughts' of absence just until we take the risk of thinking of them. Thinking *about* this possibility of figures we haven't thought of is like thinking about what we might have been after choices we never stopped to ponder. This is the anxiety in Sartre's slippage between past resolve and the present moment of what we do.[27]

A Void in Suffering

We recognise the force of feeling[28] even while agreeing with Sartre's diagnosis of our wish to *lose ourselves* in it or else to *repudiate it* as alien. For *how* we suffer, while not avoiding suffering, *is* our own business. We suffer, and we have not only to suffer but also to cope with it. Being totally possessed by feeling in the moment[29] simply happens, unwilled. But feeling carries the invitation to lose oneself in it. '*Anything less does not give full justice to this grief, elation, pride, shame!*'. With such blandishments I lose myself, left alone with grief – as with an acquisition, to be free from criticism or mockery.[30] This tendency to self-immersion and loss of autonomy (so that what the loss or gain *means* to you is not examined) is not so great with joy at success, which we are more liable to share. Grief is hard enough to bear. To grieve, and also to have to attend to another's needs (or one's own), can seem intolerable. It seems 'unfair' and, 'left to their grief', people become angry even at being comforted. Sartre's metaphysics, bordering on melodrama, has a satirical tinge:

> The suffering which I experience ... is never adequate suffering ... it nihilates itself as in itself by the very act by which it founds itself. It escapes as suffering towards the consciousness of suffering (BN, 92).

I can 'grasp' a statue of a suffering figure. It is there, given as a whole to be studied. I cannot exist at that remove from my own current experience, which I could encompass only if it were 'adequate' – excluding all else. But then I could not 'grasp' it either, since there would be no 'me' distinct from it. There *is* that which nihilates my nature and what happens to me, as

---

[27] This may include what we think about or feel, or 'actions' like conducting deals.
[28] A good moment to think of Beauvoir's *The Force of Circumstance.*
[29] A 'moment' may be of seconds or days, depending on feeling and circumstance.
[30] Leonard Cohen sings of the lover who had 'always been a stranger', who wanted only '*a card so high and wide he'd never have to play another*'.

'in itself'. This nihilation is the condition of *any* experience, so the in-itself
has to be nihilated in order that my suffering exist.

The suffering is not 'for-itself', and yet cannot exist as 'in-itself' – as
consciousness it involves consciousness (of) itself. When Sartre says that
the suffering I experience '*escapes suffering toward the consciousness of
suffering*' (BN, 92), the 'of' is not bracketed. Suffering does not 'escape'
from itself simply in that it is consciousness (of) suffering, but is ready to
escape *via* this pre-consciousness. It is ready to make a 'theme' of itself, so
that I take *it*, rather than that for which I suffer, as my object. I might fancy
that once I do attend to it, it would become a quasi-'in-itself' for me, which
I could prod, inspect and appraise. Being raised up by nihilation, however,
its *being*, as a virtual '*in-itself*', will not remain stable when it is made an
object of reflection. Inspected, nihilated against a field of other feelings and
thoughts, it loses the stability granted it by its own immediate object. As if I
held a glass sphere in the air by concentration of my will and then, to
examine this phenomenon further, I turned my attention to the *ball-as-held-
up-by-will*; the ball trembles and falls as my concentration on it is fractured.
Within such a metaphysics, so far so good. But Sartre is about to hijack his
recognition of the ungraspable character of one's own feelings:

> I can never be surprised by [the suffering], for it is, only to the degree that I
> experience it. Its translucency removes from it all depth. I can not observe it
> as I observe ... the statue, since I make my own suffering, and since I know
> it (BN, 92).

This strikes a false note. Suffering *can* surprise me: '*I could never have
imagined it could be like this.*' So far from a 'translucency', suffering
seems opaque. Sartre has distinguished my feeling as an object of primary
attention, from a pre-reflective consciousness (of) one's feeling. This pre-
reflective consciousness (of) one's conscious state does *not* give it a
'*translucency*'. Not attentive *towards* that conscious state, I have only a
marginal awareness of it that is, at best, ready to provoke some probing of
the feeling as if a thing in itself. 'I make my own suffering' in raising it up
by nihilation, but if I cannot observe my suffering, it is not because I
'know' it but because I am only conscious (of) it. Evanescent under
scrutiny, its reliance upon me '*for-myself*' gives it more power over me. If I
could see it as a given object, I might master it, but I cannot do so. Again,
Sartre is the master of lyrical satire:

> If I must suffer, I should like simultaneously to be it and to conquer it, but
> this enormous, opaque suffering, which should transport me out of myself,

continues instead to touch me lightly with its wing, and I can not grasp it (BN, 92).

The suffering now refuses to fill me and fails to exclude my responsibility for how I deal with it. What 'should' transport me out of myself appears as *opaque*. Since I suffer so much, surely nothing can be expected of me; surely I need expect nothing of myself? In such a mood I reject sympathy – '*let me alone ... you can't know how I feel*'. The suffering is now 'opaque' to my (vain) desire that it is my own feeling! Sartre assured me it is I who raised it up out of indifference. A vain desire for total possession. I raised up the *absence of Pierre from the café*, too, and, for all that, his absence is an obdurate fact.

Though obdurate, suffering *touches me lightly with its wing*.[31] Suffering can torment and yet not damage me; it takes to the air ahead of my grasp, close enough to be my suffering, separate enough that I cannot lay hold of it to deal with it. Perhaps I can let go of the contradictory desire to *be* the suffering. But my struggle to lay hold of it is in vain – a tragic comedy of isolation:

> I find only myself ... who moans, wails ... plays without respite the drama of suffering. I wring my hands, I cry in order that being-in-itselfs, their sounds, their gestures may run through the world, ridden by the suffering-in-itself which I can not be (BN, 92).

Sartre has shifted his theme. The existential moment he exposes is the desire to be nothing but my own suffering, a gravity so great that I escape through its black hole into a world of stillness, as unreachable to myself as it is by others. Such a feeling, maintained by precarious nihilation, becomes a quasi-'*thing-in-itself*'. I only enforce this self-imprisonment in the aim of being 'absolutely sincere' – so full of feeling that I am nothing else! Sartre evokes my final gesture at release in the wild image of making of my own feeling a series of moving statues, enactments of feeling which '*may run through the world, ridden by the suffering-in-itself which I cannot be*' (BN 92). Thus we abuse feeling so as to escape its origins and demands. Sartre castigated as 'bourgeois' those who perceive the world in terms of given values, needs, rights and wrongs (BN, 38). They want their values to be 'there' to raise them up, to '*touch them lightly with their wings*', transporting them beyond anxiety.

---

[31] The allusion seems to be to Jacob's wrestling with the angel – a vain struggle of flesh and blood with its own imaginary construction – too evanescent to be grasped, too much momentum to be wished away.

Conscious in an Empty Room

At a much later stage, Sartre again describes how someone's being – as their body – is revealed in their absence:

> This room in which I wait for the master of the house reveals to me in its totality the body of its owner: this easy chair is a chair-where-he-sits, this desk is a desk-at-which-he-writes, this window is a window through which there enters the light-which-illuminates-the-objects-which-he-sees. Thus it is an outline complete with all its parts, and this outline is an outline-of-an-object; an object can come at every instant to fill the outline with content. But still the master of the house 'is not there'. He is elsewhere; he is absent (BN, 341–342).

Here, Sartre expands the meaning of the description of perceiving that Pierre is absent from a café, developed earlier.[32] Now he uses it to indicate how in the absence of another we perceive their mentality as expressed in physical things. Finally, it is no more remarkable that we find the mentality of someone 'in' their easy chair and the windows of their room, than that we find it 'in' their face, or their gestures (Deutscher 1992). Consider the significance of *usurpation*. To see the mentality in the physicality of another's existence in the world is to be a pretender to their throne. There is the possibility of understanding here – a kind of projection of oneself to 'live through' the imagined life of another, particularly by placing oneself in the very physical and social position that they occupy. At the same time, this kind of empathy is, equally, misleading. What it is for *me* to occupy another's throne is a function of my past and my projected future, my skills, temperament and personality. It is a real question whether one can project oneself into those aspects of the life of another so as to empathise, even in those respects. In Sartre's vivid picture, it is in taking a position in another's 'room' to observe how it is arranged and what objects are given prominence and whether it is tidy or in disarray, that we gain an immediate feel for, and perhaps some understanding of their temperament, skills and moods. Here is another point of access to Sartre's ways of regarding consciousness in its materiality without reducing descriptions and perceptions to *objectity*.

---

[32] In 'A Void'.

5

On Lacking Reason for Desire

Specific Desires and the Fundamental Project

Life can seem like a series of pure contingencies, perhaps charming in their chaotic eclecticism. As a child I was mad on scrambling into the Australian bush, learned to shoot rabbits in a trance of horror, was pressured to show an interest in going to church and Sunday school, loved to play Bach on the piano and organ, was urged to perform in public, liked reading about ships and was besotted with the stories of Lassie. As Sartre writes, '*every desire ... if presented as ... irreducible is an absurd contingency*' (BN, 561). When adults don't like what you are doing, or friends think it's weird, they say '*Why do you do you do that? How can you really like it?*'. They elicit a few embarrassed words – or frenetic arguments. Smartly we learn the fallacies in the logic books – *ad hominem, petitio principii, denying the antecedent*. Absurd logic befits the defence of absurd contingency.

Efforts in adult life to shape the cloud of dust of our desires and interests re-enact this absurdity. Sartre summarises them neatly. To posit a pre-given set of desires that impel me towards various activities is to forget that my desire just *is* my consciousness of them as desirable. My parents and friends were closer to the mark in asking me what I found in the activities that puzzled or annoyed them. Certainly, Sartre accepts the general contingency of facts. If there is some further *reason for* my bundle of desires, this is not a self-caused cause to terminate, like the God of Aquinas, an otherwise infinite regress. Some other explanations seem utterly banal, and yet serve their purpose: '*S/he likes going rowing because it is an open-air sport!*'. '*Yes*', one might retort, '*and s/he likes cherries because they are fruit!*'. Context gives point to such empty forms. S/he is aching to get out of the study; an opportunity arises to go rowing – a friend has just bought a fine double-scull. '*OH!*' we say, '*that makes sense. It had seemed so utterly out of the blue*'. So too, s/he's been deprived of fruit for weeks, has never shown any interest in cherries before. But cherries are on offer and so, yes, '*S/he likes them (just) because they are fruit*'.

Sartre does look for a kind of unity for the self – that '*human reality, [as] defined by the ends one pursues*' (BN, 557). He diagnoses an appeal to substance as a 'caricature' of the unity in terms of which someone is *'agreeable or hateful, blameable and praiseworthy'* (BN, 561). Outside conditions won't hold together the *'dust of phenomena'*, either. Those conditions themselves disperse. It requires a tale and an image to collect them. The unity of human reality may be thought of as the conditions of writing a coherent biography – '*To be, [as for any subject of a biography] is to be unified in the world*'.[1] The conditions of the world in which we live do not simply give shape, externally to our desires. As part of our overall consciousness, our desires configure that world as attractive, repulsive, or indifferent to us.

Existentialism, based on contingency, might invoke every arbitrary fact of desire as brute fact. I like rowing. She likes skiing. Tomorrow, I am sick of rowing and she is ever more taken up with skiing. That's the world. Take it or leave it. Certainly, for Sartre, anything we do has *'all the gratuity of a free decision'* (BN, 561). Nothing can explain it, if that means to deduce it from principles of reason. And yet such desires are not purely autonomous either. Each of them has some sort of meaning within the structure of one's life. We feel the tug on the web of all our desires when we are deprived of satisfaction of such 'absurd contingencies' – rowing, sailing, saving money, being admired, being desired. Sartre searches to explain both a contingency that exists along with its causes, and he looks to find an interconnected meaning in one's desires. In Heidegger's terms, we want the secret of the subject's *being-in-the-world*. Sartre proposes the idea of a fundamental project to explain, a priori, why our desires connect in a web of meaning, while still giving full weight to the contingency of desire. There are explanations by prior causes, by classification, and by physiological reduction. None of these explanations touch the concepts and phenomenology of desire. What is the significance in one's life of desires gratuitous contingencies?

Pascal sees, in our arbitrary desires, a need to be diverted in pointless activities. Stendahl and Proust too, are hot on the trail. Love for a specific person can be understood without trivialising it in the ways Sartre has rejected. For Proust, says Sartre, a man desires to lay hold of the world *through* a woman – thus the intensity of his otherwise inexplicable choice of a specific figure. Sartre slips his metaphysical language into the problematic of desire. To be conscious is a way of *being-for-oneself*, and this involves immediate (not infallible) relations to aspects of the world. *Love* is a mode of this *being-for-oneself* in which we relate to the world through another. While rejecting the Christian diagnosis of the never-fully-satisfied nature of desire (it was really God we pursued all the while), that

---

[1] To write a biography of Flaubert is already a benchmark for Sartre!

kind of explanation at least maintains a concreteness of desire. Sartre's aim is to discover a contingent a priori that founds all desire while not threatening *its* contingency. A person, Sartre suggests, is neither merely malleable clay, nor a loose bundle of desires. It is in terms of my *initial project* that I lay claim to myself as 'I'. Sartre's aim is

> to rediscover the veritable concreteness ... [of] the totality of his impulse toward being, his original relation to himself, to the world and to the Other ... in the unity of internal relations and of a fundamental project (BN, 563).

It is not that Sartre would attempt thus to reconstruct the real or essential person from their diverse tendencies. There is a kind of transcendent meaning in each concrete choice that requires neither an unconscious level nor a noumenal level beyond experience. In acting from any one of these tendencies – to swim, to save money, to be famous – '*the person expresses themself completely, although from a different angle*' (BN, 563). The intelligibility of the choice '*can exist only as the transcendent meaning of each concrete choice*' (BN, 563–564).[2] If I am rowing on the river I am *nothing but this rowing*, and yet, Sartre will argue, the project is the totality of my being – it expresses my original choice, though in these particular circumstances. (The language of this original choice is introduced in stages.) We need a vindication of this posit of an original choice implicit in every desire, however varied and arbitrary, and we need a '*special method to detach this fundamental meaning which the project admits*' (BN, 564).

The distinction of the specific desire and original project is not Heidegger's distinction of inauthentic and authentic existence, which is '*tainted with an ethical dimension*' (BN, 564), and relies on a claim that primary anguish is at one's death. Sartre rejects this. We are anguished at death only in having some project in living. Otherwise we can welcome death. There is an anguish at death because there is an '*original choice of being*', he argues. Though there are physiological and other empirical bases for the impulse to survive, this *choice of being* takes on a particular metaphysical significance. Sartre adds an element of the a priori to the understanding of our human condition. The initial metaphysics of *being-for-itself* and *being-in-itself* now emerges to map the difference of desire and non-desire. As *for-itself* human being is constituted as desire, which, for Sartre, falling in line with an ancient tradition from Plato and Plotinus, is evidently a *lack* of being. Sartre has described freedom itself as this lack, as a thin film of nothingness that slips between past and present, cause and

---

[2] The transcendent is the *movement across*, from experience to experience. An object we see is transcendent to what we glimpse – suggesting more to be seen.

effect, perceiving and its object, oneself and another. '*Freedom is the concrete mode of being of this lack.*' In *nihilating* what there is, this '*being*', we raise up consciousness and freedom. Free consciousness. Conscious freedom.

Sartre has thus brought desire home to roost in a necessity of contingency. It is contingent that there is *being-for-itself*, but not contingent that such a being is a being of desire. It is evident that desire involves a consciousness of lack, and that consciousness itself *is* a lack of the sort of stable definition enjoyed by *being-in-itself*. The original project – the desire for *being* – *is* the being of the *for-itself*. In its being, its being is in question. It *is* the project to '*make known to oneself what one is by [what is available]*³ *to the being of the for-itself*' (BN, 565). (It is this possibility, this making use of what is available to me, which appears as value.) And, as if we might have forgotten, this *for-itself* is defined as a lack of being. What the *for-itself* lacks is the *in-itself*; the *for-itself* arises as the nihilation of it. Between this nihilated *in-itself* and the projected *in-itself*, which simply is the *for-itself*? There slips in, nothingness.

Knowing Possessively

Becoming What One Desires

Although '*every desire … [appears as] an absurd contingency*' (BN, 561), '*in each inclination … the person expresses himself completely*' in trying to realise an original project (BN, 563). Though '*if I am rowing on the river I am nothing … save this project of rowing … this rowing expresses my [whole] original [project]*' (BN, 564). This 'project' is '*the desire to be*'. In my original project I desire to be-something-in-particular – a rower, an Olympic medallist, engrossed in writing a philosophical essay or established as a notable philosopher – and yet my desire is to *be* as only a stone, a tree, the sky can *be*. '*If only I gain a gold medal I will be made – as good as gold*'. '*While I'm rowing I'm in seventh heaven – not a care in the world!*'.

Since I *am* a *for-itself*, and can in no way change the fact, why don't I take up the more realistic aim of being myself in these various activities, simply *as* a *for-itself*? Ah! I can desire only what I lack. I *am* a lack, so my original project must be to satisfy it by what does *not* lack the lack.⁴ Well, unfortunately for such a project, that is precisely what we are, 'always

---

³ This replaces the translation, '*a possibility which belongs*', which is scarcely intelligible.
⁴ The argument resembles that of Platos *Diotima*, discussing love and beauty.

already', essentially, in being conscious and having aims. I can't lack my *being-a-for-itself.* I can only *pretend* I don't exist for-myself. I *am* a for-itself. Not lacking it, I cannot desire to become it.

Why not, then, cease to desire to exist as in itself – settle down into living out my being for myself? Why desire to *become* what already I am? Why desire to become something incompatible with that? My being is God-like enough in its power to nihilate being, as a God is omnipotent in creating it. Why destroy such a state of perfection? We know the answer from early on. Well, we know well about the element that disturbs the system: as a *for-itself* I am free, and I live the consciousness of this freedom in anguish. I desire escape from this unhappy human condition. Yes, but why not settle down with a little *in-itself* then? I shall abstain from desiring it, if this desire means the absurd aim of *becoming* that existence in itself. Shan't we then live happily ever after? Alas! An impediment to this happiness exists, more disturbing to it than even my tendency to flee my own state of being for myself: To be as purely *for oneself* is not to *be.*[5] Only an *in-itself* can have being. To live purely *for oneself* is an infinite lack, a nothingness we learned in existentialist kindergarten.

There is nothing to *being-for-itself* – living for oneself. Such a failure of being will be swamped in gaining its prize of the lovely solid reassuring on-going coming-ready-or-not *in-itself* that is so utterly *being* while the *for-itself* (*to live for oneself*) is, as a nerd, *not to be.* When the infinitely desiring *for-itself* meets the infinitely desirable *in-itself*, there will be found nothing but an *in-itself.*[6] The *in-itself* has not even *consumed* the *for-itself.* It found nothing there to consume. The referee declares 'No contest!'.

> The for-itself is its own lack of being ... The for-itself arises as the nihilation of the in-itself and this nihilation is ... the project toward the in-itself. Between the nihilated in-itself and the projected in-itself the for-itself is nothingness. Thus the end ... of the nihilation which I am is the in-itself (BN, 567).

Living for oneself, aware of the absurdity of my project while incapable of being released from it, I begin to wise up: *I could desire that plain factual in-itself if she makes herself nice – more civil, a little more civilised.* The *in-itself* itself anticipates this desire in gestures of cross-dressing towards the (masculine) self-image:[7]

---

[5] Were it so, to be a *for-itself* would be the mode of *being: being not-an-itself.*
[6] 'And a she-wolf, that seemed laden with all/ cravings in her leanness and has caused many peoples to live in wretchedness' (Dante 1996: 49–51).
[7] Le Dœuff observes this double frustration in Shakespeare's 'The Phoenix and the Turtle' (Le Dœuff 1986a: 26).

> [T]he in-itself which it desires cannot be pure contingent, absurd, in-itself, comparable at every point to that which it encounters and which it nihilates. The nihilation is ... like a revolt of the in-itself, which nihilates itself against its contingency (BN, 566).

Tragic farce. In my desire to have the *in-itself*, it seems that, in living for myself I am hell bent on *becoming* what exists *in-itself*. Meanwhile, what exists *in-itself* risks the very stability for which, in living for myself, I desire it. So, on the quiet, she nihilates on *(her)self* a little, so as to approximate the world of the *for-itself* – my living for myself. She wants to be recognised, after all:

> What the for-itself demands of the in-itself is precisely the totality de-totalised – 'In-itself nihilated in for-itself' (BN, 566).

Like Narcissus, to live *for oneself* is to recognise something like oneself in looking at what one loves. We do not welcome the loneliness of Venus who, when deserted by an Adonis who refused her every word, now complains about the birds which echo everything she utters (*Venus and Adonis* I.850–853, Shakespeare 1959).

And the Desire to Be God?

Freedom and consciousness have become one and the same. The absurd desire one has – to gain solidity in being conscious and exist as *in-itself* – is equal with desiring *for* God in *becoming* God. The detached existence of a *Being*, perfectly *in-itself* and fully *for-itself*, would not satisfy the believer who desires to possess his object – to gain its desired quality. What we desire we desire to possess, argues Sartre (BN, 575–577). The desire for God is the desire to *have* this God, for only thus would *we* experience, at once, the stability of the *in-itself* and one's creative being for oneself. Like the desire of his man to make of the *for-itself* an *in-itself*, this grandiloquent, pathetic desire is a logical consequence of the initial (absurd) fundamental project. How can I have this being which has all the creativity and freedom and awareness of a god, and yet preserve the reliability, the facticity of the *in-itself*? I should have to *be* that *in-itself*. (*'I should have been a pair of ragged claws'*?)

What advantage is there if a being exists, perfectly in-itself and fully for-itself, if I cannot possess it? Why possess it unless the possession is so intimate that I take on the character of what I possess? This desire to have the advantage of the qualities of what I desire, is the original meaning of the desire for God. What I cannot achieve for myself – the union of *being-*

in-itself and *being-for-itself* – could be achieved by a being of infinite intelligence and power. This *being* might then confer its achievement upon the one who would 'draw nigh unto him'. There is correlative reading of the absurd wish (this 'useless passion') that is man. The persisting passion of a *belief* in God is otherwise incomprehensible. The *belief* has out-lived the ancient reasons for belief – our inadequate grasp of the powers of nature. As existentialist, Sartre places the source of the belief within our passions, mirroring Descartes' placement of his knowledge of God amongst the ideas within the intimacy of his soul:

> Whatever may be the myths and rites of the religion considered, God is first 'sensible to the heart' of man as the one who identifies and defines him in his ultimate and fundamental project (BN, 566).

Belief in God is wishful thinking when God is defined without austerity. It is wishful to believe in a kindly, helpful and wise One who makes things turn out for the best – to whom we appeal when all else fails. Given the everyday world, this story beats anything we hear in a second-hand car yard. The efforts to formulate God as an absolute in existence, in contrast, fail not by improbability but in the absurdity of the desire they evince. Their wishful character is not like the child's easy wish for a biscuit when the cupboard is bare. The wish for a transcendent *being* who knows us in our inner feeling is like that of a child who wants a 'whole biscuit' and cries in discovering that upon taking a bite there is now a bit missing. To vary the metaphor, those with a passion for belief – a desire supercharged rather than annulled by its own absurdity – are like Sartre's 'lover' who desires to 'be the whole world' for the one he loves 'as a free consciousness for herself'.

Sartre's analysis has a striking advantage in explaining the passion of belief in terms of its peculiar absurdity. The detached rationalist can only excoriate the believer for clinging to faith when confronted with the shiny face of reason. Sartre's analysis explains how we know what it would be like for there to be a God. If there *is* a 'fool [who] has said in his heart that there is no God' it is he who denies what he knows well as an absurd desire that he will not cancel.[8] Nietzsche's '*God is dead*' has arrested us to the progress of thought more than the sober judgement: '*There is no good reason to believe that God exists*'. Nietzsche's announcement is an oxymoron since the God Nietzsche was interested to contend with is

---

[8] Martinez and Durling wonder why Dante's narrator expresses such fear of a she-wolf. I think it is because while a he-wolf wolfs his prey and is satisfied (a simple soul that lives purely for-itself), the she-wolf, hungry on another's account, exists in order that others may consume. This breeds an insatiable anxiety for well being (Dante 1996: 36).

defined as immortal. One cannot *cease to be* immortal. We who were
shocked or delighted by Nietzsche know this implicitly. The illocutionary
force of Nietzsche's outrageous declaration is, '*God has always been an
imposter, a fraud, and a mountebank*'. We have only ourselves to blame
when we are discountenanced by his death. It was we who raised him up
from the dead (letter office) by the force of an absurd, infinite desire.

Only we who exist *for ourselves* could have so perfectly idealised the
desire and fear of the parent. We have created One who created us without
risk and pain, who knows without need of a way of knowing, who loves
without need, who suffers no hazards of materiality and yet can identify
with us in that costly business. This God knows us as creatures of flesh,
blood, bone and brain and yet without distance, in our innermost thoughts
and feelings. That last desire is that useless passion to be a *for-itself* that has
being. It is the desire that the *in-itself* should acquire, tacitly, the character
of the *for-itself* – to have conferred on itself the value we confer by our
desire and passion. We want the difference between the *for-itself* and the
in-itself and we want the power to absorb or to annul that difference. Such a
desire is for a being who is so different from us as to be an absolute creator,
perfectly knowing, loving us without hidden agenda or need for reward.

In recoil from such absurd desire and senseless existence, yet desiring
not to feel lonely when alone, we might do well to consider Plato and
Arendt's idea that to think is to have a conversation with ourselves.[9] To
think is already to be two people in one. This is not religious nostalgia. I
need not demand that when alone my interlocutor is other than myself since
to have a mind is already to exist in plurality of consciousness. We can
overcome the insistence on an *infinite* difference between locutor and
interlocutor in the gesture by which we would 'differ' a God from
ourselves. If I do not have to present my thoughts and feelings externally
for this God to read them, then that Being is *within* my mind. As
interiorised, there is no difference between a God and a multiple self,
capable of self-fission. A pluralised being that has to be divined by others is
simply oneself. Luce Irigaray resolves this tendency to find the divine
within the soul. She would have us regard each other as *to be divined*
(Irigaray 1993b: 55–72).[10] Sartre thinks of this Spectre as imposed by
absurd desire – a medium between selves as conscious and as bodily
beings:

---

[9] See the *Sophist* and *Theaetetus* (Plato 1953) and *The Life of the Mind* (Arendt 1971: 73–
83, 179–193).
[10] This idea will be taken up in the final essay in the present work.

Thus ... the God, which we find in Leibniz ... is the negation of interiority; it is concealed in the theological notion of creation: God is and is not both myself and the Other since he creates us.[11] He must be myself in order to apprehend my reality without intermediary and yet ... he [must] not be me in order that he be over there both to be and not be the Other (BN, 232).

Desire's Lack

Desire's Lack of Being

The lack of reason for desire is now reflected in desire's own lack of being, and on this ontology, stemming from Plato[12] and Plotinus, Sartre founds his existential psychoanalysis:

> Desire is a lack of being. As such it is directly supported by the being of which it is a lack. Thus the being of human reality is originally ... a lived relation (BN, 575).

While desire is for something one does *not* yet possess, or for *not* losing what one has, there is also a fullness of being in desire that Plato, Plotinus and Sartre take no account of. To lack desire is a greater lack than desire's lack of its object, but Sartre wants to depend upon, rather than unsettle this tradition of desire as lack. Like the object of perception, the object of desire 'directly supports' its desiring consciousness and creates a lived relation between desire and world. This gives Sartre a pivot to lever up his account of value in terms of the *in-itself* and *for-itself* and, at the same time to press his vision of the *for-itself* called man, as *not-being*:

> The limiting terms of this relation are first the original In-itself, fixed in its facticity, and second the In-itself-for-itself or value, which exists as the Ideal of the In-itself ... Man is neither the one nor the other of these beings, for, strictly speaking, we should never say of him that he is at all (BN, 575).

Sartre points out how any desire is a complex of the sub-desires involved in what we want. This relation explains the ease with which we find reasons for our desires – they are part of, or means to, more fundamental aims. He designates one's desire to *appropriate* as essential to the process. Desire as a lack smoothes the way – in filling the lack, it

---

[11] This argument depends on God's intimacy with his act of creation. God creates as an author creates his characters, knowing their every thought because he wrote the script. But God as our author demotes us as figments of Divine imagination.
[12] See, for instance, Plato's *Symposium* (Plato 1957, Vol I: 531–532).

becomes one's own. To desire a picture is to desire to buy it, or otherwise to appropriate it, to secure it as object of one's gaze or grasp. Sartre alleges inextricable links between 'to do', 'to have' and 'to be': all *doing* signifies the desire to *have*. The desire to have mutates into the desire to be. Even the desire to create certain activities is the desire to *have* them as one's own creations, since to desire to have them is the desire to be them.

The issue becomes fraught when Sartre argues that to know, also, is to appropriate. Something which *I* had not previously encountered becomes *my* knowledge, but this knowledge refuses to remain *my* property:

> [T]he thought which I form ... pursues ... its own independent existence to the extent that it is thought by everybody (BN, 578).

This knowledge revealed to me is a thought that relates *me* to others. At the same time it is *'doubly closed to me'*. I recognise how things are as how things are for me, and yet as beyond myself, capable of anonymity. Sartre might have argued in the same way that the object I desire pursues its own independent existence to the extent that it is *desired* by others.

Sartre's tale of thought takes a new turn: *'in addition the idea of discovery includes an idea of appropriate enjoyment'* (BN, 578). Purists may banish this reference to 'appropriate enjoyment' as irrelevant to knowledge, and others may suspect egocentricity. But Sartre is right – it is unreal to exclude enjoyment as intrinsic to discovery. It is when he says, as if putting it in other words, *'What is seen is possessed; to see is to deflower'* that critical reflexes spring into play. To *deflower*? Man as knowing violator of innocent feminine Nature? Le Dœuff complains that Sartre has no right to assume any 'we' who would recognise that

> the comparisons ... are represented as being a kind of violation by sight. The unknown object is given as immaculate, as virgin, comparable to whiteness (BN, 578).

Rather than satirising these fantasies he buys into their market. We have to ask whether this image of perception and knowledge as *defloration* is now only an exhibit in the philosophical museum? Yellowing, curling at the edges? Or a trace yet at work beneath our iconography of knowledge? Sartre might have satirised, rather than inscribed and re-employed it. Beauvoir, working with Sartre then, exposes the picture, still visible, in order to mock it in *Le Deuxième Sexe* a decade later.

This ancient connection of the gaining of knowledge with the loss of innocence, and of sexual innocence in particular, is still maintained by the religious institutions in their desire to control the education of children. The

State, too, in its control of education, wants to protect the innocence of children in denying them knowledge of the shameful along with the honourable events of their nation's past and present. And there is only what we might laughably call reason to think that the permission of free access to knowledge should be figured as a *woman's* loss of innocence. What does it mean, to collapse the gaining of knowledge into the gaining of sexual experience, itself represented as a deflowering, with all that term implies about a loss of bloom and beauty? (Downhill all the way from there!) Sartre's free use of imagery can prompt us to raise these questions, but his theory, image and story reinforce each other, prefiguring the answers.

We can guess what happens next – to know is to destroy the innocence of its object in the same act as the tyro knower loses his.[13] The desire to know is a desire to appropriate, but the object resists, for it speaks of '*its own independent existence to the extent that it is thought by everybody*' (BN, 578). This discourse between appropriating subject and never-to-be-quite ensnared object is played out in the ensuing revival of another great old tradition of epistemology and ontology – the struggle between the revelation of the object in its qualities, and the object itself as always already hidden under or behind those qualities. And so we come to the final stage of this excursion into images of knowing and the known, in its relation to desire's lack and its lack of reason.

The Question of Qualities

Perceived qualities of things reveal being says Sartre:

> In each apprehension of quality, there is ... a metaphysical effort to ... pierce through the shell of nothingness ... to penetrate to the pure in-itself. But ... we can apprehend quality only as a symbol of a being which totally escapes us, even though it is totally there before us ... we can only make revealed being function as a symbol of being in itself (BN, 603).

How things are for us opens up what the world is. If there were no ways the world was for us, we should know nothing of it. Yet as fast as the world shows itself we become suspicious of what we have been permitted to see, fearing that we have come to know the *world-as-it-is-for-us* rather than *the-world-as-it-is-in-itself*. This is what Sartre means in his cryptic remark, '*quality [is] only a symbol of a being which totally escapes us even though it is totally there before us*' (BN, 603–604). The qualities in terms of which we perceive are functions of what *we* are like as well as the qualitied thing

---

[13] 'His or hers'? Is knowledge attributed to women and men with an even hand?

in itself. If we stand beside a chimpanzee or swim beside a whale, the world we see is the same as the other animals perceive, but is not *qualitied* for a swimming chimpanzee as for a cruising whale, or for us. It will not even be *qualitied* in just the same way for every human. The one world, differently *qualitied* for the beings that exist in their different manners of perceiving it, has been symbolised by the way it appears, qualitatively.

We perceive this neutral world, which we take to possess in its own right the qualities it presents. We must perceive it as *qualitied* – we cannot describe it as un-described or theorise it as beyond theory; we cannot perceive it other than in the ways *we* find it as perceivable. We cannot describe and theorise it without concepts, and we must use the concepts *we* have – we describe this world as it is for just these human beings of this culture and sexuality that *we* happen to possess. Our concepts have been made possible by our experience, and by particular processes of abstract thought in the light of that experience. Other beings, with different modes of perception, would no more produce our physical theories than they would see the same qualitied world we find so evident. The differences do not remain entirely mysterious, though. The lives, customs and responses of the other animal species indicate to us something of their world.

Thus, we claim a feasible objectivity, accepting this *partiality* in our appreciation of the world without losing confidence in what we have discovered. Secure in this, we are ready to modify our acceptance of the qualities our world presents. Eager to expand on what is presented, we bring all that we infer from experiments and understand theoretically. We extend objectivity as a nuanced way of handling varieties of subjectivity, but we do not engineer self-defeat by claiming, by such means, to uncover the world itself as a reality behind *any and all* the qualities exhibited to us. To uncover *anything* about the world is to encounter or to make manifest new qualities. The world itself, but not the world in-itself. How we see the world in terms of its qualities (bizarre or normal) and how we see the world as it is involves forms and senses of subjectivity. Our ways of being subject are intrinsic to perception and thought, but to accept that as intrinsic to an approach to reality does not entail that all views are equally true, or equally false. Without a common world of our differing investigations we should not find ourselves differing.[14]

Imagination and Perception

We can use these reflections in dealing with what Sartre says about lack in relation to desire. Dissociating his writing from the work of imagination,

---

[14] I have argued this position in detail (Deutscher 1983: 214–247).

Sartre aims to describe what he perceives, but his poetic phenomenology of *quality* and *being* relies on how *we* see the world, and we are not one unified group.[15] His narrative 'I' sees the *'feminine and masculine poles of the world'* (BN, 601), the *'secret meaning of snow'* (BN, 582, 584, 601), the *'sliminess of a smile'* (BN, 604), the *'hysteresis of honey'* (BN, 608). Those who fail to see the *for-itself* slide towards the *in-itself* when sticky honey flows from a spoon, when breasts flatten against the body in repose, do not have a failure of eyesight but of metaphysical imagination.

Sartre can claim that *'to perceive does not mean to assemble images by means of sensations'*, but he surely he exaggerates in adding, *'perception has nothing in common with imagination'* (BN, 600). Certainly we perceive *imaginatively* and are led by our modes of imagination in how we take what we see. Sartre's own description of seeing *someone* rather than some *thing* near a park bench (BN, 254) depends on imaginative perception as vital to seeing what stands before the eyes. I see *somebody* (rather than some body) not by peering, but by imagining the park from a point of view not my own.

Sartre has chosen the phenomenon of the *visqueux* to make us question the distinction we make so swiftly between an objective state of nature and our subjective reactions to it. We do not just *'project our affective dispositions on the thing, to illuminate or color it'* (BN, 604). One cannot just dismiss Sartre as describing things 'only as they seem to him', since each of us make good our claims of how things are by relying on how they appear. Each of us must accept that the qualities we find indicate the significance things have for us. Though Sartre cannot assume a unified *we* who find the given qualities in things, it remains possible that these differences in the ways we find and take the world may involve common factors. These may be open to our differing perceptions, to being experienced and discussed, contestable by any observer.[16]

Even as we proceed to contest and augment what is given to us at any phase we regard qualities as a revelation of being. It is this readiness of engagement and critique which enables us, whether scientists, poets, artists or philosophers, to understand the world itself and our projects within that world through qualities that speak of our responses. At the extreme of imagination and metaphor, the body becomes drizzling honey and drizzling honey is an agony of water that takes its revenge upon free consciousness. Sartre is maintaining imagination as central to understanding what we perceive. Snow melts in our hands. Money slips through our fingers or burns a hole in our pockets. We melt away at a fearful sight.

---

[15] Sartre argues this himself (BN, 413–430).

[16] See a discussion of perception by animals in *Theaetetus* (Plato 1953, Vol III: 258–260).

There is a fascination in fairy tales for the precariously adult reader no less than for the child to whom they are read. It is in order to understand desire for which there can be no adequate reason that Sartre took up our involvement with the hidden liquidity of what is solid.[17] He had the effrontery to read this fascination ontologically, elaborating it in terms of the *'in-itself'* and the *'for-itself'*. Our fascination[18] with the ambiguously liquid and solid is reckoned to signify our horror at the possible reversion it signifies – a reversal of the process by which the inert *in-itself* has transformed itself into the mobile *for-itself*. Since the *for-itself is* the *in-itself* in the process of nihilating itself, this horror is at the same time a fascination with a hidden motility within the inert. And, as we read earlier,

> in each apprehension of quality, there is in this sense a metaphysical effort to escape from our condition so as to pierce through the shell of nothingness about the 'there is' and to penetrate to the pure in-itself (BN, 603).

He continues,

> But obviously, we can apprehend quality only as a symbol of a being which totally escapes us, even though it is totally there before us; in short, we can only make revealed being function as a symbol of being-in-itself' (BN, 603–604).

Here Sartre takes up his theme of the *visqueux*, translated as the slimy or sticky.[19] The viscous as the slimy is what makes us uneasy; it is what is undependable, what is both more and less than is presented for our acceptance. Since Sartre holds to a theory of knowledge as appropriation, it indicates how what we seemed to have known securely, may slip from our grasp. The slippery is a quality of metaphysical argument itself. This lack of dependability is the customary sense in English – 'slimy handshake', 'slimy smile', 'slimy thought'.

---

[17] There are connected themes in Irigaray's writing here, too.

[18] In later parts of this work I contrast Sartre's 'nausea' with Irigaray's 'wonderment'.

[19] The translator notes that Sartre's 'visqueux' is rendered simply by 'sticky' or 'viscous', but prefers the emotional connotations of 'slimy'. The *Petit Robert* gives the descriptions 'qui est épais et sécoule avec difficulté; qui est mou et adhère en formant une couche gluante'. Practical synonyms include *'collant'* (*clinging*), *'poisseux'* (*sticky*), *'gras'* (*fatty or greasy*), *'huileux'* (*oily*) and *'sirupeux'* (*syrupy*). Sartre's own writing has become the benchmark for *'visqueux'* as meaning an untrustworthy character: 'un sourire est visqueux, une pensée, un sentiment peuvent être visqueux' (a smile, a thought, a feeling can be visqueux').

Imagination and Absence in Desire

Eluding Appropriation

Sartre has already elaborated his idea that, in our involvement with things and people, and in our most disinterested knowledge, what we humans want is to *appropriate* what we deal with. It is 'superficial', he says, to explain our horror at the slimy simply by some brute quality of the substance, and equally impossible to make something merely psychological out of the phenomenon in terms of pre-existing attitudes. Rather, our repugnance at the *visqueux* arises because semi-fluidity challenges our fundamental desire to engage with the world by appropriating it. That which is neither properly solid nor properly liquid foils that desire, and thus foils the desire to know an object, if to know is to appropriate something without the chance of its slipping out of one's grasp. The *visqueux* does not slip away to be held in its own container as does a pure fluid – liquid or gas. Nor, as does a solid, will it remain to be firmly grasped or consumed, whether in being eaten or in becoming known. (With what great satisfaction and recommendation we speak of solid issues, solid arguments.) What is fluid can be safely contained within solids ready for ingestion – a cup of tea, a glass of wine, a tumbler of water. If the fluid is a medium like the sea or the atmosphere within which we exist, it sustains or buoys us up ready for our appropriations:

> [A] being without danger and without memory, which eternally is changed into itself, on which one leaves no mark, and which could not leave a mark on us, a being which slides and on which one can slide, which can be possessed by something sliding (BN, 584–585).

Le Dœuff steadies our reading of this. We are in the realm of the dream here, she says. Yes. When I awake I realise that it makes a lot of difference whether I go to take a tumbler of water or, inadvertently, of gin. If a fluid leaves no mark, I would do well to make an early check whether the 'water' I am about to splash on my skin is not nitric acid.[20]

Sartre's *visqueux* – the slimy, the viscous, the gluey, the tacky, the slippery, the oily cannot be appropriated as can the solid that remains at hand. Nor does it keep to its own domain like the fluids that sustain or envelop us. The '*visqueux*' sticks to us or sucks down the solid, which attempts to take hold of it, rest on it, or slide on or through it as we would a

---

[20] To lodge chemistry against the phenomenology of fluids disrupts the flow of metaphor – like standing up during a play to cry out that none of it is real.

fluid.[21] In a bizarre figure, Sartre declares that '*slimy [the viscous] is the agony of water*'.[22] In viscosity, liquids and solids are in agonistic combat – the liquid becomes sticky and the solid slips. It is the 'death' of both of them, but, as in the Greek/Hegelian notion of the agonistic struggle, something more is revealed about each in this death.

Scene and Ob-scene

Most commentators blink (Manser 1966, Naess 1968, Grene 1971, Morris 1976, Caws 1979, Catalano 1986, McCulloch 1994) when they come to Sartre's metaphors of vaginal obscenity. They are silent at or silenced by these images of the female sex as something that 'gapes open', making its metaphysical appeal to *being* as do all *holes* (BN, 613). The text purveys what Warnock described as 'pornographic' images of women (Warnock 1965).[23] Le Dœuff has observed the section too, more precisely, mocking her own impending 'nausea' at the terms and tones of its portrayal of the female body. There are passages that one must '*handle with tweezers*' she says (Le Dœuff 1991:165). There is no licence for the private nightmare of a 'Monsieur Sartre' to be passed off as general propositions about the character of the world and of knowing and of perceiving it, she implies. Le Dœuff is concerned not only with what Sartre is doing here, but at the tacit currency given to Sartre's ideas for some decades – those who criticise his philosophy stay silent about the metaphor he makes of a woman's body. Le Dœuff proposes that his philosophical dealing with things sexual approaches, in its 'verbal violence', everyday aggression towards women.

Certainly, Sartre (or his narrator's 'I') is obsessed with the female form in all of this discussion of what threatens the achievement of freedom by the *in-itself*. Le Dœuff's irritation at his description of breasts settling against a reclining female figure is not only at a voyeur's attitude. The semi-solid, now taking the form of breasts, has already been loaded with qualities of repugnance and threat. But now there is more. The narrator's anxiety about semi-solids has been projected onto the woman – displaced, surely, from his own body. Anxiety over erection and detumescence. Now the *visqueux*, threatening his living for himself, is described as feminine, and that in turn, (implied as well known to any reader) can pull down any careless traveller into its swamp.[24]

---

[21] The marshy swamp, rather than the pool in which one can swim.
[22] The notion of an agonistic struggle derives from ancient Greek thought (revived by the 19C Hegel) in which those who struggle discover their true natures.
[23] It was the tone, not the sexual explicitness that attracted her adverse comment.
[24] And would the threat be any less to a travelling woman?

Sartre links the quality of the *visqueux* with that of spaces, fissures, or holes, and connects that fantasy of a lack in being with the female sex. Is it his image of the female sexual form, endowed with a deep ontological significance, that inspires the dream-like philosophising which follows? Or is it his abstract image of *being-for-itself* and *being-in-itself* that inspires his image of the feminine as lack or hole in *being*? He writes of the 'obscenity of the female sex'. If the *ob*-scene is what is performed out of its proper place, what is the 'proper' scene of sex, then? Irigaray contends that for such a philosophy, woman is 'that sex which is *not* one', an expression she inflects to her purposes as 'that sex which is not *one* (Irigaray 1995b: 23).

Masculine, Feminine, For-itself and In-itself

'*A strange image*' says Glaucon to Socrates after hearing the first announcement of the allegory of the cave (Plato 1953, Vol II: 376). Yet it is the story of all of us, Socrates dares reply, and it describes the predicament in which we all find ourselves before achieving philosophical enlightenment. Sartre constructs '*a strange image*' of the masculine and feminine to portray his metaphysics of the *in-itself* and *for-itself*. We should recall what generates it.

Concepts of *being-for-itself* and *being-in-itself* were introduced in *Being and Nothingness* at the outset, with no discernible distinction of masculine and feminine or between everyday men and women. *Being-for-itself* is the possibility of a conscious being that takes account of itself by its power to *nihilate* – to distinguish itself from its objects of perception and thought, from itself as mere object, from other objects, and from other people. This is supposed to be of the essence of a human being. It has been supposed that the theory of that *being* should be *epicene*, either applying to either sex indiscriminately, or applying as to something asexual.

The stories in *Being and Nothingness* that have been told in counterpoint to theory have represented women as liable to lose themselves in the *in-itself*, dragging men down in the process. Sartre's story-telling, metaphors and imagery permit the sense of his theory to appear. The metaphysics of a *for-itself* as threatened by an *in-itself* emerges finally in the form of the female body sucking away the male's self-determination. Sartre juxtaposes two threatening phenomena. Each helps to explain the force of the other. The first is the *visqueux*, which represents the death of the solid, graspable, knowable, material and solid. Equally it is the death of existence as unscathed liquid or gaseous forms, which can buoy up solids so that they can glide, ski, skim or fly. If the *visqueux* is a swamp in which the sturdy *for-itself* is unable to swim, and on which it is equally unable to stand, it is also *the agony of water*. How are we to read this symbolism?

The *visqueux* threatens the distinction of *in-itself* and *for-itself* in another way. Now, in connection with anxiety about *fissures in being*,[25] Sartre attributes to us an anxiety about the places where being fails to be complete. We find gaps, holes and drains in things. We are supposed to feel compelled to fill them, to stop them up.[26] Perhaps this compulsion bears no relation to what we need in these things, or what they need for themselves. Perhaps, as Sartre implies, we stop up gaps because they represent to us a primordial lack in *being* itself. Or we may read this metaphysical lack as a free-floating anxiety about the fissures in specific things that have highly charged meaning for us. But, whichever way this anxiety is read, Sartre claims that we see the female body as radically incomplete. Le Dœuff points out, acidly, that women, equally with men, should perceive women's bodies as incomplete. But it is only Sartre's little *boy* who feels compelled to fill up holes and cracks.[27] As if gesturing to a well-known painting in the public gallery, Sartre declares that a woman's sex is 'obscene' in its open-ness. Le Dœuff refers to the passage including this imagery as 'megalomaniac ravings' – nightmares and fantasies of a mind bent on maintaining a sense of control over the proper image of the human body, at no matter what cost:

> The nightmare then moves on to the image of the hole, of which the female genitalia are a notable example. The hole originally appears as a nothingness to be filled with my own flesh, in a sacrifice of my body so that the plenitude of being may exist, in other words to preserve the totality of the In-itself (Le Dœuff 1991: 81).

Sartre does not try these images for validity in the marketplace; he does not check his phenomenology with those whose bodies are involved in this traffic (*l'imagerie*). If the existence of fissures, and a general lack of closure is an existential threat – a too disturbing reminder of lack in being – then on the same basis the mouth is obscene – not only women should wear the chador. The ears are worse. We can't even choose to close them.

* * *

It should not be surprising that a reader should be conducted once again through these thoughts. The body is a cause of anxiety as well as pleasure.

---

[25] Perhaps Sartre runs them together.

[26] The same symbolism would apply to incompleteness in situations and in events.

[27] But is the male body is regarded – (by men? by women?) – as complete?

For each of us, the body is the primary organ of our knowledge of things and people and the universe at large. Hence, it will be at least subliminally involved in all of our imagery and concepts of what is being achieved when we know anything. To enter into these images of body, and our anxiety and pleasure in regard to it, is to enter the land of fantasy, of dream. Not to enter into these images, however, is to allow such dreams and partial truths to operate without scrutiny. We have to defuse Sartre's assumptions, but it is not enough simply to close down his distorted discussion of the human body as lacking propriety. Repression produces only further uneasiness.

Let us stay with Sartre's 'ravings' (as Le Dœuff calls them) for another short term. What of this open or incomplete character to the female sex that he deems to be obscene? And what happens when we recognise the improprieties of the male body? It is not his observation of an absence of complete closure in the female body that we should challenge, but the obscenity of that lack of propriety. The image of the human body as creviced becomes a surreal metaphysics. It is a crevasse, not a crevice; obscene rather than capable of reciprocity; sexually threatening rather than marking a proper sense of difference in propriety.

Sartre was remarkably confident about his and the reader's native powers of interpretation. In the prior section, in connection with the project of an existential psychoanalysis, he says that it is possible to '*decipher the empirical behaviour patterns of man*' because of the

> fundamental, pre-ontological comprehension which man has of the human person'. [For] although people can ignore the indications ... in a gesture, word, a sign ... each human individual possesses a priori the meaning of the revelatory value of these manifestations and is capable of deciphering them, at least if he is aided and guided by a helping hand (BN, 568–569).

Sartre points out that no one has a privileged access to the meaning of their own gestures. While he rejects an *un*conscious mind, to *know* the *always conscious*[28] project of one's life does not come easily or naturally. It requires the observations of others upon my gestures, and the advantage of concepts that I, as subject, may not possess.

---

[28] One is not therefore *conscious of* one's project. To make an explicit theme of it is a new task. The point is that, prior to reflection, the project is *part of* one's conscious being.

Reasons for Desires

Sartre makes a double claim both that the fundamental project that informs our every action, attitude and feeling is a conscious one, and that each needs an observer's view to challenge their avowals of their project. It is not access to a buried unconscious that we need, according to this existential psychoanalysis, but knowledge of what we are *doing* in choosing, acting, feeling and interacting. This is a process of description and interpretation. I may not know what I (or someone else) am up to in my (their) various acts and feelings. The character of what one does is a 'mystery in broad daylight' (BN, 571). The consequence is that in describing a (sexual) phenomenon 'just as it is', Sartre has to contend with observations by others upon his own project in describing it. Furthermore, every 'phenomenon of being' – every appearance of something as it *is* – is transphenomenal. Every such description alludes to an open class of phenomena of that thing, every member of which may be relevant to the description. In consequence, any description of a phenomenon is provisional, pending other descriptions by other perceivers about phenomena concerning the same being. That provisional status must remain, even within a systematic phenomenological ontology.

This is why Sartre, with Beauvoir, had a framework that can contain a feminist critique, though his narrative and imagery now appears misogynist. There is power in the method. His own stories inform and support his metaphysics – they do not merely colour in a pre-determined outline of abstract theory. Like Cézanne or Matisse, shape is created by areas and gradations of colour, but as an elusive and shifting space. The weakness is that he tells his stories and paints his pictures as if he thus clinches his issues. The images and stories that ought to have invited open interpretation adopt instead the dogmatics of an Aquinas. In style and manner his is the voice of '*l'unique sujet parlant*' (Le Dœuff 1991: 177–194).

No less than over-forceful abstract argument, the entertaining story or the memorable image may be abused to produce a sense of closure. The preferred image can arrogantly proclaim totalisation – as if everything has been presented out in the open, making argument and differing observations seem unnecessary, improper. Yet neither argument nor imagery *need* do this. Argued considerations invite other considerations, and one image provokes another. Le Dœuff has shown how we should probe the illustrative, the picture or story, itself liable to be the neuralgic point of a theory. If the story is told or the image painted in probity we should hear a pause as the raconteur concludes or the painter finds some space to hang the canvas. The painter, the storyteller, will be holding their breath, awaiting the story or image or moral the other is dying to tell.

Sartre's style is, however, marked by the absence of such an interest in the criss-crossing stories from the unexpected sources in unfamiliar concepts. Le Dœuff calls such a discourse that shuts out or co-opts its surrounding voices, that of a 'unique' or 'sole' speaking subject (*l'unique sujet parlant*' Le Dœuff 1991: 82–194). The image sketched in probity seeks not to capture the essence of a scene or a subject but to show how it cannot have been captured. It shows a reality as beyond its representation. Those who paint or philosophise in such probity present an image not as readied for simple consumption. The world itself gives the materials by means of which a viewer, and the painter, can see and image what was in process for this image to be presented. Painting itself, as part of the world, is part of the provision of such materials. Famously, Cézanne promised Émile Bernard *the truth in painting*. '*I will tell it to you*', he swore (Merleau-Ponty 1964: 159–190, Derrida 1987: 1–13). And part of the *truth* in his painting lies in how the painting demonstrates the incompleteness of the picture it creates. The viewer can wonder what is so special about Cézanne's work, feeling vaguely impressed, interested, a little uneasy – '*Am I missing something? What am I supposed to see?*'. Cézanne accepts and shows in painting the partiality and instability of a picture of the solid world. This suggests the possibilities of using story and image as strategies of philosophical reason, as part of a mobile phenomenology.

PART III

ABSENT AND INTIMATE OTHERS

6
In Parks and Corridors

How do I know what another thinks and feels? The problem arose for modern philosophy from Descartes' method, which raised up a bright self-awareness against a dark backdrop of always 'dubitable' physical matter. His scepticism involves an image of myself as observer of another, feeling an 'infinite distance' between 'myself' who *perceives* them and the bodily dispositions and actions that another might observe in me. Then, I contemplate their dispositions and actions and wonder about what thoughts and feelings lie behind them. These images arise in everyday life, without need of a philosophical method. In evoking my vulnerability to the gaze of another Sartre is foremost amongst those who break up the picture within which this conundrum is structured.[1]

From Perceiving to Being Perceived

On Being for Yourself

It is in bad faith, says Sartre, that we sense an unbridgeable gulf between being conscious and being actively disposed in one's body. Using '*being-in-itself*' and '*being-for-itself*', he describes how 'bad faith' arises and becomes entrenched, if meta-stable.[2] '*Being-for-itself*' is not merely a phrase to replace '*conscious*'. As related to '*being-in-itself*' it undoes knots in the notion of consciousness.[3] *Being-in-itself* can have no regard for itself; it has no regard for anything else; it establishes no 'distance' within itself, nor any 'distance' of itself from other things. *Being-in-itself* takes a view upon itself and its situation, its past and its environment. In taking regard of these things, it gives us a kind of freedom, but afraid of our own being – afraid to be *the one who acts and values things* – we lapse into an absurd state. In 'bad faith' we act as if we were incapable of deciding how to value one thing over another.

---

[1] Author's construction of the 'dualist' tradition that Sartre means to undermine.

[2] The production of philosophical 'dualism' would be part of this entrenchment.

[3] Expositors commonly say that *being-for-itself* just means 'conscious'.

A person is not only an object at a distance from, or in contact with, other objects. As 'somebody', I *distance* myself from objects, take myself as 'not the object over there', and the object over there as 'not myself'. I distance myself also by thinking of objects as they would look from elsewhere. We are *people* in 'distancing' ourselves from bodies, becoming beings that are 'no-thing' beyond our brainy bodies. In 'nihilating' we are 'no-things'.[4] Consciousness is 'constituted in our flesh', Sartre says.

We are people – we have being *for ourselves* – not simply in 'having' fears, pain, pleasures, and hopes. We *fear, suffer, enjoy and hope*, take up a stance, engage with or bracket off feelings and tendencies. We make our states of mind the medium of involvement with others and with ourselves. *Being* is a mode of existence, not a *thing*. We have *being-for-itself* in that feelings are modes of 'taking in' what we encounter. They are the manners in which, pre-consciously, we approach and perceive things. We look sadly at our wrecked car; it is the *car* we consider, sadly, not our sadness that we attend to. And yet, we may then set our distress apart as its own object of attention. We may come to judge – '*Stupid to be upset about the car when we got out without a scratch!*'.

On Being for Others

There is a limitation in consciousness as a *being-for-itself*. From that point of view everything exists as if *for* it. Before me stands a tree; a wide beach stretches beyond it; in the distance a ship appears on the horizon. At one end of the beach someone is about to go into the surf. This all exists as for me who observes it. Someone taps me on the shoulder – '*This is a private beach*'. I am angry, embarrassed at this scrutiny.[5] I want back my innocent possession of the beach and sea and ship on the horizon, these things that I still sense in the background through my mortification. My very right to take in the world through my senses is under challenge. In such a changed world I have *being-for-the-Other*.

I lose something in being subject to another's gaze, but I gain something too. In becoming the one observed, I understand the difference between my seeing someone as an object of my perception and seeing them as a centre of their own world. The person I saw getting ready to go into the surf was not just *to be perceived*. The visual 'portrait' that forms on my retina and within my brain/mind only suggests the picture of what they are. What it is like to *be* the surfer 'for his or her self' is not a matter of 'looking to me

---

[4] Sartre's brief account in 'The Reef of Solipsism' (BN, 233–252) is extended in 'The Look' (BN, 252–303).
[5] This shift could occur within pride but still there is embarrassment.

like a surfer'.[6] The world *for* the surfer is not that of the one who looks at the surfer: the surfer's world is of being in the surf, or on a beach offering the promise of good waves, or of a solitude disturbed by someone gawking. As I continue I discover that I have to take things in for myself as someone whose own way of being present in the scene is open to observation and appraisal. The world becomes more than 'something for me' as observer or user of it.

In being regarded by others I discover that my own being as conscious is constituted not only as *being-for-myself* (to coin a phrase), but as *for-others*. In realising this, I begin to understand the limits of my own control over what I am and can be and how others see me. I can think of myself as thought about or judged by people at some later time, as becoming older, or having been younger. I realise the *vanity* of Descartes' notion that he understands his whole nature as a conscious being simply in his immediate acquaintance with his own mind, and with what passes through it. To think in that way is to overlook, in the midst of one's egocentricity, that I am observable to others as a conscious being, and that these others can call attention to the ways in which I am conscious. As *being-for-myself* these aspects escape me – my distance from myself lies in my imagination. Only others can make me an object of *observation*.

Sartre shifts from story-telling to theorising. In being discovered looking through a keyhole, his philosophical narrator 'goes red'. The 'colour' of his shame is not something he can observe with detachment: '*Shame ... realises an intimate relation of myself to myself*' (BN, 221). As intimate, it is shocking that this shame comes to him from how he is viewed by someone else – with full force as from *outside*. He would be more comfortable to engage in his own soul-searching about it. The shame produced by another's look is a reflex, an '*immediate shudder*' that '*runs through [him] from head to foot*'. In one blow, his own world that absorbed him as he peered through the keyhole is taken over by someone else. A critical glance is enough to overtake the voyeur's egocentricity.

Shame and guilt is not essential to Sartre's stories. In the midst of making up a tune a child might become aware of someone listening with admiration. The child's immediate surroundings and half-heard sound of their musical phrase is replaced by a world in which they are the '*budding musician*'.[7] The child flushes with pride rather than shame, happy perhaps to relinquish a solitary musical consciousness, but Sartre's point about how the view of another changes one's own sense of being remains. The quality

---

[6] The professional surfer says of the poseur – 's/he's only interested in how s/he thinks s/he looks', having a more disinterested interest in their own style.

[7] Sartre's grandparents discover his stories; he becomes 'the little writer'.

of the child's musicality becomes something s/he can frame externally – an 'objective fact' known primarily by others. When I, narrator of my own story, am caught looking through the keyhole, I realise something unpredictable from within consciousness as only for myself. My awareness of another's regard shows me 'I' am not lord and master of my own conscious life, that life has a life of its own, an ontological 'thickness'. I discover that a conscious life I lived pre-reflectively has an outside to be seen.[8] Worse – for my sense of being master of my soul – I discover that this 'outside' is the intimate self I had taken to be my own possession.

Public Exposure of Dualistic Realism

The (dualistic) 'realism' which Sartre is seeking to expose, treats mind and body as separate and real things. That can still sound like sturdy common sense. Like Hume before him, Sartre argues that it leads to scepticism, or the empty certainty of solipsism. A realist would take for granted the existence of physical things including his own body and that of others. Of course he would not doubt that he himself is conscious; he is quite certain about his own states of mind. Yet such a 'realist' is beset by a problem:

> Neither from observing what they do, nor from listening to what they say, can I know what another person thinks and feels and intends. How do I know that the sounds I hear from them have the same meaning I attach to them when I utter them? How can I know that they mean anything at all? If I can have no idea what another person thinks, feels and means, why should I fancy that another person thinks, feels, and means anything at all?[9]

Sartre's '*It is strange that the problem of Others has never truly disturbed the realists*' constitutes a radical critique of this tradition. For, if it is doubtful whether other people think and feel, then it is doubtful whether there are *other people*. To accept the reality of others as thinking, feeling beings 'given to us in sense'[10] is at odds with the image of mind and body as two different things. If the mind is a thing separate from the body, 'immaterial' where the body is material, I could only dream that another body had a mind connected with it.

In the latter part of the twentieth century it became a commonplace to suggest that the mind is a *material* thing – the brain. This removes the gulf between body and mind but does not resolve the question of how I have *being-for-others*. The theory still places the conscious being whom others

---

[8] Wittgenstein has similar reflections. Neither appears to have read the other.

[9] Author's construction of a typical 'realist' point of view.

[10] Sartre uses Kant's term 'intuition' to mean such 'direct sensory awareness'.

appear to meet 'in the flesh', as an unobservable entity within and behind my expressions. As a process in the brain, consciousness remains, in its own way, 'separable' from the body. That a neurophysiologist might have a working theory of what is going on 'in there' does not help me recognise another's thought and feeling. Physicalist theories place thought and feeling within the body, and insist that though they *can* be withheld from expression,[11] they are not necessarily private – not 'intrinsically inner'. However, just as thought and feeling are not intrinsically within a non-bodily mind, they are not intrinsically within the brain, either. On the view that emerges from Sartre's phenomenology their alternative site is neither an immaterial soul nor the brain but rather the body at large. Within Descartes' method of doubt, though I do eventually find reason to accept that there are bodies in motion and at rest, thought and feeling remain *essentially* different from their bodily expression. My sensory awareness of objects does not include my (everyday) sense of others as expressing thoughts and feelings and as making observations of me. Prior to accepting others as *observably* conscious beings I can only *hope* that my observations justify an inference that these other bodies are driven by minds – whether 'physical' or 'non-physical'. This 'vain hope' is the only reasonable attitude for the (dualist) realist, for whom,

> my body ... and the Other's body are the necessary intermediaries between the Other's consciousness and mine. The Other's soul[12] is therefore separated from mine by all the distance which separates first my soul from my body, then my body from the Other's body, and finally the Other's body from his soul (BN, 223).

So, if 'realism' rests on our consciousness of others only in their *objectity*,

> it cannot lay claim ... [to] the reality of the Other's soul, since the Other's soul does not give itself 'in person' to mine. In a philosophy based on intuition [sensory awareness] there is provided no intuition of the soul of the Other ... [I]f we are not to play on words, this means that realism provides no place for the intuition of the Other (BN, 223).

How can I conceive of this 'other' whose experience I cannot experience? The realist (and idealist) conceives of the Other as a being who is 'not-myself' and indicates this by an 'external negation', thinking that 'not being me' *'derives its being'* as from a third party. If we assume that we know *what* an 'other' would be, the question becomes 'Are there *others* at

---

[11] The withholding of thought involves *some* outer expression – a guardedness.

[12] 'Soul' has Descartes' sense: 'That immaterial entity whose essence is to think'.

all?' If those other bodies cannot be known to be conscious, they cannot be known to be *others*. For realist as for idealist, the difference between others and myself is a 'given fact', independent of the relationship between another and myself. Sartre argues this to be their fundamental error:

> The realist[13] who believes that he apprehends the Other through the body, considers that he is separated from the Other as one body from another [as if] 'I am not Paul' is [like] 'the table is not the chair' (BN, 231).

But my expressing myself can have an impact on another – 'in their being':

> If my relation to the Other must be in the mode of indifferent exteriority,[14] then I cannot be affected in my being by the upsurge ... of the Other any more than the In-itself can be affected by the appearance ... of another In-itself' (BN, 231).

This *mode of indifferent exteriority* had to be re-established against an immediate sense of the 'Other', given in the voyeur's rush of blood. Sartre loops back to resume the story of others within this extended frame.

Perceiving Others

From a Pavement Café

> This woman whom I see coming toward me, this man who is passing by in the street, this beggar whom I hear calling before my window, all are for me objects – of that there is no doubt (BN, 252–253).[15]

In depicting these simple encounters, Sartre's phrases – '*this woman whom I see coming toward me*', '*this man who is passing by in the street*', '*this beggar whom I hear calling before my window*', express three different 'modalities' of relationship. All lie beyond *objectité* ('objectness', or 'objectity'). The narrative differently frames these people and the observer of them. I could place the narrator at a table of a pavement café as he wrote of '*this woman whom I see coming toward me*' – someone possibly attractive to the (male) writer. And I could leave him there as he records, as a matter of indifference, '*this man who is passing by in the street*'. Perhaps

---

[13] The 'realist' is a dualist, or a materialist for whom thought is *inside* the body.

[14] 'Indifferent exteriority' is the relation one non-conscious object has to another.

[15] Like Descartes: '*I ... look out of the window and see men walking in the street ... but what can I 'see' besides hats and coats, which may cover automata?*'

the narrator looks up from writing at his outdoor table. He can't be inside; he is not placed, like Descartes, *inside his house looking through his window down at the world of life below him.*

The third figure, who calls out to him for money, places Sartre's narrator as elsewhere. (A shift that would be evident in cinema.) The first two people have appeared without a barrier – *'coming towards'*, *'passing by'* him.[16] When it is *'this beggar whom [he] hear[s] calling'*, the narrator is framed from within a more secure place. The beggar, *le mendiant*, already makes that 'upsurge' we shall hear a good deal more about. *Ce mendiant* projects the *chantage* that proclaims him as needy. He does not pass by neutrally; he appeals for response. The text places a 'window' between him and the narrator.

In a Park, Unnoticed

The spectator explores the world of others with no fear of confrontation:

> I am in a public park. Not far away there is a lawn and ... benches. A man passes by those benches. I see this man; I apprehend him as an object, and at the same time as a man. What does this signify? (BN, 254).

If I were to think of him only as an object – as a puppet – his

> relation with other objects would be of the purely additive type; this means that I could have him disappear without the relations of the other objects around him being perceptibly changed (BN, 254).

When I perceive him as a person, as a human being,

> I register an organisation without distance of the things in my universe around that privileged object'. [Certainly] ... the lawn remains two yards and twenty inches away from him, but it is also as a lawn bound to him in a relation which at once both transcends distance and contains it ... [This] distance is unfolded starting from the man I see and extending up to the lawn' (BN, 254).

Sartre is depicting how in seeing another as *someone*, tacitly, I go beyond egocentricity. As conscious only of other objects, all things 'come to me', perceptually, but when I notice that Pierre has looked at his watch or that Jean has glanced out the window, I realise that something of what is thus

---

[16] Any 'windows' in the image could have been only of 'the windows of his eyes'.

'*given in sensory intuition*[17] ... *entirely escapes me*' (BN, 255). Another's perceiving is not mine.[18] I can imagine myself in their position. I picture what it is like to perceive from where the other is placed, but when I walk across the park and glance from where the 'Other' had stood, still I do not take in the scene as they had done. I had already perceived a distance 'unfold' between them and what they looked at '*as a pure disintegration of the relations which I apprehend between the objects of my universe*' (BN, 255).

In a Corridor, Through a Keyhole

The narrator had gazed at the objects in the park, including the man reading a newspaper, not thinking of anyone looking over his shoulder. But now, set in a public space (a hotel?) where he cannot know who might arrive in the corridor, he stoops to look through a keyhole into a room that is not his own domain. Again the narrator is absorbed – what he sees 'presents itself' as 'there to be seen'. Then there is a more dramatic perceptual change than when he gazed at the park where he sat and it dawned on him that what he saw was a 'park-for-others' as much as for himself. Living out a new drama, the narrator again makes the reader live in his world: '*I hear footsteps in the hall. Someone is looking at me!*' This 'I' finds itself to be a subjective object for another who is also conscious. A radical change in consciousness has been brought about and 'I' am not responsible for it. Not only does the world 'escape me' and flow towards others. That much was learned in the park, without confrontation. Now 'I' learn again in shock, that '*I am conscious of myself as escaping myself*'.[19]

When Sartre described seeing others who, though given 'in the modality of thinghood' were 'given' as people, he had no need to attribute an aggressively objectifying gaze to himself (BN, 252, 254). The scene was gentle, the observer not intrusive. Sartre could inquire, without prejudice, 'what this might signify'. Being in no danger of being observed, he did not objectify the Other. The Other was simply within his view. Sartre assumes that if he were the one to be looked at, this would petrify his being. This is, therefore, less than just. When he was the observer he did not regard the other as a mere object. Why should he not be looked at, then, without being threatened? When he was that 'Other' looking at someone reading, he was interested in their status as *for-itself*. That there was another centre of consciousness introduced a movement of perspective into an otherwise

---

[17] A way of thinking of sensory perception that Sartre has absorbed from Kant.

[18] Syntactically, 'I see them perceiving', but not 'I see their perceiving'.

[19] The Other has 'escaped me' in the active sense of causing my '*escaping-myself*'.

uniform world. Sartre describes, with lyrical beauty rather than in 'fear and loathing', the world that is also the world of an Other to myself:

> The Other is first the permanent flight of things towards a goal which I apprehend as an object at a certain distance from me but which escapes me inasmuch as it unfolds about itself it own distances (BN, 255).

In contrast, the dread of the 'look' to which he is subject in the hotel corridor arises because he is aware of the other as observing him. But not only this. As victim of another's 'look' he is petrified by it because he cannot or will not make his own response to it. But capacity and courage is no use to the victim. Sartre strips away, *by authorial fiat*, one's capacity to look back, for if I do, a role reversal is written into my script. I now am 'condemned' to objectify my erstwhile observer and, in the same act, I cease to be observed:[20]

> The Other cannot be the goal of attention; if in the upsurge of the Other's look I paid attention to the look or to the Other this could be only as to objects, for attention is an intentional direction towards objects (BN, 268–269).[21]

Sartre describes one kind of situation – a real one – where I break out of being objectified by objectifying my oppressor. He generalises this 'oppression by being perceived' and 'release by reverse oppression', however, as the conditions of my being open to observation, and having the power to observe, respectively. Being objectified is the price I pay in order to realise another's free consciousness:

> Thus, in the look, the death of my possibilities causes me to experience the Other's freedom ... I am inaccessible to myself and yet myself, thrown, abandoned at the heart of the Other's freedom (BN, 271).

'Then what is the Other?' Sartre attacks a reduction of the Other to a Kantian 'regulative category' of (my) experience, and yet his 'Other' seems to lack its own being. Someone is 'Other' *only in that* I do not turn my attention to them:

> [The Other] is the being toward whom I do not turn my attention. He is ... the one who delivers me to myself as unrevealed but without revealing

---

[20] Sartre proceeds to describe returning the look in the presence of a 'third'.
[21] Sartre is alluding (BN, 269) to a 'Kantian' idealism that reduces the Other to a regulative principle of my perception. This omits my *encounter* with another.

himself, the one who is present to me as directing [attention][22] at me but never as the object of my attention; he is the concrete pole [though out of reach] of my flight (BN, 269).

I return the look – the 'Other' disappears. Indeed, *'the world is haunted by the Other'*! If spectral, this 'Other' is described in material metaphors:

> [T]he Other-as-object is an explosive instrument which I handle with care because I foresee ... the permanent possibility that they are going to make it explode ... I shall suddenly experience the flight of the world away from me (BN, 297).

This sense of the Other as 'explosive' evokes the tension in a philosophical treatment of the Other, as in daily life. Treat another as a pure spirit beyond Berkeley's 'stupid inert unthinking matter' and s/he will erupt with their physical presence and material demands. S/he will identify with the powers and needs of a body/brain. Treat another as 'mere matter' on the other hand – to be probed, scrutinised, subject to the laws of the land or of science – and s/he will explode again. We each refuse thus to be objectified. Like the bad faith by which I undo my tense transcendence of facticity, my being *'for myself'* is itself evanescent.

Not only does the Other 'explode' in protest at being settled into either *transcendence* or else *facticity*. I must live with this tension, 'care' for the responsibility my situation reveals. The 'explosion' sends debris scattering from where I am – *'I experience the flight of the world away from me, and the alienation of my being'*. As Sartre shrewdly observes,

> my constant concern is to contain the Other within his objectivity ... But one look on the part of the Other is sufficient to make all these schemes collapse (BN, 298).

Being and *nothing* abstract from *life* and *death*, as *in-itself* and *for-itself* map on to *obdurate object* and *free subject*. And these signs reverse, at a touch:

> [T]o die is not to lose one's objectivity in the midst of the world; all the dead are there ... around us ... [T]o die is to lose all possibility of revealing oneself as subject to an Other (BN, 297).

---

[22] *'Celui qu m'est présent en tant qu'il me vise et non pas en tant qu'il est visé'* is mistranslated. A principal sense of 'viser' is 'regarder attentivement'. 'Directing an object' instead of 'directing attention' produces a spooky effect.

Even that 'security in death' slips away. After a writer's death others may learn to read them – as if only in absence can the Other be immediately present. Furthermore, Others may reveal themselves as the persons they were, only after death. This is the power of the trace and the power of the new 'I' who, in reading, finally 'makes nothing of' an 'obscurity'. As readers, we feel our responsibility to a work now that the writer is '*in the hands of the Other*'. In addition, we feel their continuing responsibility to us. This is what they took on in writing. As do we.

The Disappearing 'Other'

When the One Who Looks at Me is Absent

I cannot doubt the presence of the Other who shames me, but it may turn out that no one was there. Descartes' scepticism echoes in Sartre's text:

> [T]hose eyes which are fixed on me ... [might] be only 'artificial ones' resembling real eyes [and thus] ... our certainty of the Other's existence [seems to] take on a purely hypothetical character (BN, 275).

Sartre insists that each human existence is utterly contingent. Though, with Hegel, he emphasises that any coherent mind with categories of objectivity is structured by internal points of view of 'self' and 'other', the reality of another person does not reduce to the internal status of a category. Sartre's 'Other' is not given refuge, as a necessary structure of mind, from my doubt. Now, a doubt about *specific* others does not amount to the '*purely hypothetical*' character of my every recognition of them. Sartre's stories have evoked the immediacy of the presence of others. Misapprehensions occur, but do not touch this immediacy. Empiricism reads the possibility of illusion and error as proof that consciousness delivers packages of information for the mind to contemplate as 'always and only its own images and ideas'. From the outset Sartre has rejected such internalisation of the objects of consciousness. He will not have internalised the Other merely because mistakes in identification can occur.[23]

Sartre counters dualistic 'realism' no less than idealism. He employs images, narratives and arguments to show people as immediately, though not infallibly, present to each other as conscious beings. Non-conscious

---

[23] Natanson chides Sartre for not following Husserl's 'transcendentalist' line against empiricism (Schilpp 1981: 326–345). But Sartre is right to reject representationalism and yet to question Husserl's *noemata*, which, as intentional objects, are present even if the 'world' is not as it seems. They may not reveal 'the things themselves'.

objects, too, are immediately though fallibly present to each of us. The conscious, intending, desiring Other is *none other than the body of the Other*. That body is present not only in *the modality of object-ness*, but as *for-itself*. I can see another as the centre of their own conscious world, configuring its elements. The world ceases to revolve around myself who watches both this other observer and their angle on the park. When thus musing, disengaged, I can think how I might be mistaken even while the person remains present to me as a conscious centre of their own life. Their presence as a conscious being is full and real like that of the trees, grass, birds and statues – the *in-itself*, in short. No solipsistic frame of mind can guard against this immediacy.

Bodily Presence and Absent Consciousness

It is in bodily presence and behaviour that someone is present to me as conscious. At the same time, this presence *emphasises* my sense of the 'absence' of their consciousness. We have already begun to see how the dualist would turn this *absent awareness* into a substantial being on an equal footing with the bodily substance of the other, and how the materialist feels that the 'absence' to me of another's awareness will have to be denied. Confronted with this *absence* when gazing at someone, Sartre has pondered:

> In the midst of the world I can say 'man-reading' as I could say 'cold stone' and 'fine rain'. [This] reading remains blind and mute and seems to be related to the rest of the world by a purely indifferent externality (BN, 256).

Though potentially obdurate in its 'objectity' ('objectness') this mute 'man-reading' is a *'crack in my* universe', which may be likened to the perceivable absence of Pierre when I entered a café. I am related, at least at the level of an object, to this man reading. The reality of *'this ... absence'* of his world in reading the paper, though I perceive it directly, *'is only probable'*, says Sartre (BN, 256). This is for the simple reason that there is an 'objectity' to the existence of anyone as a conscious being, so that my perceiving cannot, must not, guarantee that existence.

Sartre takes an interesting but questionable step. Assuming that 'probability' contrasts with the certainty on which we estimate it, he asks *'To what original presence of the Other does this [objectity of the Other] refer?'* Sartre appears to take a mis-step here from the 'mere' *probability* of the presence of the perceived Other to the *non-immediacy* of his presence. For a moment at least, in his search for the 'original encounter' he is on a wild goose chase for a certainty within immediacy. A demand for *certainty* about the Other would lead to internalising others. Does he demand certainty in this promised 'original encounter'?[24]

When simply observing someone I have been given an inkling of the consciousness of an Other. I can imagine the world he sees from where he is. I 'see' the presence of an Other – as potentially more than an object – precisely *in* the 'crack' that appears in my world. I see that their world is not (quite) the same as mine. Correlatively, therefore, *I* am the source of a crack in *his* world when, in looking at me he sees someone who looks out at the world from 'elsewhere'. Thus I recognise something about *myself* as if seen from elsewhere. Sartre edges his way across the lawn towards the Other. By osmosis, he would gain the sense of his *being as subject*. Just as that Other made a crevice for him, he must, in turn, be an object that 'cracks' another's 'massive' world.[25]

> For just as the Other is a probable object for me-as-subject, I can discover myself only[26] in the process of becoming a probable object for some subject (BN, 256–257).

Sartre indicates how deeply the Other's subjectivity is implicated in this realisation. However much I would like to objectify the other's 'look', I cannot *'discover myself as object'* in the 'face' of what is no more than an object. Sartre satirises the fantasy of their being such a reified 'look' – a heat-sensitive missile that would seek me out:

> This revelation can not derive from the fact that my universe is an object for the Other-as-object, as if the Other's look after having wandered over the lawn and the surrounding objects came following a definite[27] path to place itself on me (BN, 257).

The bizarre image makes a simple and powerful point. I cannot be an object *for* what is merely another object. If I can regard something, then I too can be regarded – as an object and as an observer. My imagination of the status of s/he who would regard *me*, is at least a self-possessed understanding of my own ambiguous status in the world, as an object that surpasses its object status, both 'for itself' and in the eyes of another:

---

[24] Consciousness as 'nihilation' implies that I encounter another as mode beyond the *in-itself* even if I objectify them; *no in-itself* could be objectified in that way.

[25] 'Opening a crack in the solid world' is ambiguous. *Being-for-itself* makes being 'lighten up' but it makes fear and pain possible.

[26] '*Je ne puis me découvrir en train de devenir object probable que pour un sujet certain*' (Sartre 1943: 314): 'a probable object for only a certain subject' makes no sense.

[27] '*en suivant un chemin défini*' suggests an *ordained* or a *specific* path.

Thus this relation which I call 'being-seen-by-another', far from being merely one of the relations signified by the word '*man*', represents an irreducible fact which can not be deduced either from the essence of the Other-as-object, or from my being-as-subject (BN, 257).

And so we are brought to Sartre's version of the idea, from Hegel, that being seen by the Other is the *truth of* seeing the Other.[28]

Reading a Face when Faced with a Book

In the pictures that Sartre summons up there is material for a philosophy of reading. We have read of how someone, absorbed in the 'face' of their book, is obdurate to the observer like 'fine rain', 'cold stone'. Again we are shown someone reading. Pierre is said to give a 'particular objectivity' to the face of the book turned to him, but '*on a face which belongs to the world where I am and which consequently by a magic bond is connected beyond distance to Pierre-as-object*' (BN, 272). Sartre finds 'magic' at work in the operation of emotion: You are on a bus looking at someone reading the newspaper, unable to see the 'face' of the newspaper story with which s/he is conversant. This 'face' belongs to the 'world where you are', however. It is the face of what is presented to me as an *object*, just as Sartre's 'Pierre' himself appears as '*Pierre-as-object*'. I am equally at a distance from each of the 'faces'. I can't read the 'face' that presents the news story; I can scarcely read the 'face' that reads it. The bond between reader and printed face is 'magical' in issuing from a doubly inscrutable source; the bond is 'connected beyond distance' because the *distance* between reader and print is measured not in centimetres, but by the reader's absorption.

The 'Other-as-object' might have been an empty 'reinforcement of objectivity' in the Husserlian fashion Sartre criticises. Sartre insists that the Other's 'look-looking' undoes, not *reinforces* my world. But his Other *does* undo the fantasy of its being peculiarly *mine*. This deconstructive 'undoing' could help to rebuild that world – not as *purely mine*, but as mine no less than anyone else's. '*It is re-integrated over there, but is denied to me*' (BN, 272). But only as *purely* mine is it 'denied to me'.

Presence in Absence: Absence in Presence

Sartre returns repeatedly to the problem that while '*we confer on the Other an indubitable presence ... it is only probable that the Other is looking at*

---

[28] In this kind of expression Sartre is following Hegel, of course.

me' – '*our certainty of the Other's existence is purely hypothetical [in] character*' (BN, 275). (Sartre describes hearing the 'Other' in a footstep or in the rustling of branches.) He deals with the problem by claiming that the Other's existence is *guaranteed* by the radical shift in my consciousness that occurs when I experience the 'Look'. In answering in this way, Sartre threatens his insistence on others as separate centres of consciousness, apart from mine. The Other is more than a kind of uneasiness *I* suffer.[29]

Sartre says that the 'convergence of the eyes of the Other' (by which I see that I am being looked at) '*are a pure monition*'. The archaism in English matches the French 'monition' – an ecclesiastical warning in advance of outright condemnation. These signs I notice are purely the '*occasion of realising my being-looked-at*'. Sartre is uneasy, nonetheless, lest he has cut the connection between the bodily presence of the Other and my consciousness of the Other as *someone*. If, having shuddered '*at having been seen*', I look up and see a '*deserted corridor*', '*don't I breathe a sigh of relief?*' (BN, 277). If the other turns out to have had no material presence, I was *not* looked at. And so I may allow *own* being as 'for the other' to melt away. Some resolution is needed.

Public Performance

Sartre says that what he means about the appearance of the Other-as-subject

> will become more concrete if we recall an experience ... of appear[ing] in public [for] we never lose sight of the fact that we are looked at, and we execute the ensemble of acts ... in the presence of the look (BN, 281).

In concentrating on a public performance, '*attentive only to the ideas which we wish to develop*', I am not aware of specific individuals and how they receive what I am saying – '*the Other's presence remains undifferentiated*' (BN, 281). Sartre observes, acutely, that when

> I want to verify that my thought has been well understood and ... I look at the audience ... I shall see heads and eyes appear ... but the look has disappeared (BN 282).

Sartre argues that those who looked at me '*can never be apprehended as object*' since the Other '*immediately disintegrates*' (BN, 282). This observation, however, blocks other possibilities. A member of the audience asks a salient question of the lecturer as s/he goes on to verify that *their*

---

[29] Perhaps I am conscious of being seen if *at some time* I am seen by someone present.

question has been 'well understood'. The critical 'look' has *not* disappeared. The unspecific 'Look' has been replaced by *someone's* act of questioning. Now, only in being subject to questioning by specific others can I 'verify that my thought has been understood'. It is not as a general 'Other' that the audience asks a question. If a member of the audience who does so becomes an 'object' as soon as s/he questions the lecturer, the 'audience' cannot exercise its right, and its proper power. Sartre's thought about an audience has allowed the difference between a generalised and a particular 'Other' to slip out between the lines.

Reasserting Mastery

What the 'Other' Owes to Me

Suddenly, as rabbit to duck, as duck takes to water, the Other to whom I had owed the *objectity* I cannot recover, owes its *being-Other* to *me*:

> I can not not-be the Other unless I assume my being-as object for the Other. The disappearance of the alienated Me would involve the disappearance of the Other through the collapse of Myself (BN, 285).

Sartre is making a 'double gesture' – ceding the impossibility of grasping for myself the object that I am for another, and laying claim to 'escaping the Other' by disclaiming my 'alienated Me'. It is as if he wants to treat that being of mine that another perceives, as nothing but my 'tattered outer garment' after all. In the same gesture I would reclaim the territory I had lost to the Other:

> I escape the Other by leaving him with my alienated Me in his hands. But as I choose myself as a tearing away from the Other, I assume and recognise as mine this alienated Me (BN, 285).

And, having thus instated the Other as internal to my awareness, Sartre now develops the theme of '*wrenching away*' from this Other. It is essential to my own structure that I make '*an assumption as mine of the Me which the Other refuses*' (BN, 285). And yet the 'Other' is necessary. In depicting the futility of trying to 'apprehend myself' as a subjectivity as 'for the Other' Sartre uses a quite brilliant figure:

> [A] good comparison ... might be found in that sphere described by Poincaré in which the temperature decreases as one goes from its centre to its surface. Living beings attempt to arrive at the surface of this sphere by

setting out from the centre, but the lowering of temperature produces in them a continually increasing contraction. They tend to become infinitely flat proportionately to their approaching their goal, and because of this fact they are separated from the surface by an infinite distance (BN, 286).

Poincaré evokes how, as interiorised, we feel that as *being for another* we might break free of our surfaces. Sartre uses his physical metaphor to place the reader as an outside observer of *being-for-itself*'s struggle to externalise itself. Yet the picture does not alienate us from our own struggling ego, that 'worm of nothingness' within *being-in-itself*. Although the desire of the ego to live upon its own outer surface is absurd, there is such an outer surface nevertheless – it is manifest to any Other, since '*this limit beyond reach, the Self-as-object, is not ideal, it is a real being*' (BN, 286).

This yearning to arrive upon the outer surface of one's own (actual) boundary suggests a new possibility. The 'Other as subject' disappears under the Other's gaze, only to be recovered as an interiorised presence in their absence. This explanation sets the interiority of the Other at a distance that I *can* traverse within the 'infinite density of the world'. This would be the accessibility of an interiority that Sartre previously accepted as perceptible to a spectator, but registered directly in one's encounter with the other in reciprocal behaviour, disposition and expression.

The Diminishing Force of the 'Other'

Precisely when I appear to regain ground I had lost to the Other, I lose it :

In fact nothing can limit me except the Other. [H]e appears as the one who in his full freedom ... puts me out of play and strips me of my transcendences by refusing to 'join in' ['*mit-machen*'] (BN, 287).

An interesting phrase has slipped in – 'refusing to *join in*'. That is precisely what it feels like when subject to the appraising look, the critical word, the cautionary touch. That dreadful thrill of being torn away from yourself, that torn part still living on *as you* while yet beyond your power to look after it. If only the other had 'joined in', you might have been observed without being objectified. Someone *joins in* when in tune with your kind of awareness of something. No need for disruption and alienation. Sartre excludes this possibility by his formula of *being subject* or *being object*, but, prompted by an example he will flourish to support that formula our hopes for a sometimes shared consciousness '*start up like a partridge*'. Sartre is aware of the diminishing force of the Other as a figure that disrupts one's egocentricity. The description of the Other's presence approaches, asymptotically, a description of my own emotions. Only the oscillation between reading the 'Other' as my inner disturbance, and as revealing the Other as an object I cannot co-opt, prevents the collapse. Sartre is aware of this imminent loss of the independence of his Other, for initially, he had prized it for its disruption of philosophy's egocentricity:

> The motivation of this passage [between emotion and its object] is of an affective order – I realise [it] in fear, in shame, or in pride. But the feelings are ... our way of affectively experiencing our being for others. Shame is only the original feeling of my being engaged outside in being ... without any defence ... in an original fall (BN, 288).

What is revealed in the emotions is thus on the side of the *object* of consciousness, and that 'fall' reiterates my *'need [for] the mediation of the Other in order to be what I am'*.[30] This 'need for mediation' can be met only if it is possible to 'join in' – to share one's consciousness with another.

A Vain Image of Sensations as in a 'Hollow Box'

Sartre has not cleared his chest of the congestion of the Other's presence:

> From the moment the Other appears to me as an object, his subjectivity becomes a simple property – the Other-as-Object 'has' a subjectivity as this hollow box has 'an inside' ... [T]hus subjectivity is degraded ... into a pure [mere] image of me in the Other's 'consciousness' (BN, 291).

In evoking the wrong way to think about the consciousness of another, Sartre's language prefigures Wittgenstein's image of sensation as a 'beetle in the box'.[31] Sartre, before him, developed a satire of sensations as entities inside a 'hollow box'. He found vanity as the clue to the fantasy – I want to 'burrow into the heart of this object' that I have made of the Other in order not to be at the mercy of his differing view of me. If I know as if from their own interiority where the difference comes from and what it consists in, I can forestall and disarm his/her power to make me a 'being-for-another':

> I attempt to lay hold of the Other so that he may release to me the secret of my being. Thus vanity impels me to get hold of the Other and to constitute him as an object in order to burrow into the heart of this object to discover there my own object-state (BN, 291).

---

[30] Sartre approaches Hegel's Other as an 'intermediary between me and myself'.
[31] Wittgenstein mocks the image of sensations as 'hidden' in one's private container (Wittgenstein 1953: 100).

This 'vanity' in which I would be my only scrutineer and yet outside of myself in order to achieve this, links with Sartre's location of shame as at the heart of one's recognition of the Other. Both in 'pride' and in shame, as structurally akin, I recognise the Other as the subject through whom I gain my object-state. It is the realisation of my 'object-state' before the eye (or the word) of another that threatens the pretensions of vanity and seduces me with the dangerous rewards of admiration. I would therefore 'burrow into the heart' of this Other made object within the classical dualist fantasy:

> [B]ut this is to kill the hen that lays the golden eggs. By constituting the Other as object, I constitute myself as an image at the heart of the Other-as-object; hence the disillusion of vanity. In that image which I wanted to ... merge with my own being, I no longer recognise myself (BN, 291).

The pleasure of being admired by another ('pride') may confer 'beauty' upon me without vanity, but it is risky. The Other may not admire everything about me, may change their mind or vision. In Sartrean terms – beauty is a quasi-object state that disintegrates (BN, 290–291). Thus I tend to 'degrade' the role of the Other by using all my stratagems to supplant his/her independent position. Thus I turn towards conceit or vanity.

Nausea, Self and World

At the end of 'The Body' Sartre makes a new remark about what the body is *for me*. The over-familiar linking of 'Sartre', 'being for oneself' and 'nausea' might have inoculated us against this remark's taking effect:

> This perpetual apprehension ... of an insipid taste that I cannot place ... is what we have described elsewhere under the name of *Nausea* ... [which] perpetually reveals my body to consciousness. Sometimes we look for pleasure[32] or for physical pain to free ourselves from this nausea; but as soon as the pain and the pleasure are existed by consciousness, they in turn manifest its facticity and its contingency; and it is on the ground of this nausea that they are revealed (BN, 338).

Sartre's sudden reference to *nausea* has a strange air, carrying a world of imagery from his novel of that name that disturbs the hermetic quality of *Being and Nothingness*. Though imported from 1938 across a period of only five years, *nausea* shimmers within like the flash of a movie clip.

---

[32] The English translation reads 'we look for pleasant or for physical pain', which is a slip. The point is that whether it is in pleasure or in physical pain that I look for diversion from this nausea, it is in this nausea that I recognise the body as such.

Sartre has made only one prior reference in *Being and Nothingness* to *nausea* as a sensation intimately connected with our apprehending the world as the sheer fact of its existence – and therefore of our own existence as bodily beings.[33] The intimacy – because of the self-consuming character – of the sensation of nausea grabs at us here. The sheer fact of my own existence can be predicated only upon the *lack* of separation of myself as thinking, intending, creative being, and as a bodily (brainy) being. Sartre's *being-in-itself* and *being-for-itself* do not divide us into separate 'realms of being'. The distinction can be used, rather, as the basis for a seamless identification of conscious and of bodily self, since *being-for-itself* is an *absence* of being, thus adding *nothing* to *being-in-itself*. Reading Sartre in this way leads us, thus, towards identifying *being conscious* with *conscious physicality*.[34]

I myself am exposed to the glance of another – registered and figured in *shame*, or some other disconcerting but involving emotion. Even though 'being for myself' and 'being for another' are irreducible concepts, in being for another what is exposed is the fancy that I exist purely *for myself* in my feelings and intentions. That conceit is not securely harboured in the realm of the *for-itself*. It is overtaken when I am revealed by another's observation, in a gesture or appeal that compels my response.

Immediacy of access is what connects the theme of 'in-itself' and 'for-itself' with Sartre's intrusion of *nausea*. The body 'in-itself' is something to which I do not have *privileged* access. I know relatively little about my own body – others may know much more. But the same can be said of my thoughts, feelings, and the intentionality of my behaviour, even though these, though partially and fallibly, are *immediately* accessible to me. This *immediacy* has to do with thought, feeling and intentionality[35] rather than with a *privileged access* to my own conscious modes, since these may be also immediately (though partially and fallibly) apparent to another. This shift in the paradigm of *immediate acquaintance* is achieved by attention to the mentality of one's expression and behaviour as 'gaping open' to another's gaze.[36] My *shame* in being caught out by another in what I am really doing and feeling is the shock of recognition of the publicity of these 'private' feelings. They are real – they have ontological 'thickness'. Particularly in the 'privacy' of my mentality I am answerable to the 'objectivity' of others.

---

[33] In opening the *Introduction* he lets slip into his abstract argument that '*being will be disclosed to us by [an] immediate access – boredom, nausea, etc.*' (BN, xxiv).

[34] In preparing for departure from the project, I look for cues and clues for further work.

[35] It has been argued by Elizabeth Anscombe that one knows immediately (though of course not infallibly) about the position and movement of one's limbs (Anscombe 1958: 14-15).

[36] See a letter of Sartre's to Beauvoir, cited by Le Dœuff (Le Dœuff 1991: 180–181).

It is thus according to a similar pattern that *nausea* is a shock in which I realise the otherness of things. (Perhaps not *the* unique shock, but still, paradigmatic of the shocks of the otherness of things, just as *anguish* is paradigmatic of the shock of the otherness of people.) This realisation of 'otherness' includes the existence of my body as a thing, which is at the same time the very 'thing' which is my conscious self. The nausea we have at first upon seeing a dead body, then to be opened up as a cadaver in an autopsy, is *epistemic*. The nausea registers a profound and total shift in our understanding of the dear familiar body with whom we had conversed, dined and fought. There is a similar heedful reaction in someone who first learns, in one hit, that the one they love is now involved with another, and that the one they had lived with as if fully intimate had been living a 'double life'. Quite simply, in my nausea at this sheer obdurate fact that undoes my constructed world I 'throw up'. In 'throwing up' I lose control of the body and what it can 'digest'. It is not an irrational or a physiologically extraneous reaction. It is epistemic, marking, precisely, the fact that I have lost control of my world. It is my knowledge that the world I had is to be ejected in being rejected.

Being Immediate and Being Doubted

In the midst of these subtle observations about perceiving and being perceived by others, we may lose sight of a problem that has been brewing since Sartre first described one's access to other beings for themselves, as founded on a 'relation of being, not of knowledge'. What he says does strike a chord. It is not merely that in being involved with someone, doubt is suspended for the time being. What it is for another to be there as a conscious being is revealed in the reciprocity. I refuse this '*what it is to be a so-and-so*' when I remain at the level of detached observation. If we have trouble in 'knowing what it is like to be a bat' (Nagel 1974), it is not because the interiority of another conscious being is inaccessible *as such –* as if the inscrutable life of a bat just dramatises that fact for us. We don't know how to get along with bats – how to do anything beyond looking at them in pleasure or disgust, or examining them scientifically. If Nagel had asked what it is like to be a *dog*, he would have provoked informed responses rather than the spectacle of metaphysical pondering doing battle with materialist carping.

In an otherwise subtle contribution to understanding Sartre in relation to Husserl on the question of one's awareness of another's consciousness, Frederick Elliston asks, pertinently it seems: '*If I can be mistaken about the emotions through which the other is disclosed, can I not be mistaken about the other?*' (Silverman 1980: 166). The answer is that one can be mistaken, and that Sartre discusses the implications of this in detail. Elliston is poised to take a mis-step, one already made by A.J. Ayer within three years of publication of *Being and Nothingness* (Ayer 1947: 101–110). It remains a common trap. Elliston proceeds to add, '*Sartre's certainty cannot be the infallibility of a claim to know*' (Silverman 1980: 166) and thus begins to walk at a tangent to the area of Sartre's position. His specific criticisms only emphasise what Sartre has insisted upon – that I can be mistaken in thinking that I am being observed at all – and thus could be mistaken about the 'look' I am subjected to even when someone *is* looking at me.

As Natanson (Silverman, 1980: 327) more clearly perceives, Sartre is claiming that *being* is prior to *knowing* in our dealing with another as conscious. To write in the manner of Gilbert Ryle (Ryle 1949: 25–61) or J.L. Austin (Austin 1961: 90–103), '*being for another*' is not some superior sort of 'knowing' that is on the same scale as more and more reasonable belief, so well founded that it is beyond all possible doubt. There is no belief that could turn into infallible knowledge. To approach Sartre's language, to '*be-for-another*' is a mode, not of knowing, but of *living* or *existing*.

Not that *being-for-another* has nothing to do with knowing, or requires no knowledge. And yet, it is no more a piece of knowledge, nor even knowledge in action, than is confidently driving a car at high speed on a winding hilly road a series of items of knowledge, nor even a series of them in action. It is a manner of *being towards the road*, you might say. Though we could not succeed in that 'mode of being' without various items of knowledge, and could scarcely be imagined to engage in such a mode of being for some time without using and gaining a good deal of standing and passing knowledge, this is not what *driving* is. There is no question of *doubt* here – no question of doubting whether I am in a car, on a road, subject to constantly changing momentum by which I gauge how fast I can enter each corner and crest each hill. This does not mean that I have entered a sphere of infallible certainty of belief or knowledge. I have entered into a broadly conscious skilled interaction between self, speeding vehicle, changing terrain and sporadically appearing fixed obstacles that would threaten life if I did not respond within the same flowing movement. It *is* thinkable, after the event, or prior to it, that I might have 'just this experience' if in a laboratory with some millions of connectors to my afferent and efferent nerves connecting brain with limbs, being 'given the drive of a lifetime' by some sophisticated computer. But this does not mean that my '*being towards the road*' was a *very* reasonable set of beliefs that might, all the same, have been mistaken. This is not because that mode of being was knowledge so certain as to be beyond doubt, but because it was not knowledge (or ignorance) in the first place.

Nor was this mode of being some mystical process beyond the reach of science – some non-rational intuition or semi-divine mode of apprehension that *'passeth all understanding'*. Sartre shows how he apprehends the likelihood of these mis-turnings when he reminds us that one's direct being for others is not in the realm of 'ineffable experience' but is the common stuff of everyday life. So Elliston is moving far of Sartre's mark when he says that *'the semblance of an unshakeable belief about the existence of the other is maintained by two restrictions never defended'* (Silverman 1980: 166). He maintains that Sartre's first restriction

> confines the experience to the pre-reflective level where it has never been subject to critical reflection, [while the second] confines the experience to emotions such as shame or pride, thereby excluding all rational appeals to evidence in support of truth claims about them (Silverman 1980: 166).

Elliston's error is instructive. To recognise it is to better understand the real possibilities of Sartre's thinking at this point. *'Being-for-others'* is in the 'realm of being', not of knowing. It is not a belief, 'unshakeable' or otherwise. And Sartre need not confine the experience (of being for another) to the pre-reflective level. The primary experience of being for another *is* pre-reflective, but this does not preclude the critical reflection that Sartre proceeds to undertake. Most importantly, emotion does not *preclude* reason, neither in fact nor for Sartre. Emotion is the 'adverb' of perception and thought, not some alternative to those cognitive processes. We think and perceive hopefully, fearfully, passionately, or in boredom.[37] Thus, in no way does this (pre-reflective) *being-for-another 'exclud[e] all rational appeals to evidence'*. It is in precisely in being involved with others, in emotion, but informed by what we think and perceive, that we place ourselves fully in the field of evidence.

---

[37] The next chapter will develop these considerations about the immediacy of uptake with others, and one's knowledge of their thoughts, feelings and motives.

7
Coping with Others

Cousins

A young child, an 'only', brought up with close attention and love, content and capable of coping with situations, internalises his view of himself and of others in relation to these situations. He has a younger cousin, also confident, articulate and more immediately vocal and expressive. The younger idolises the older, and the older is infinitely protective and aware of whatever might put the younger at risk. The older has been sick for most of a week – there were traumas associated with having moved house for the first time. They have moved to a very modern apartment block, from an old suburban house. It has an indoor heated swimming pool. The younger cousin is wild with excitement about going there to swim. He has had to wait until his cousin has recovered. He must be still uneasy at the thought that he might not have fully recovered, for upon seeing him enter the door of the new apartment, now in full health and vitality, the younger cries out 'You're not sick any longer!' The older, not entirely displeased because of the demonstrative affection, is nevertheless discomfited. 'Uuh ... well' he says. The excited, loving and relieved younger can't contain his re-iteration. 'You're not sick any longer!'

The moment passes. They go down with the adults to swim.[1]

* * *

In Sartrean terms, the older was taken by surprise by being subject to the 'look' of the younger, made to feel the object of that look, to realise his 'being-for-another' in a new way. Of course he is used to his status as a 'being-for-his-parents'. He knows they appraise him, decide whether he is at risk from anything, and push him into doing things for his own good. In 'being-for-his-parents' he is used to recovering his subjectivity in 'objectifying' them, and he knows how to place their sporadic outbursts. Sometimes he can re-subjectify this behaviour, which might otherwise alienate him even as it occurs, and comfort or divert them. Sometimes not. But almost all of their conduct towards him, closely generous,

---

[1] Author's adaptation of an observation of Phyllis Perlstone's.

comprehends him so that he has learned by bodily empathy[2] to be a caring subject in relation to someone younger. We can surmise that he didn't want to go into his trauma of moving house and that consequently he has scarcely admitted to himself that he has been ill for most of a week – vomiting, depressed, not wanting to talk. Sartre would describe him as embroiled in something sternly named 'bad faith'. Conscious (of) his recurrent bouts of nausea, retching and listlessness the child keeps this 'pre-reflective' consciousness on the periphery; he is 'not conscious' that this is his state of things. He 'nihilates' each event as it occurs.

The older cousin finds himself subject to 'the word' of the younger and treated as 'object', as an 'object of loving concern'. This being objectified is, because of the tender age of his cousin, quite inadvertent, and remains benign because his cousin speaks in unselfconscious pleasure at seeing him well – fun to play with, no longer to be worried about. The older is gently objectified – 'found out', or, 'brought back to himself'. Though not therefore discovered in 'shame' as part of a sado-masochistic ritual, he *is* discomfited since he cannot say, 'No, I haven't been sick at all!' And he can't say 'Yes, I'm O.K. now' without admitting to himself that, yes, he has been sick for most of a week, and why is this? So, in being-for-another, he discovers something object-ual in what he would have carried off as purely 'subjective' – according to his wish or fancy. At the same time, though embarrassed, he could not sustain an outright falsehood in the face of such affection. The event of the younger child's remark constitutes a shift in the gently dispensed power that the older cousin exerts, being already three years into school, able to win at games, speak in public, and give an account of himself. The younger, though verbally precocious, is scarcely beyond his 'nursling dependency'. That is part of the shock and the reason why he feels his 'being-for-another' before his little cousin, as he does not in the face of his parents or teachers. The sphere of captaincy of his soul, where his ego is finding a place, is turned inside out by this 'word' – '*You're not sick any longer!*' – too spirited and good-natured to be resisted. Feelings that had been tautologically 'his' become a state of his body – anyone's to see and to diagnose – though in the same instant their subjectivity for him intensifies – his sickness is his feeling too.

Handling Exteriority

Sartre proclaims the Other as a *being-for-itself* whom we encounter directly as a conscious being – but also interiorise. This tension arises within his

---

[2] Edith Stein's *Zum Problem der Einfühlung* (Sawicki 1997).

deconstruction of idealism *vis-à-vis* the consciousness of another. If, as he has argued, (dualistic) realism leads to idealism about the minds of others, might Kant's noumenon, that which exists in itself behind appearances, serve as the distinct 'otherness' of the Other? This is a useless move, as he points out. When I deal with another it is a specific 'life of the mind', not an abstract and inexperiencable reality, with which I am concerned. To treat the Other only as a condition of one's intelligible experience is to refuse the other as an individual. It is true that we make sense of another's behaviour only by interpreting what they do as the expression of consciousness[3] – we cannot read their behaviour except on condition of thinking of it as exhibiting some mentality. But, unlike a Kantian condition of the possibility of experience, *'the Other as such is given in experience; he is an object and a particular object'* (BN, 225). Furthermore, in thinking of a being *other than me*, I cannot just *invoke* the 'Other':

> [I]t is necessary even within a rigorous Kantianism to ask how the knowledge of the Other is possible; that is, to establish the conditions of possibility for the experience involving others (BN, 225).

When I make reference to the conscious life of another, I 'aim at' that conscious (*phenomenal*) life itself. Sartre writes that *'what I aim at in the Other is [only] what I find in myself'*[4] and while *'the perception of the Other-as-object refers [us] to a coherent system of representations'* (BN, 226), the point is that this system is not mine (BN, 227). We can read the 'Other' within the frame of this more concrete Sartrean metaphysics. At the same time, his phenomenology is already embedded in the argument. The confidence that one *is* 'aiming at' a consciousness other than one's own is based on more than common-sense:

> What I aim at across my experiences are the Other's feelings, the Other's character. This is because the Other is not only the one whom I see, but the one who sees me. I aim at the Other as a connected system of experiences out of [my] reach (BN, 228).

So far this might be a Kantian interpretation – but Sartre turns the point:

> [T]o the extent that I strive to determine the concrete nature of this system of representations and my place there as an object, I radically transcend the field of my experience. I am concerned with a series of phenomena, which on principle can never be accessible to my intuition (BN, 228).

---

[3] In many ways we are in the same position *vis-à-vis* ourselves.
[4] The Other as only a condition of coherent thought cannot bridge specific individuals.

This is not only an argument that the Other is no mere regulative category, but also delineates Sartre's 'realism'. The immediacy of the 'Other' is felt in their 'upsurge', even though the reality of this 'Other' can be no more than probable. This tension between immediacy and probability produces Sartre's tendency to interiorise others. Being more than a regulative concept, the Other's externality is set against their interiorisation:[5]

> The Other is real, yet I cannot conceive of his real relation to me, since I cannot stand outside the two of us so as to comprehend it from elsewhere.[6]

> I construct the Other and yet he is never released to me in intuition; in seeing another as such, I 'aim across' my own experiences towards those radically other experiences.

> I posit him as a subject, and yet it is as the object of my thoughts that I consider him.

To refuse the presence of others in favour of the category of the 'Other' as a condition of understanding leaves me standing alone, suffering worse than doubt about other subjects of experience. In the event, Kantian idealists will reject solipsism too, but on the basis of 'common sense' rather than by searching the phenomena. So 'transcendental idealism' returns full circle to a dogmatic realism, insisting that we accept the Other as a separate centre of consciousness. Sartre has shown how dualism collapses into idealism about the reality of the conscious life of another – both dualistic 'realism' and idealism about others are unstable. So, in order to approach a more realistic outlook Sartre re-works dualistic realism, softening the dualism and scaling back its pretensions to 'realism':

> It is in fact by this position[7] with respect to the Other that we suddenly explode the structure of idealism and fall back into a metaphysical realism (BN, 228).[8]

Neither idealism nor metaphysical realism furnishes Sartre's room but idealism, in falling back into dogmatic realism, gives Sartre a key to the door. He has shown that faced with our awareness of the world of conscious others, dualistic realists are driven into idealism about those inaccessible lives. In parallel fashion, idealists are driven into dogmatic

---

[5] Here I proceed to reconstruct Sartre's argument.

[6] But, can I stand outside the in-itself and myself, to 'conceive of' that relation?

[7] We encounter others who show their presence in an 'upsurge', in their *being*.

[8] Metaphysical realism denies idealism, not the dualism Sartre criticised as 'realism'.

realism about the minds of others. Not able to reduce conscious life to other terms, idealists have to

> posit a plurality of closed systems which can communicate only through the outside, [and while] these are only systems of representation ... their reciprocal exteriority is an exteriority in itself; it [exists] without being known (BN, 229).

That is to say, idealists have to be realists about systems of mental representation, for

> even if consciousnesses are only pure conceptual connections of phenomena, even if the rule of their existence is the *percipere* and the *percipi* ... the multiplicity of these relational systems is a multiplicity in-itself (BN, 230).

Although the would-be idealist is concerned '*not with a relation between a phenomenon and a thing-in-itself*',

> if one of the series of the phenomena resides in the Other and the other series in me, then the one series functions as the reality of the other, and the realist scheme of truth is the only one which can be applied here (BN, 230).

So idealism inherits the whole ontological problem of 'the Other', but lacks the wherewithal to deal with it. The dualistic realist cannot cross his 'double-chasm' of bodies that lies between one consciousness and another, and the idealist cannot alleviate the trauma by refusing the body as a thing in itself. So now we enter Sartre's space, where we encounter each other as conscious beings in everyday immediacy, recognising that the one cannot appropriate the difference of the other.

'I' and the 'Other'

Sartre is not just clearing his throat to utter the obvious when he writes that '*the origin*' of the problem of the existence of others is that '*the others are Other*' simply in that '*the Other is not myself*' (BN, 230). Someone is 'Other' not simply in *being for themselves*. Michèle Le Dœuff criticises Sartre for the metaphysical weight he puts on the 'Other' (*autrui*). His humanism neglects the 'dispersion' of humanity and, like that of Pico della Mirandello, emphasises 'man' rather than specific people as the end for 'man'.[9] She links the use of *autrui* with this raising up of 'man' as the end of ethical life, and the appearance of 'I' as a 'solitary and unique being' who would speak for humankind.[10] The category of *autrui* makes all others to be the 'same' – all those who happen to be 'not' the one who is currently issuing the discourse in which *autrui* appears are thereby united as 'Other'. Thus 'I' gain a (spurious) uniqueness as the one by whom all others become *autrui* – 'Other'. As equally 'Other' how can the others have anything to say about themselves? When the field is structured by 'I' and 'the Other', 'I' get to do the talking:

> Life suddenly becomes a stage on which 'I-me' and 'not-I-me', called 'other people' or 'autrui' meet in a duel ... *[A]utrui* ... was coined as a philosophical concept at the cost of a linguistic blunder. For it is a genitive or dative ... used as such for centuries, *les biens d'autrui* being 'someone else's property' (Le Dœuff 199: 190).

This is not only a linguistic but also a philosophical blunder, Le Dœuff suggests:

> [W]e make our students turn pale with the classic and lapidary essay subject: *Autrui*. So ... tell me about a person who is defined as anyone-not-me ... a half-'you' whom I discuss half as 'he' or 'she', a 'you' whom I distance into a 'he' or a 'she'. Ultimately any essay on *autrui* ends up being ... a waffle about 'I-me' ... since the category is constructed simply as a contrast to 'I-me' (Le Dœuff 1991: 190–191).

Le Dœuff indicates the legitimate use of *autrui* as '*someone who is not me*' (Le Dœuff 1991: 190) – that is, anyone other than the assigned subject of discourse. Theft is the taking of property from *autrui*. The stolen property of this 'Other' is not that of some abstract and generalised 'other', but simply of the 'one-it-does-not-matter-who' who is 'not-the-one' who took it. Le Dœuff notes, shrewdly, the discomfort in converting into a noun-form, the easily used '*of* any other' or '*to* any other' (the 'genitive' or 'dative'). The conversion is not actually illicit, for if I should not take '*les biens d'autrui*,' then '*l'autrui* (the whoever-it-may-be from whom I may have taken '*ses biens*') may have legal recourse against me. '*L'autrui*' slides easily from dative or genitive, to the nominative. This clarifies both the truth and the distortion in Sartre's discussion of oneself and 'the Other'. There is an obscurity in Sartre's perception that

---

[9] Mirandello 'retains man in general and him alone, a unique being' (Le Dœuff 1991: 191).

[10] See her studies of Shakespearean characters, and Descartes' definition of himself through doubt (Le Dœuff 1986a, 1986b).

[a]t the origin of the problem of the existence of others there is the fundamental presupposition: others are Other, that is, the self which is not myself (BN, 230).

This produces the tension between the 'Other' as someone else I encounter and the 'Other' as 'looking' even when no one is there to look. It is for the idealist no less than the realist, Sartre insists, that an 'external' negation between one person and another is *'the foundation of all relation between the Other and me'* (BN, 230). Yet, he declares, such an external negation is in fact *'a primary absence of relation'*. This is obvious in the case of the dualistic realist *'who believes that he apprehends the Other through his body [and] considers therefore that he is separated from the Other as one body from another body'* (BN, 231). The idealist, too,

> without being aware of it is resorting to a 'third man' in order to effect the appearance of this external negation ... Thus for the idealist as for the realist ... the Other is revealed to us in a spatial world, [so that] we are separated from the Other by a real or ideal space (BN, 231).

In supplanting *space* by *ideas of space* the idealist is like the dualist in treating his relationship with another as 'external'. Each picture their meeting with another as the reception of sensory impressions of another's body experienced as *'in its objectity'*, which has a 'serious consequence':

> My relation to the Other [is] in the mode of indifferent exteriority ... I can not in my being be affected by either the upsurge or the abolition of the Other any more than an In-itself can be affected by the apparition or the disappearance of another In-itself (BN, 231).

If the negation of the Other were only external, the truth of my image of the Other could be decided by an observer of both of us. A regress threatens. If that outside observer can know each of us only 'in this mode of indifferent exteriority' then the truth of *that* observer's judgement is known only by one who observes them, me and that Other. And so on.[11] This leads Sartre to discover, in the absurdity of a traditional Christian requirement of its 'God' – that It 'sees into the inner heart' of Its creatures – something about day-to-day relationships:

> God as the intermediary between me and the Other presupposes the presence of the Other to me in an internal connection; for God ... as the

---

[11] 'Realism' about the Other as 'irrespective of being knowable' is *de facto* solipsism.

Other ... must maintain an internal connection with myself [to validate] the Other's existence for me (BN, 232).

A *'Being'* which could know the life of my mind 'in an internal connection' would be the 'third man' who knows me and any other mortal with whom I would relate. Sartre's observation presents a dilemma: If such an 'internal connection' is absurd, then we cannot think of any Being as securing it. But if such an internal connection *can* be made, why should it not exist between mortal beings? Must another know my conscious life *as from living it* – an unthinkable and yet necessary internal connection with me? In that case, indeed (to parody Heidegger) *'Only a god can save us now!'*. It is neither as a third person observer nor by (impossibly) living another's life that one understands another.[12] To commandeer the internal relation of one with another is an act of philosophical desperation.

Certainty about the 'Other'

The Elusive Other

In making me respond, Sartre's Other leaves me no room for doubt, not permitting me to treat them as an 'object of inspection'. But no sooner does Sartre evoke this than he loses the sense of a direct encounter. Frederick Elliston notes Sartre's 'Other' as ethereal:

> [W]hat a strange creature Sartre's other as subject is. One moment he is on the creaking stairs, the next moment he is at the rattling window, and at no moment was he at any of the intervening places: he comes to me from 'beyond the world' as a presence 'without distance' (BN, 270). Indeed to refer to the other as 'he' is misleading, for the other has no gender. Because the other's ties to any particular object in my world are radically 'contingent' (BN, 277). I may discover nothing whatsoever when I turn to oppose the other's stare: I was looked at, when no one was looking! Anonymous, elusive, and sexless, the other is a totally undifferentiated presence without locus (Silverman 1980: 166).

Like the Scarlet Pimpernel, 'you seek him here, you seek him there, you cannot find him anywhere'. All the same, Sartre catches the irruption of the Other to confront his consciousness, and just when this 'Other' appears and observes me – vulnerable to their appraising gaze, their physical and social identity almost disappears, as he says. When someone I know irrupts with a

---

[12] In Tom Stoppard's *Jumpers*, a philosopher cites ethical theory to his suicidal wife!

'look' that throws me into disarray I scarcely recognise them. Those we know intimately surprise us with their unpredictable observations upon our repetitive acts and scarcely felt feelings. (Readers may not recognise a writer's look; the writer must unsettle and resettle them.)

François George has also diagnosed Sartre's 'intrusive' Other – it detaches from s/he who first intruded and becomes a ghost haunting consciousness:

> L'autre est un intrus parce que du fond de ma solitude je *rêve* le monde, et il me tire brutalement de ce rêve. Il est un gêneur avant tout parce qu'il est *réel*, et vient se substituer à cet autre imaginaire avec qui j'ai mes habitudes. C'est pourquoi il est toujours un Tiers intempestif. Le regard, en outre, est vécu comme possession: autrui façonne mon corps, le fait naître, le produit comme il est, bref, tout à la fois me donne et me confisque mon être réel, alors qu'auparavant je possédais toutes les apparences et entretenais à ma guise des images d'autre (George 1976: 307–308).

> The other is an intrusion because at the heart of my solitude I dream the world, and he drags me roughly out of this dream. He is an intruder first and foremost because s/he is real, and is about to take the place of that other imaginary system with which I am familiar. That is why he is always an untimely Third. The look, furthermore, is lived as possession: the Other shapes my body, brings it to birth, and produces it as it is. In short, in the one hit s/he both gives me my real being and takes it over, where previously I owned all appearances and looked after images of the other as I pleased (Author's translation).

Sartre's 'Other' and Descartes' 'I'

For Sartre, the necessity in recognising the Other is not an a priori 'condition of experience', but 'factual' like that of Descartes' '*I am, I exist [which is] necessarily true each time I utter or conceive it in my mind*' (Descartes 1954: 67). It is not necessarily true that I think or exist, but my declaration of it is bound to be true.[13] Sartre recognises a similar necessity – to doubt another is conscious when subject to their 'look' is to doubt my own mode of conscious existence.

Since any existence is 'a contingent and irreducible fact' I can doubt whether anyone was there to 'look' at me, but not doubt my being as 'for another' – irreducible to being 'for myself'. Even if no one looked just then, my being has shifted irrevocably from '*being-for-myself*' to '*being-for-others*'. Just as Sartre's certainty about his 'Other' is not a certainty

---

[13] Here I offer my own expression of this 'factual necessity'.

about a specific individual, so too, Descartes' certainty concerning '*I think*', '*I exist*' is not about anyone in particular. Curiously, the charge of a 'ghostly' existence is also laid at Descartes' door,[14] though he notes that I know myself as body even in thinking it away:

> [I]t is I who have sensations, who perceive corporeal objects as it were by the senses. Thus, I am now seeing light, hearing a noise, feeling heat. These [may be] unreal, for I am asleep; but at least I seem to see, to hear, to be warmed (Descartes 1954: 71).

Thus in a world given as material with myself as embodied, I live in the possibility that I am, precisely, this material existence. With equal certainty, in a world of being perceived by others, I live in the possibility that this 'Other' is a conscious material existence like myself. The melodrama of Descartes' doubt made him forget that he who doubts his body may be nothing other than it and that he is something that is *being perceived*. The 'Other' who can see him as conscious is part of his elemental world of sensation, whatever the pressures to interiorise that Other in order to guarantee its immediate presence.

Saying Adieu to Predecessors

In departure, summing up Husserl and Heidegger, Sartre rejects both

> that we have to *prove* that the Other exists,

and

> that we *do not know* that the Other exists (BN, 250).

Rather, we have to *describe* what it is for the Other, as conscious subject, to exist. Where a proof requires premises that do not take the existence of the Other for granted, a description shows us a world in which '*at least we seem to see light, seem to feel warmth*', and, equally, in which we seem to see and to be seen by the Other. The lack of proof of the existence of the Other is not a lack in logic or experience, but registers the primacy of the Other within the experience of being a self and perceiving a world.

Sartre also rejects

> that we can stand *outside* the point of view of Descartes' cogito (BN, 251).

Such an emphasis on the point of view of consciousness does not set us apart from the world, or from the Other. Consciousness launches us into the

---

[14] Famously, by Gilbert Ryle in *The Concept of Mind*.

world, delivering us those things *of which* we are conscious – what has being *in-itself, for-itself*, and *for-others*. That from a detached point of view we can imagine a doubt about the reality of any instance of these things does not change anything. The 'cogito', when examined,

> must throw me outside it by disclosing to me the concrete, indubitable presence of a particular concrete Other, just as it has already revealed to me my own incomparable contingent, but necessary and concrete existence (BN, 251).

Implicit in Sartre's presentation is that the being revealed by the 'cogito' is *ostensibly* material and social, though contained within a doubt which 'sets aside as if false' all material things, '*I am conscious*' is an *apodictic*[15] performance of the social materiality of thought. Furthermore, Sartre rejects that consciousness reveals the Other only as object, claiming that consciousness reveals the Other as a conscious subject. This is because, if consciousness revealed the Other only 'in its objectity' we would have to merely *suppose* that 'consciousness' was attached to other bodies. In fact, while we must sometimes 'inspect' people impersonally, their demands compel us into reciprocation so that we experience them as *beings for themselves*. Sartre presents the Other as a conscious body, given as a subject in connection (*rapport*) with me. The immediacy '*refers to no mystical or ineffable experience but to the reality of everyday life*' (BN, 253). Sartre evokes the immediacy of the *rapport*, resists *proving* the existence of the Other – that would lead to some sort of reduction of the Other. Yet, though he resists a reduction of the Other to a structure of 'my' mind, his text interiorises the disruptive Other. For, how am I to grasp the Other in their interiority? Can I experience another without objectification when the Other is present only in bodily form? Perhaps 'interiorisation' is simply candid phenomenology.

Another's searching look can recognise my subjectivity so that I am not provoked to 'make an object' of them.[16] Sartre's descriptions are done 'by the book' – an alternating command of each by each does occur but this falls short of reciprocity. To capture the attention of another only ambiguously causes their objectification as 'listener'. For the listener the speaker is all speech; for the speaker the other is *all ears*. Yet each can retain an awareness of each other's subjectivity. Their readiness to adjust

---

[15] 'Apo deiktikos' – 'demonstrative' – to cause to 'stand out'. Mathematical 'demonstration' is but one *mode* of making things stand out as evident.
[16] '*Subjectivity is the tissue of knowledge, opinions, feelings and tastes, which yields the flavour and style of his or her approach to things*' (Deutscher 1983: 41).

what they say or hear in the face of incomprehension and disagreement makes them parties to a reasonable, if passionate, discussion.

On Being Present to Others

> The Other's look as the necessary condition of my objectivity[17] is the destruction of all objectivity for me (BN, 269).

Reciprocity as Revealing Others

How like Hamlet sounds Sartre, as he laments, with some effect, that *'all the world's density is needed if I make myself be present to the Other'* (BN, 270). Not so much like the Antonio who declares – *'I hold the world but as the world, Gratiano;/ A stage, where every man must play a part;/ and mine a sad one'* (*The Merchant of Venice*, Act I, ll.77–80, Shakespeare 1959: 193). For, that possibility of making oneself known in 'playing a part' might be one way of juggling with the 'infinite density' of the world. No! Sartre is the Hamlet of '*Oh! that this too too solid flesh would melt, / thaw and resolve itself into a dew*' (*Hamlet*, Act I, ll.129–130, Shakespeare 1959: 873). One hears *'adieu'* in those words – the flight of *'being-for-itself'* into an insubstantial future. The desire for self-sufficient interiorisation emerges in the next Act – *'Oh God! I could be bounded in a nutshell and count myself a king of space'*, the desire being held in check by *'were it not that I had bad dreams'* (*Hamlet*, Act II, ll. 264–266, Shakespeare 1959: 882). There is the same kind of check (*'but in that sleep what dreams may come'*) to the fantasy expressed by the *'To be or not to be'* that preceded it – the fantasy of a state beyond bodily confinement, a vanishing into vanishing interiority as one's *'flesh thaws'*. Sartre steadies his text with his mantras about this Other who *'fixes'* my possibilities:

> I can be an object only for another freedom ... [When] I naively assume I can be an objective being without being responsible for it, I thereby implicitly suppose the Other's existence (BN, 270).

Yes, this reminds us of how Sartre's phenomenology of consciousness does not 'bracket out' the Other as in a Husserlian reduction, but finds them in the business of their being conscious:

---

[17] 'Objectity' rather than 'objectivity' more properly translates *'objectité'*.

This pure subject I cannot know is always there when I try to grasp myself as object ... In experiencing myself as an unrevealed object-ness, I experience the inapprehensible subjectivity of the Other directly ... and ... I experience the Other's infinite freedom (BN, 270).

In counting myself an object, I am located in universal time, located as by a third party. I am given externality by the Other's 'internal negation':

Only a being which temporalizes can throw me into time ... [O]nly his freedom separates the Other from me[18] (BN, 271).

'I' depend upon the 'Other' at the 'heart of my being' without therefore being able to co-opt this *autrui*. This lies at the foundation of the common-sense objection to solipsism:

[T]he Other is given to me as a concrete evident presence which I can in no way derive from myself and which [cannot be] doubted nor made the object of a phenomenological reduction or of any other *epoché* (BN, 271).

Sartre here concedes that '*I am conscious of being an object*' when someone looks at me – a consciousness that is given through the existence of the Other. I am not in a position to *appropriate* the gift of my objectity. Sartre's metaphor of a gift 'wraps up' the present too much; the Other may give me their confidence and express their feelings without reserve. While I cannot be in the position of the one who offers the gift (of *objectity*), the gift can be offered and received. To say this cannot be done is to say a gift cannot be received because it cannot be for me what it was for its donor. For all Derrida's delicate impossibility of the gift we do swap presents.

Sartre says that I cannot *represent* the Other to myself (BN, 271), as if to say, '*If only I could see the very interiority that makes me an exteriority I could see how I am an object as from the point of view of the Other!*' In his prohibition 'I cannot *represent* the Other to myself' Sartre reveals our desire to do just that.[19] In *representing* the Other we make an object of them but for all that, we receive a gift from the Other's position even if we deconstruct the conscious '*being-for-itself*' that initiates the gift. I make the Other an 'object' by perceiving them but they are not, therefore, made peculiarly 'my' object. The *objectity* I accomplish makes relevant what others perceive and think about me. Each uses 'I', but Sartre turns this into being a 'unique speaking subject' (Le Dœuff 1986a: 24–5; 1986b: 89, 104). The other undoes only the fantasy of its being peculiarly *mine*. To criticise

---

[18] Must I obliterate this freedom? An 'immediate presence' might obliterate it.

[19] Sartre is like Wittgenstein, admonishing us against the 'temptations' of thought.

this impossible interiority is to deconstruct the thought, '*It is re-integrated over there, but is denied to me*' (BN, 272). Only as *purely* mine is it 'denied me'. I may concurrently rebuild the world as 'mine' – and 'as-for-others' – as does anyone else. Sartre extends his analysis of shame to a general account of being conscious of an object:

> Shame is a revelation of the Other, not as consciousness reveals an object, but as one moment of consciousness implies another ... The 'cogito' [consciousness as revealed by systematic doubt] would still be haunted by an inapprehensible presence ... It is not in the world that the Other is first to be sought (BN, 272–273).

Any reader of this may well burst out – '*The Other is not to be first sought in the world*'! Shocking! *This is to slip back into solipsism!*'. An admirable warning. Yet, what is this 'immediate revelation' of the Other? Sartre claims that if shame revealed the Other as an *object* of consciousness then the Other would not be present to me as a subjectivity. He insists that an Other must be present '*as one moment of consciousness implies another*'. Sartre apprehends the risk of solipsism in this:[20]

> [I]s this not simply because the Other's look [is only] the meaning of my objectivity-for-myself? ... [S]o we shall fall back into solipsism (BN, 273).

Sartre's imaginary critic sees the impending collapse of the Other's otherness. Sartre's devil's advocate proposes that

> when I integrate myself as an object in the concrete system of representations, the meaning of this objectification would be projected outside me and hypostatized as the Other (BN, 273).

Sartre is aware of the risk of solipsism. He is running close to the wind but is sure he is still making headway. To countenance a plurality of conscious beings that can recognise each other as such, requires a being that can negate that which is not my consciousness. So the Me which is *object-for-myself* is a 'Me' which is *not-Me*. Objectification ('*l'objectivation*') is a radical metamorphosis. Sartre extends this explanation:

> If I could see myself as an object ... I should see ... the objective apprehension of my being-other, which is radically different from my being-for-myself, and which does not refer to myself at all (BN, 273).

---

[20] Thus Sartre's interiorising of the Other has a motive. It is not just a slippage between the 'immediacy' of the Other's presence to its 'indubitability'.

Sartre exaggerates in saying that my 'being-other' does not refer to myself *at all*. This denial is the 'bad faith of transcendence' that he has so shrewdly diagnosed – to identify with my power to 'nihilate' what I am in itself. My facticity[21] is involved in my being for another.

Being Responsible for the Reality Conferred Upon Me

Sartre seems to take on Cartesianism, no longer allowing that 'I myself' in my intimacy was discovered to be on view to another. He says, '*I am my own detachment ... [my own] nothingness simply because I am my own mediator between Me and Me*' (BN, 274). What he would deny, here, is that the Other can see me *as a conscious subject* when I look at them. Sartre denies that I can see someone as a conscious being at the very time that I see him looking at me. A 'modal' change of consciousness occurs or I should not be *aware* that I was being looked at. This, however, does not mean that the Other *is* this perceptual modification. That 'modification' might require a *reference* to the Other to describe it, but my consciousness is of its *object*. And its object is *another person* as a conscious being who can see what I am up to.

The 'me' which is seen is neither my '*I am I*' nor some 'empty image which the Other makes of me'. Sartre puts it irresistibly: '*The fact of the Other is incontestable and touches me to the heart*' (BN, 275). I am this new 'me', but I am not *this* '*nothingness which separates me from myself*' (BN, 274). I can 'nihilate' *for myself* but this does not give me the power to nihilate the distance (to 'differ') between what I am for myself and what I am for the Other. I am not the Other that 'nihilates' my world and me; I am subjected object of that Other.

Sartre tries again to express the situation – '*My being for others is a fall through absolute emptiness towards objectivity*'[22] (BN, 274–275). Alienation is something that must *happen* to me. I am alienated by the very fact that it requires another to alienate me. A neat point. But what is this we hear? '*The Other does not constitute me as an object for myself, but for him*' (BN, 275). This might slip by as part of the Sartrean litany. You know:

Either   I am subject, in making an object of the Other
Or   I am object in being subject to the Other.
Ergo,   Though made object by the Other I cannot be object for myself.

---

[21] The resistance offered by my objectity to what I would make of it.

[22] The right word is 'object-ness' or 'objectity'. It is not a question of 'objectivity'.

Sartre thus shies away from his discovery of an intimate interiority that exists *for another*, irrecoverable by me. I exist as an object for her/him, whether as 'mere object' or as conscious subject but I can gain an appreciation *for myself* of myself as object. The Other does me this uncomfortable favour of being made an 'object for the Other', and so long as this obtains, I gain *for myself* this sense of objectity. This is precisely what happens when brought up against myself by another's scrutiny. If the Other's intention to 'bring me to myself' is to succeed, I must gain an 'appreciation for myself of myself as object', though it appears impossible in Sartre's terms. Sartre 'differs' my *being-for-myself* as it is for another, and my *being-for-others* as it is for myself, claiming that '*I apprehend nothing but an escape from myself toward* – ' (BN, 275). Nevertheless, as he shows, I can be brought up short before the exteriority; I have to take responsibility for it, just as I am accountable for my 'inner life'. We could read the following description as tracking the paths of interiorisation rather than as a reduction of the reality of the Other:

> [M]yself-as-object is neither knowledge nor a unity of knowledge but an uneasiness, a lived wrenching away from the ek-static unity of the for-itself, a limit which I can not reach and which yet I am (BN, 275).

As it turns out, the Other bounces back, instantly. She or he was already there within the 'wrench':

> In fact my wrenching away from myself and the upsurge of the Other's freedom are one ... [T]he fact of the Other is incontestable and touches me to the heart (BN, 275).

From being someone who might challenge me, this 'Other' falls away to

> [appear] as a being who arises in an original relation of being with me, whose indubitability and factual necessity are those of my own consciousness (BN, 275).

We may recall from the opening pages of *Being and Nothingness*, that '*consciousness exhausts itself in its positing*' – we find 'nothing in' consciousness except what we are conscious *of*. Are we safe from solipsistic collapse then? Though perceived within emotion, in uneasiness, in my '*falling away towards* – ' it is still the Other of which I am aware. Only subliminally or peripherally am I aware (of) my mode of awareness. But we are not safe. There is violent ambivalence in the text. The boat of theory and phenomena is tossed and drifts back towards the 'reef of solipsism'. An image of how the Other may be *some kind of object of consciousness* for me even when s/he looks at me, could steady the movement between *me-as-subject and Other-made-object*, and *Other-as subject-making-me-object*. This differing has, however, become a dichotomy. No room is left for both 'I' and the Other to be present equally as conscious subjects, albeit within the distance that perceivable objects maintain for each other – being 'at least in the mode of objectness'!

A 'patient' phenomenology and a thoughtful psychology can discern the varieties of 'being object'. To recognise and use them would steady the rush from side to side. Critics have been liable to upbraid Sartre morally or else to announce that the buoy both Other and I need equally was steadied, already. To invoke Otto Neurath,[23] this vessel of phenomena and theory into which we all are thrown has to be reconstructed on the high seas. In recognising the other as subjective object we find ourselves – seen as objective subject. We rock on.

Upsurge and Absence

Persisting in maintaining 'immediacy', Sartre's narrator makes a second sweep through the corridor. There I am again, bending at the keyhole. I 'hear' a footfall. It turns out that no one was there but I remain in the frame of mind of one under outside scrutiny (pounding heart, hyper-alert). Even if I do proceed with looking through the keyhole, knowing I am not observed,

> I continue to feel profoundly my being-for-others. I am already in the state of being-looked-at. What falsely appeared [was] ... the Other's facticity ... that concrete event ... of ... the Other's *being-there* (BN, 277).

Something new is happening in the text. The central question has become '*What is this absence of the Other?* It is now someone's *absence* that best conveys their own separate subjectivity; this recalls how Sartre described finding Pierre to be absent from the café, making *absence* the key to understanding creative consciousness. He showed then, that absence consists in more than the nominated thing or person's 'not being there'. Pierre might be 'absent' for a quarter of an hour from the hotel corridor, but the non-presence of the Aga-Khan is, as idiom has it, simply 'neither here nor there'.[24] And yet, more than someone's *presence in absence* was conveyed by the image of being surprised by another when peering covertly. 'The existence of the Other as *implied within* one's shame'

---

[23] I have the allusion from W.V.O. Quine (Quine 1960: 3f, 124, 210).

[24] In writing another's outlook to take form – 'emotion recollected in tranquillity'.

emerged, but also the story evoked the power of another separate centre of consciousness to de-centre one's own.

This image of an observer bursting in upon my private scene set up an expectation of an encounter that involves more than Sartre has allowed for in his metaphysics of an 'indubitable Other' who is there even when I am alone. He is lessening the tension between the external and the interior *Other* by emphasising the power of an absent, imagined Other. '*For Pierre to be absent from Thérèse is a particular way of his being present*' says Sartre, and we recognise some truth in this (BN, 279). But what *is* Pierre's way of being present to her? By letters? Telephone? E-mail? Perhaps he thinks of her as he awakes?

Is his 'presence' to her only that *she* has him in mind? He may have forgotten her entirely. What of the different 'presence' he has, physically, elsewhere? What might his actions – that she cannot imagine – mean to his *presence-in-absence* to Thérèse? Sartre provides Pierre excuse for infidelity because he can now say, '*I am never so present to you, my dear, as in my absence.*'! Since absence is more than 'not being there', there must be a reciprocity between Pierre's presence to Thérèse when he *is* with her, and his presence when he is not. Sartre has been seeking an 'immediate presence' of 'I' and 'Other'; the bodily presence of another would hinder rather than facilitate this immediacy, he thinks. As he says,

> [w]hether the distance is small or great, between Pierre-as-object and Thérèse as subject there is the infinite density of a world ... between Pierre as subject and Thérèse as object there is no distance at all (BN, 279).

We are situated, not '*by means of degrees of longitude and latitude*' but are 'placed' by our modes of being – *between* '*the Guermantes way and Swann's way*'. In consequence of this,

> [a]t London, in the East Indies, in America ... Pierre [can be] present to Thérèse who remains in Paris (BN, 279).

In a distortion of this nice observation, Sartre places 'man' at the centre and 'woman' on the dependent margin. He adds, as if to mark an evident corollary, that '*he will cease to be present to her only at his death*' (BN, 279). But this is not up to Pierre! She will cease to be present to him only at *his* death just so long as she remains a 'significant other' in his life. It is up to him to make such a vow. But whether Pierre will remain significant for Thérèse until his death – and after it – is Thérèse's affair. In that Pierre can be 'present to' Thérèse while roaming the world, he can remain present *after* his death. 'Presence in absence' may continue, though, unless she believes in a psychic realm, it is not bolstered by his possible return.

Though someone's proximity to another cannot be measured simply in terms of geographical distance, physical proximity is still a factor. Whether you achieve proximity by e-mail or in person has a good deal to do with what can happen when you 'arrive'. What happened in physical proximity before you parted weighs heavily upon the kind of absent presence that can be maintained, too, and upon whether continued absence will make a crucial difference to one's 'presence'.[25] Sartre avoids these issues in generalising his reference to the 'Other'. He states that

> every human reality is present or absent on the ground of an original presence ... [which] can have meaning only as a being-looked-at or as a being-looking-at-for-the-Other (BN, 280).

While this defines the Other as a category for consciousness, it does not describe the involvement of some particular (even if unspecified) 'other'. Sartre is severing the *presence* even of any particular person from any physical encounter with them:

> I can ... believe that it is Annie who is coming toward me ... and discover that it is an unknown person; the fundamental presence of Annie to me is not ... changed (BN, 280).

Annie's presence as interiorised Other survives unchanged despite her failure to appear in person.[26] That interiorised presence was established, nevertheless, in the narrator's encounters with her – that is, where she is present 'at least in the modality of objectness'. This principle holds even if the relationship has been established only by letters, telephone conversations or on e-mail. These involve material mediation. There are other implications when it turns out that the one approaching is not Annie.

Had we run into each other an 'infinite density of a world' would have separated us even as it brought us together,[27] and since we are separated by that 'infinite density', we employ arts of expression, listening, deciphering and co-ordinating our ways of 'being with' each other. Certainly, proximity to another is no simple geographical matter. We maintain a presence for each other even when separated by a wall, an ocean or a national boundary. Even death can only change the character of presence in absence. For all that, we do have to describe how 'subjective objects' meet *by means of* the

---

[25] Paul Auster's *New York Trilogy* explores Sartre's theme of 'making nothing of'.

[26] Unless her failure to appear was a breach of trust, this would seem correct.

[27] That is, what are the possibilities in our being with, or 'knowing' each other?

world's 'infinite density', if they are to meet at all. Sartre, however, sees the Other as failing to be present *as a subject* when bodily present. His vision has skidded over what it is to be an object, with the consequence that the Other as present *even when absent* has been converted into the Other as *immediately* present *only* if absent.[28] If this means the Other has being only in one's thoughts, it does appear that Sartre has said what he wished to say. He claims, as a natural consequence, that

> [I]n every Look there is the appearance of the Other-as-object as a concrete and probable presence ... [O]n the occasion of certain attitudes of that Other I determine myself to apprehend my being-looked-at (BN, 281).

The 'Other' at whom I look, not to objectify but in reciprocity as with a thoughtful feeling 'object', has been lost. There has been too loose an idea of 'object' and of 'objectification'.

'External' and 'Internal' Negation

Reasserting Mastery

We noted earlier Poincaré's image of breaking out of our interiority, of *'living beings [who] attempt to arrive at the surface of [a] sphere by setting out from the centre, [where] the lowering of the temperature [as they approach the surface] produces in them a continually increasing contraction'* (BN, 286). Sartre's most intricate attempts to relate *in-itself* and *for-itself* in their encounter, work in counterpoint with this image:

> [My being object for-another] is not in-itself, for it is not produced in the pure exteriority of indifference. But neither is it for-itself, for it is not the being which I have to be by nihilating myself. It is precisely my being-for-others, this being which is divided between two negations with opposed origins (BN, 287).

This introduces a significant degree of precision beyond the common reading of a 'dualism' in his *in-itself* and *for-itself*. 'Divided between the two negations' of my nihilating of my own facticity, and negating the Other as 'not-me', this being foils the dichotomy. It makes conceptual space for a manifestation of one's conscious life to an Other who would be in reciprocal relation with me. Is this reciprocation possible between conscious bodies, separated by the 'infinite density of the world', or is it

---

[28] As *for-itself*, it is necessarily 'absent' for any other (conscious) *for-itself*.

only after interiorisation that the Other (not me nor any aspect of nor mere shadow of me) can be in an immediate relation?

> For that Other is not this Me of which he has an intuition, and I do not have the intuition of this Me which I am. Yet this Me, produced by the one and assumed by the other, derives its absolute reality from the fact that it is the only separation possible between two beings fundamentally identical as regards their mode of being and immediately present one to the other (BN, 286).

This is how Sartre pictures the indubitable immediacy of 'I' to 'Other' while claiming that the conscious *for-itself* is the 'nihilating' activity upon what exists in itself rather than being some entity beyond it. I am a nihilating *for-itself*; the Other is the same. The question is not *how* 'I' can be internally related to the 'Other' but how there could be any alternative to it. Each conscious being *is* alike as *nihilating upon an in-itself*. Because of this internal relation to the *in-itself*, how one bodily consciousness relates to another is always open to question. The internal relationship ensures only that the body as *in-itself* is neither essential obstacle nor alien intermediary between one being and another. In nihilation, the body becomes *for-itself* and this is what ensures that the relation between 'I' and 'Other' can be *immediate*. And yet, while it is neither intermediary nor obstacle, the situation (of one nihilating *in-itself* meeting another) has the implication, Sartre thinks, that the Other can be known 'only as object'.

It is better to inflect and enrich his expression than to combat it head-on. For Sartre, this *'Other' the other sees is not this 'Me' of which I have an intuition*, which makes it difficult to describe a reciprocal relationship between one conscious subject and another. The 'Other' *has an intuition* of me as an *'Other-for-them'* who is not, however, *'me-as-I-am-for-myself'*. I have no intuition *of* this *Me-which-I-am-for-the-Other*. (But does the 'Other have an intuition of 'me for them' *as a conscious being*, or only *as in itself?*)

I am said to 'have no intuition' of myself for myself since I am in no position to make an object of myself – there is no 'nothingness' to mediate 'I' from my own 'other'. At the same time (according to Poincaré's image) I have to accept the 'object' that I am for another: '*It is the only separation possible between two beings fundamentally identical as regards their mode of being and immediately present one to the other*' (BN, 286–287). The desire to represent myself as in immediate and reciprocal relation with another has led Sartre to a point where the problem is to differ[entiate] us. While this 'object' which I am for the Other is not reducible to the level of the 'in-itself', it is not a *for-itself*, either. It is my *in-itself-as-nihilated-by-*

the-Other.[29] For Sartre, 'I' am immediately and indubitably related to the 'Other' when I find myself being scrutinised. Even if I only imagined I had been seen, that immediacy is not brought into question. But is there any facticity in my *being-for-another* if the immediacy of my exposure to the Other is thus preserved from all possible doubt?[30]

What can Limit Consciousness?

'I' have no immediate consciousness ('intuition') of that very 'me' of which the 'Other' is aware (BN, 286). Indeed, we 'differ' only because each 'refuses' to be merely what we are for the other (BN, 285). If neither of us can be conscious of the other as 'for themself' it cannot be by consciousness that we 'differ' in ourselves. Yet, the Other touches me to the quick by their 'look'. Am I really in no way conscious of what I am, as 'for them'? How *do* we 'differ' our conscious selves, then?

Sartre brings the point to crisis in his open declaration that '*consciousness alone can limit consciousness*' (BN, 286). This is not merely Berkeley's refrain that consciousness cannot depend upon 'stupid unthinking matter'. Sartre's difference is subtle and effective. He uses '*only consciousness can bear upon consciousness*' to show that my *being-for-another* (which I cannot appropriate for myself) must lie between *being-for-itself* and *being-in-itself*. If this *being-for-another* can 'differ' us then it must be safely within the province of the *for-itself*. I cannot appropriate this *being-for-another* for myself, and the Other can appropriate it only as perceivable object, perceived nevertheless as irreducible to the *in-itself*. I now recollect that it was I who 'negated' the Other in the first place – the Other depends *on me* for being an Other,[31] to the extent that it is up to me to '*deny that I am the Other*'. I might seem to have some control over this '*Other ... [who] can be manifested only as ... a subject beyond my limit, as the one who limits me*'. But this control vanishes as it appears. Though '*nothing can limit me except the Other*', this One can, '*in his full freedom ... [put] me out of play ... by refusing to "join in"*'[32] (BN, 287).

For all that the 'Other' can negate me, I can define myself against them as *for myself* – not only as a being *for* this Other whom I cannot grasp:

---

[29] Though, in the park, it is also an '*in-itself*' nihilating itself, too.

[30] That I am 'for the Other' in *some* way, is indubitable. Yet one *can* doubt that I am 'for the Other' in just *this* way.

[31] And is the idea of someone as 'the Other for me' the idea that someone is *an* 'Other, or that someone is *this* Other'?

[32] That another might 'refuse' to join in suggests the possibility that s/he might agree to!

In the very apprehension of this negation [which does not come through myself] there arises the consciousness (of) myself as myself. [And] thus I gain … an explicit self-consciousness inasmuch as I am also responsible for a negation of the Other which is my own possibility (BN, 287).

This 'consciousness of myself as myself' must be of myself as object – an interiorisation of the way I can be seen as object by the Other.[33] Desperate manoeuvres surround the encounter between 'I' and 'Other' which is becoming, not just a 'duel' (as Le Dœuff put it), but a downright wrestling match. 'I' press my initial slight advantage over the Other, laying hold of my own 'being put out of play' by the Other, on the ground that they obtained this power only on licence from myself in 'wrenching myself away from the Other by assuming my limit'. After all, 'I' am the one who 'put the other out of play':

[I]f there is an Other who puts me out of play by positing my transcendence … this is because I wrench myself away from the Other … [Thus] I am already putting the Other out of play. To that extent I am responsible for the existence of the Other … [It is] by the very affirmation of my free spontaneity [I] cause there to be an Other (BN, 287).

The Other had burst 'already a legend upon the scene' (Baez, of Dylan).

[Now] since the Other finds himself out of play … [they] now appear to me as a degraded presence [because] the Other and I are in fact co-responsible for the Other's existence, but it is by two negations such that I can not experience the one without immediately disguising the second (BN, 287).

The negation that I experience by 'disguising' another is the negation of myself *by the Other* as *being-for-itself*. The negation is my co-operative gesture that permits this *being-for-itself* to be an 'Other' to me. Sartre appropriates the 'Other' as 'his responsibility', which is incommensurate with its first, primary role in de-centring the 'I' (BN, 221).

Experiencing Behaviour

Engagement and Instrumentality

After three hundred pages of existential philosophy, 'engagement' appears as a theme:

---

[33] Perhaps this is a salutary warning rather than an arrogant appropriation.

> I exist only as engaged and I am conscious (of) being only as engaged [and] apprehend the Other-as-object only in a concrete and engaged surpassing of his transcendence (BN, 291).

This is what is so promising. The philosopher who would take us beyond the role of disengaged spectator:

> [T]he Other's engagement appears to me as a real engagement, as a taking root – I am engaged to a particular person ... to return that money (BN, 291–292).

I discover another conscious being not in the way that I know an object in detachment. I am involved with another as 'being to being':

> The being-in-the-midst-of-the-world which comes to the Other through me is a real being ... not like a subjective necessity which makes me know I [thus] exist (BN, 292).

Ambiguity disturbs my involvement with this 'real being', however. For my part, I '*exist[ed] as engaged*' only in an '*engaged surpassing of his transcendence*'. By the same token, another's 'engagement' with me appears only '*in so far as it is transcended by my transcendence*'. Because, in Sartre's imaginary, one is 'engaged' with another only in *surpassing* them in one's *transcendence*, still I apprehend '*the Other as object*'. Engagement is no escape from one's objectification of another. It is no surprise, then, to find a new theme of '*degradation*' that signals the dying fall of the promise of '*engagement*':

> But when I grasp the Other as object his engagement is degraded ... [to something 'engaged'] in the sense that 'the knife is engaged in the wound, the army is engaged in the narrow pass' (BN, 292–293).

As soon as I act, my (personal) engagement 'degrades' into an instrument engaged in a task. Images of damage and war overtake the promise of reciprocity. So just why did I *have to* strive to 'surpass' the 'transcendence' of the other person? Her 'transcendence' was simply that she, like myself, lived for herself even in living with me. Sartre feels that in my engagement with the Other as '*in a concrete and engaged surpassing of his transcendence*' I still '*apprehend the Other-as-object*'. How do we read this (vanishing) moment of 'engagement' against Sartre's preceding story of how I encounter the 'Other' in their absence – in the immediacy of my own consciousness? Sartre discovers someone as a subject in isolated detachment, not by immediate engagement.

The Impossibility of Conceiving of the Other as Subject

Sartre rules out the possibility of my 'knowing or conceiving of' the Other-as-subject, basing such ontological difference on inaccessibility:

> The difference of principle between the Other-as-object and the Other-as-subject stems solely from this fact: that the Other-as-subject can in no way be known nor even conceived as such (BN, 294).[34]

He explains afresh why he is so confident in saying this, elaborating the meaning of *being-object-for-another*:

> [T]he objects of the world do not refer to his subjectivity; they refer only to his object-state in the world as the meaning – surpassed toward my selfness – of the intra-mundane flow (BN, 294).

This inflects the initial simple and calm image of seeing a man in the park – I 'see' his subjectivity in the way my perception of the park is shifted. This is no egocentric reduction of the other's point of view, but a way to *'register an organisation without distance of the things in my universe about that privileged object'* (BN, 254). Engagement has set the Other in motion:

> What I apprehend as real characteristics of the Other is a being-in-situation ... The Other becomes the instrument which is defined by his relation with all other instruments [including mine] (BN, 292).

This instrumentalism also has its ambiguities. The impersonal 'vase' of the 'mere instrument' flips over into the more homely 'pair of faces' – my perception of another's world. I understand another in comprehending how he organises a world: *'it is to apprehend this enclave-order and to refer it back to a central absence or interiority'* (BN, 292). I think, here, of Simon Schama's *Rembrandt's Eyes*. Schama evokes the interiority of paintings and of Rembrandt, not by a pretended knowledge of 'inner thoughts and feelings' but by the intense detail of his words. His words mime a painterly rendering of the world into which Rembrandt was born and then of the world as Rembrandt organised it around himself and his intimate (Schama 1999). There is no particular limit to how far this 'enclave' of instrumental connections extends; the philosopher's imagination swiftly sees that

---

[34] He had some success when regarding people from his café, and in the park.

> it is from the standpoint of the entire world that I arrive at the Other-as-object. Around this man ... who is reading in the subway, the entire world is present ... It is not his body only ... which defines him in his being; it is his identity card ... the direction of the ... train he has boarded ... the ring on his finger (BN, 293).

This 'what is not visible' within 'the visible', all lies within the parenthesis of an unspoken thought – the inconceivable 'central absence' of the Other's interiority. Sartre is led to connect his *being-for-itself* and *being-as-object* with a behavioural reading of the 'Other':

> [T]he anger of the Other-as-object as it is manifested to me across his cries, his stamping ... is not the *sign* of a subjective and hidden anger; it refers to nothing except other gestures and other cries (BN, 294).

In articulating consciousness through the concept of '*for-itself*' and '*for-others*', Sartre ran close to behaviourism. But these 'cries' and 'stamping' do not exist only '*in-itself*'. I can misread behaviour – '*in relation to other gestures*'. Sartre also insists that anger lies in these gestures in terms of the subject's world, within which emotion is perceived as a '*disposition ... around a presence-absence*'. Also,

> the behaviourists have lost sight of [man's] characteristic principle, which is transcendence-transcended ... [man] is understood only in terms of his end (BN, 294).

Sartre wants no mystique about subject and object, though. The *nihilation* that effects *transcendence* of my condition is *transcended* by the Other who 'makes nothing of' aspects of what I have configured. This 'making nothing of' is not some activity unknown to science. By understanding us as we live 'for ourselves', Sartre, like Heidegger, deconstructs 'material' and 'mental', undoing the pseudo-scientific image of 'man as a machine':

> [T]he hammer and the saw are [understood in terms of their 'ends'] ... because they are already humanised ... If we can compare the Other to a machine, this is because the machine ... presents the trace of a transcendence-transcended, just as the looms in a mill are explained by the fabrics which they produce. The behaviourist point of view must be reversed, leav[ing] the Other's [objectity] intact (BN, 295).

Behaviourism treats gesture and conduct as *less than* feeling and perception, stripped of what we understand in reciprocation with others:

[T]he objective fear we apprehend when we perceive the Other-as-object is not [merely an] ensemble of physiological manifestations ... [F]ear is a flight; it is a fainting ... not only the desperate running through the brush, nor ... the heavy fall on the stones ... but the total upheaval of the instrumental organisation which had the Other for its centre (BN, 295).

Sartre's soldier had had the Other in his sights; now *he* is in flight:

[T]he presence of the enemy surrounds him and presses in ... that land in the background ... against which he was leaning as against a wall ... opens fan-wise and becomes ... the welcoming horizon toward which he is fleeing for refuge (BN, 296).

I describe another's life *for-itself*, not as a '*hollow box inside him*' but from his engagement in a world that brings his life within perception:

All of this I establish objectively, and it is precisely this which I apprehend as fear ... [F]ear is given to us as a new type of internal haemorrhage in the world – the passage from the world to a type of magical existence (BN, 296).

The 'magical existence' conjured up by fear suppresses '*by incantation the frightening objects which we are unable to keep at a distance*' (BN, 295). As *feared*, the 'Other' is kept at a distance in fantasy, which makes a wry comment upon the Other as 'immediately present to consciousness only when absent'. The present Other, feared, is removed to a magical distance. Sartre tries to deal with the tensions:

The Other-as-object is an object, but ... I could always ... produce from him another experience ... on another plane. [I have] knowledge of my past experience ... and on the other hand [I have] the dialectic of the Other [which] I make myself not-be (BN, 297).

Origins and Contingencies

'*But why are there Others?*' asks Sartre. I might live an entire life without recognising the 'Other', dealing with others as scientists used to treat animals in Descartes' time – their pain not being recognised because their responses were observed only in detachment. Sartre senses danger in this:

[T]he Other-as-object is an explosive instrument which I handle with care because I foresee ... the permanent possibility that they are going to make it explode ... I shall suddenly experience the flight of the world away from me (BN, 297).

Why these 'explosive devices' that litter the world? *Why* these 'others' that fracture complacency? Sartre points out that *'the "Other" is not an ontological structure of the for-itself'*,[35] while warning us not to be overwhelmed by its contingency: *'An original contingency? Any metaphysics must conclude with a "that is" – a direct intuition of contingency'*. A kind of explanation exists, however, for the Other is not an optional extra. Is the contingency of the Other *'derived from a fundamental contingency?'* (BN, 297).[36] The origin of the 'Other' lies in a series of self-transformations of what exists *in-itself*. The first of these of these pre-reflective stages[37] is the familiar *'"wrenching away" of the for-itself from all that is'*. The second stage reveals irresistible bad faith – I try to establish as a fixed fact, my 'differing' of myself as subject and as object – as if to be master of my being a free embodied mentality. Sartre describes the metaphysics of this impossible project[38] as *'a wrenching away of [the initial] wrenching away [from what has being only 'in-itself']'*. Using the biological notion of *scissiparity*[39] as metaphor, he diagnoses our *'vain attempt to take a point of view on the nihilation that the for-itself has to be'*. The attempt is 'vain', *'because I am my own transcendence. I can not use it so as to constitute it as a transcendence'* (BN, 298).

This leads *'to a [third] more radical ekstasis'* in which I am 'lost' to myself in *being-for-others*. What I look for is to be established *in the form of an external negation*, as if I could see my differing myself-as-for-myself from myself-as-in-the-eyes-of-the-other.[40] Able to compare what I am *for-myself* with what I am *in-itself* I could then exist as *'in the spatial exteriority of indifference'* (BN, 298).[41] Alas! *'The goal is never achieved … The for-itself … can not [realise] itself'* (BN, 298) as differed by an outside party. My differing of another from me is internal. *'It is a nihilation which the for-itself has to be, just like the reflective nihilation'* (BN, 299). I have not established the difference as seen by a third party.

The chickens have come home to roost. It is the 'internality' of the negation by which 'I' differ myself from the 'Other' that gives a sense to the question of the 'origin of the Other' – not the evolutionary process by which the human species arose, but the origin of one's concept and experience of being 'Other'. An 'I' cannot meet the 'Other' merely in terms

---

[35] Leibniz assures us we can question the origin of any contingent existence.

[36] One could read Derrida's 'traces' for 'origins' and *différance* for *néantisation*.

[37] *'Ek-stases* – as in ecstacy I am 'taken out of myself'.

[38] *Reflected-on* and *reflective* each wants a life of their own.

[39] 'Scissiparity' – schizo-genesis: reproduction by fission of an individual.

[40] *To see myself*, not just *as others see me*, but *as if to be the other in seeing me*.

[41] I thus neutralise an appeal and observe myself as an object 'beyond entreaty'.

of the being of each in the external mode of 'object-ness'.[42] The 'negation' – that differing by which I encounter another immediately – is 'internal', already differed (*'nihilated'*) by the 'I' who accepts the challenge of the Other. As *internal*, this 'differing' achieves 'objectity', since even an imaginary Other is encountered as an *object* of thought.

An Other as only another moment in my consciousness could not be *encountered* and would not satisfy the condition of being *'present to me as objectness'* (BN, 253). And yet the Other as present within the being of my shame is an interiorised Other that might threaten this 'objectity'. Sartre points out that *'the negations are effected in interiority'* and concludes that *'the Other and myself can not come to one another from the outside'* (BN, 299). But this *'not from the outside'* just means that the relation is not established as by an uninvolved third party; *'the "I-and-the-Other" ... [is the] reciprocal scissiparity of [being] for-others* (BN, 299). This self-reproduction by self-fission is provoked 'from outside' and takes the self beyond itself. The *self*-fission emerges, reflectively, after the irritant.

So when Sartre claims that *'my selfness and that of the Other are structures of one and same totality of being'*, one should not conclude that the *totality* is purely *mine* (BN, 299). After all, I recognise (in shame or delight) the Other who sees me, as beyond oneself, appearing as another conscious body, or as someone I deal with in their absence, or as an imaginary character. In any case the 'Other' is 'external' to my being conscious of myself or my own states of mind. Hamlet, Odysseus, Emma, scrutinise my ideas and outlook.[43] Also, the 'otherness' in the absence of someone I know encourages or restrains me, in continuity with their walking through the door to correct or upset that 'other' that operated in their absence. I may not understand the 'Other' better when they are present but, contra dualism, the Other *can* be 'immediate' in their bodily presence.

The Return of the Repressed: a Plurality of Conscious Beings

'I' and 'Other' must fail in our desire to constitute a couple fully grasped by each partner, but the attempt does not 'go gently into that good night':

> [T]here is this perpetual 'explosion' of the totality that is a kind of origin of the being of others and of myself as other ... as a kind of shattered totality, always elsewhere ... never in-itself (BN, 300).

---

[42] A surgeon operating on a patient has related 'purely in the mode of objectness'.

[43] Though formed by history and culture their presence is 'immediate' – there can be nothing *between* them and me. They are present purely in their absence.

This imagery of 'explosion' speaks of a 'return of the repressed' from the solipsistic frame of mind. Interiorising the Other intensified its suffocation by *being-in-itself*. An escape from that has animated the 'pursuit of being' and Sartre achieves a new release by a strategy akin to Husserl's *epoché* in which any 'I' sees that the 'Other' operates in the same self-frustrating way, thus gaining an empathy that resists the self-absorption of each:

> [S]imultaneously with my negation of myself, the Other denies concerning himself that he is me. These two negations are equally indispensable to being-for-others, and they can not be reunited by any synthesis (BN, 300).

The impossibility of such 'reunion' signifies the intransigent difference of the Other even though we are related by 'internal negation' and despite the fact that we meet within the immediacy of two moments of consciousness. This fact *'represents the negation of any synthetic totality in terms of which one might understand [as if from the outside] the plurality of conscious-nesses'*. The plurality *'is inapprehensible because produced neither by the Other nor my myself nor by any intermediary'*. Each conscious being that experiences the other as conscious, experiences that other *'without intermediary'* (BN, 300–301).

This phrase, *'without intermediary'*, precipitates the idea of each conscious being as existing *for itself* in having nihilated (differed, made nothing of) the only possible mode of *being* – its *being-in-itself*. This means that we *are* our bodies *tout court* – in the mode of 'making nothing of them'. Sartre himself has come as far as he can in explaining the contingency of one's being as *for-an-another*. It arises with the eruption of an Other and occurs as within 'moments' of consciousness. Whether the 'eruption' occurs as between separate conscious bodies appears to be left undecided, but the 'bodied' character of *living for oneself* is implied by the everyday character of the immediacy of encounter. Not ineffable, its 'mystery in broad daylight' is that of a contingency that places it beyond explanation:

> [S]ince there is nothing which can found it, neither a consciousness nor a totality exploding into consciousness, it appears as a pure irreducible contingency. [M]y denial that I am the Other is not sufficient to make the Other exist, [and] the other must simultaneously with my own negation deny that he is me. This is the facticity of being-for-others (BN, 301).

Sartre has come to a terminus in describing the interiorised exteriority of the Other. Though I exist as *for-others* even when I only imagine another perceives me, that contingent *being-for-an-other* must 'deny he is me'. The contingency speaks of the difference of the Other that challenges my self-centredness. The 'scandal' of a plurality of others confounds Hegel's 'interiorised' Other as intermediary between 'I' and 'I'. As a *category of thought* a Kantian 'Other', too, fails to challenge one's *being-for-oneself*:

> In one sense ... a plurality of consciousnesses can not be a primary fact and it refers us to an original ... wrenching away from self, a fact of the mind. But in another sense ... this plurality seems to be irreducible [since] from the standpoint of ... the plurality, [the mind] vanishes. Then we can answer only 'That's how it is' (BN, 301).

Concluding Remarks

We have come close to resolving the status of the Sartrean Other, and in so doing, have begun to sketch a credible story for ourselves. How is another present without intermediary to challenge my mode of being as from an unbridgeable distance, immediately present to me though I cannot represent their standpoint? The tension in these demands reflects an actual state of affairs, a partial description of life with others and oneself. We *refine* our understanding of interiorised exteriority in order to act and speak with others as separate, allied to us in consciousness. And yet no one of us 'comprehends' another if that means to 'encompass' their mode of conscious life within one's own or to translate their use of terms into one's own without loss. In this situation it achieves nothing merely to insist on the Other's exteriority, to congratulate oneself on repudiating a solipsistic mentality. Without an internal image of others to nuance our reactions and responses to their behaviour and expressions, we 'handle' them more or less efficiently for purposes of business. Closer interaction from that mode produces not intimacy but a descending spiral of anger and accusation.

In taking his departure from the problem Sartre alludes to the Cartesian tradition which represents in terms of one's having a 'mind' what is special about *being-for-oneself*:

> Can we say then that the mind is the being that is and is not, just as the *for-itself* is what it is not and is not what it is? The question has no meaning ... It supposes we could take a view of the totality from the outside (BN, 301).

Sartre has taken the measure of this proposed 'totality of others' in terms of a totality of mind taken up with its concerns. It is an 'ek-static'

> totality ... appear[ing] to us as a shattered being concerning which we can neither say that it exists or that it does not exist (BN, 301).

There is no outside point of view from which I can survey it, since a plurality of conscious beings *'appears to us as a synthesis and not as a collection – a synthesis whose totality is inconceivable'* (BN, 301). Like trying to represent another's living through their life, such a synthesis

> is impossible precisely because I exist as myself on the foundation of this totality and to the extent that I am engaged in it. Not even God could do this (BN, 301). [44]

Sartre reiterates what we can take with us to the next stage:

> [T]he Other ... was experienced ... through my [objectity] ... [M]y reaction to my alienation for the Other was expressed in my grasping the Other [in their objectity]. [I]f I experience the Other with evidence, I fail to know him; if I know him, I only reach his being-as-object (BN, 302).

Sartre propounds this new enigma to replace Descartes' 'body and mind' and Husserl's 'natural and transcendental attitudes', but he entrenches his own difficulties in treating us as living 'for ourselves' and 'for others'. As 'for myself' I discover a 'body for me' that cannot be synthesised with my body as for another, just as *being-for-myself* cannot be co-ordinated with *being-for-others*. This raises a new question about

> the object which the Other is for me, and this object which I am for him are manifested each as a body. What is my body? What is the body of the Other? (BN, 302).

The body as *in-itself*, nihilated as *being-for-itself*, is a conscious body. This result might promise a synthesis of us as bodily conscious both for ourselves and for others. [45] On this conception there is no gulf that would thwart reciprocity between one conscious being and another. The 'infinite density' of the world is the means of encounter even though comprehension will be partial at best. This is life, as we know it. Only Sartre's insistence that as a conscious body living 'for itself' I can be seen only as 'object' by another, obstructed him in taking his theory further down that path. We can set out, in our own thinking, from the scene with which we began these three studies of perceiving and interiorising others. The world changes for me when I see 'my' park as being scrutinised and enjoyed by another. My sense of my self changes irrevocably when I become aware of myself as

---

[44] The Christian god of salvation, an impossible being, effects the transaction.

[45] It is Sartre's development of Husserl that first established the body as the site of conscious life for European philosophy. 'The Body' prefigures Merleau-Ponty.

open in my interiority to the canny observation of another. The other sees me as more than body, by sensing the absence, for the other, of the consciousness the body signifies. Our presence to each other as conscious bodies has been a constant image provoked by the same gesture that reinstates reciprocal bodily consciousness as impossible. One might say that Sartre's contradictions mean that for him *les jeux sont faits*. I think that he has not played out his hand.

The Other's Body

What emerges, strikingly, in 'The Body for Others' is an idea of knowledge that is not specifically my knowledge.[46] The possibility of impersonal knowledge arises from the fact that *'the Other's body* is radically different from *my body-for-me'* (BN, 340). To translate freely into the twenty-first century the passage that follows:

> I get a new grip on what I am by framing, for myself, the way in which another views me. I go past simply being an object for the other, and establish my own point of view upon the way I have been framed. It is in this way that I can frame the way someone has been framing me that I get beyond myself, as it were, so as to see knowledge, as if from the point of view of others, as simply there (Author's free paraphrase).

Sartre sums up his line of thought: *'The senses of the Other are senses known as knowing'* (BN, 341).

At the end of his chapter on the body, Sartre asks, *'Why is it astonishing that my hand touches my eyes?'*. What we find astonishing now is that he found a way of representing such a commonplace fact, known to any infant, *as* astonishing. That what can't see itself, being taken up by what it is doing, can be surprised by its own hand – as surprised as 'I' might be by a stranger when peering (or leering) through a keyhole in a hotel corridor. *'We ought to see here the necessity of a concrete and contingent existence in the midst of the world'*, concludes Sartre. Any part of the book has its surprises, but with familiarity, most of these appear as unwinding each stage of the dialectic from the previous one, with an almost fated inevitability. However, the language and mood of 'The Body' stand out from the rest. The person, being a body – albeit first and foremost the body that they *live* – loses the aura of their existence as an heroic struggle against what exists merely *in itself* – an aura typical of earlier sections.[47]

---

[46] In *Knowledge*, which concludes *Transcendence*, Sartre sketches how a world is revealed to what exists for itself. We might ask how we *know* of this relation.

[47] This *being-for-oneself* against the *in-itself* finally emerges as 'psychoanalysis'.

Here, Sartre's narrator is given the stance of being a body that can 'live' itself and frame itself. Hitherto, the narrative voice was unlocated, based in nothing other than what it had raised up as a significant structure in the first place. Here, even if sporadically, Sartre is possessed of an outlook more accepting of the sciences or of other studies that lie outside phenomenology or the various branches of philosophy. It becomes simply a matter of fact that one hand can touch the other, that one eye cannot see the other except indirectly. And it is simply a matter of fact that the hand as instrument of touch *is* in touch with what gives us vision. The object of vision is not peculiar to vision, since vision is no longer a 'private' process that just happens, somehow, to give us clues about an 'outside real world'. The object of touch is not peculiar to touch, for the same reason, and it can cease to be a (metaphysical) surprise that one can be in touch with the very process of vision. '*What can we hear but sounds?*' asked George Berkeley, rhetorically, in mocking the notion that sounds might be airwaves (Berkeley 1972: 153; 161–164). '*What can we see but sights?*' he might have asked in the same vein, to mock a material view of the senses according to which we might 'see' the process of hearing. Sartre is coming to identify the body we 'live' with the body others observe, and the body that I too can observe as if I were its own third party. His notion of *void*-ance ('nihilation') assists this identification. It points us towards our own current unresolved attempts to understand this identification without imposing a reduction to 'objectity' of the various levels of description of the conscious bodies we call people.

At an early stage of *Being and Nothingness*, in 'Transcendence',[48] Sartre's remarks about knowledge had begun to deconstruct public (objective) knowledge and to set it up as (to speak after Derrida) an 'impossible possible'. This shifting perspective on knowledge accepts its reality as something we hand back and forth to each other, even while making clear that we are bound to give it our own touch and to receive it back, differently, as from another's hand. This is to accept public knowledge, even though it is located within a phenomenology that is still centred, textually, on '*my consciousness*'. And this is how Sartre sets up the possibility he exploits later in his work on the body as, at once, *in itself*, as *for others*, and as *lived by me*.

It is not that these sections are *inconsistent* (as if *contradicting*) those large sections in which the 'other' is seen as necessarily a threat to oneself, and 'nihilation' as a desperate struggle *against* what exists in itself. Rather, these passages on knowledge, and the body, have the lack of consistency in relation to the rest that one finds in preparing a mix for baking. The lack of

---

[48] '*Framing*' is more apt for what Sartre means, in contemporary terms.

consistency appears as an interesting lumpiness. Some of the original ingredients have not been taken up smoothly within the rest. If this is considered, technically, as a fault in writing, it is certainly capable of revealing how the text works. To smooth out these lumps would be too much like a detective's wiping out awkward clues at a crime site. It is from such perceptions, in fact, that we can work such earlier forms of language as that of Sartre and of Beauvoir into our contemporary life. The various junctures in the text where sexually biased perceptions, language and theory reign supreme are other lumps that resist absorption. They are typical of the sites where the systems require further deconstruction – and elaboration.

8
Intimate Bodily Consciousness

Promise and Seduction

A New Promise of Immediacy

Beauvoir investigates the myths and idols of sexual intimacy that she displays for sometimes gentle and sometimes savage mockery. If there were one more play that Sartre might make in describing a free and reciprocal recognition of another as a conscious subject, it would be in conjunction with this investigation of hers. Sartre describes the objectification of another in observing them, as if it were a matter of ontology, while she demonstrates this objectification as embedded, sexually one-sided, fantasy. It is true that Sartre describes how, left to its own devices, the *for-itself* is solipsistic, and that the irruption of another on the scene is designed to disturb this self-confirming self-centredness. We recall how Sartre evoked this within an autoerotic narrative:

> Absorbed with what I see in looking through a keyhole, I live the metaphysics of a being-for-itself when I find myself being seen 'for what I am'. I shudder from head to foot. In this masochistic orgasm, I discover that my mode of being conscious was already a bodily state of being[1] – not a pure mentality totally 'exhausted' in its intentional object. In that same shudder I discover that in my very intimacy of being conscious to myself, I exist as a being for another, a being of which I cannot divest myself. I can no more regard what the other sees of me as a mere 'outward display' than I can escape my conscious 'being for myself'.[2]

This image depicts the indignity of philosophy itself. Peering through a keyhole at the fascinating 'real world' the philosopher, oblivious, projects his body into the corridors. The activity of writing eludes the author's sight or grasp, unable to escape conceit. Sartre's embarrassing image depicts how the observer's point of view upon the world cannot be equivalent to

---

[1] The tie between solipsism, autoeroticism and *being-for-itself* remains implicit.

[2] Author's compression of the 'shame' (BN, 221–222) and 'keyhole' passages (BN, 259, 277).

that of others – not only upon the world but also upon one's mode of viewing it. Thus another's response to what one does cannot be encompassed within one's own terms and attitudes. The reader, 'observer' of the philosophical writer, appraises in their own terms not only what that 'lover of wisdom' *says*, but what they were *doing* in writing what they did.

There is tension between Sartre's evocation of another's immediate perception of one's conscious acts and demeanour, and the gulf that is set up by the 'fact' that each, in observing the other, sees them as 'object'. I have described Sartre's tendency to internalise the 'other' as a response to this tension – a response that he himself finds unsatisfactory. If I am 'glued' within this metaphysics then the promise that the consciousness of each partner in a couple 'rises to the surface' of the body in sexual intimacy is particularly seductive. It is not only Beauvoir who evokes love's 'generosity' of spirit that permits each to be open to each – as subjective and as discerning bodies. Sartre too has his moment of almost lyrical metaphysics:

> Whereas before being loved we felt our existence as a mere protuberance ... we now feel that our existence to be taken up ... in its tiniest details by a ... freedom which ... we condition by our existence and which we freely will ourselves (BN, 371).

Assuming Neutrality Enforces the Other's Separation

How easily this newly re-born vision relapses into an age-old sexually skewed fixed one! It was a super-saturated solution from the start, ready to crystallise around a speck called sexual difference. Beauvoir, and then Irigaray showed how the masculine voice, in assuming neutrality, appropriates to itself the whole territory of *the positive and the neutral*. Such an assumption does not entail an outright denial of value, freedom and consciousness to the 'feminine' – or to the status of women. The appropriative 'masculine' presents what it says as if to be read by anyone, as if addressed to anyone capable of reason and thought. It is, nevertheless, constructed, *enunciated* and performed within an imaginary of a masculine subject who stands (in) for each and all. When that is how it works, we find 'woman' symbolised on the margins of the theory's world. Women, those actual people who think and perceive and have something to say about any issues including the theory itself, are liable to be erased from sight or audibility. An imaginary category of the 'feminine', or of 'woman', finds a place, half hidden, within the world of the appropriating theory.

When Plato (or should I say 'Greek society') excludes women from the business of philosophising[3] he then sets up Socrates as *mid-wife* in relation to the young men, and woman irrupts within the young men's bodies.[4] (I think of how in the movie *Aliens* Ripley fought to keep that 'other form of life' on the far side of an impregnable space craft, then dreamed of one bursting from her own body within the 'sealed space'.) Socrates delivers the ideas, the *cherished infants*, of his own young ones. And always the neonate is stillborn!

Beauvoir's Re-vision of the Other

For Sartre, someone is other simply in being 'looked at'. From Beauvoir's opening declaration, '*L'histoire nous a montré que les hommes ont toujours détenu tous les pouvoirs concrets ... [et] ont jugé utile de maintenir la femme dans un état de dépendance*', she establishes the 'look' within a domain of power and of strategy. While the effect is described in terms that resonate closely with the third Part of *Being and Nothingness*, far from an objectified 'Other' appearing as an inevitable ontological consequence, we read of the disastrous effects of an absurd error. An attitude towards a reified, feminised 'Nature' is an error that becomes violent when worked out in relation to women themselves:

> [M]an's life is never abundance and quietude ... [since Nature either] appears as ... an obstacle and remains a stranger, or 'she' ... permits [him to] ... [take] possession of her only through consuming [and thus] destroying her. In both cases he remains alone; he is alone when he touches a stone, alone when he devours a fruit (SS, 171).

We can speculate on whether Beauvoir is criticising this phenomenology of 'Nature' – implying that loneliness would be less acute if objects and plants were more to us than mere 'obstacles' and 'consumables'. She states, overtly, that 'my' life will never be one of simple 'abundance and quietude' since 'I' have need of others, who must exist also for themselves:

> There can be no presence of an other unless the other is also present in and for himself ... true alterity ... is that of a consciousness separate from mine and substantially identical with mine (SS, 171).

---

[3] Plato allows that after men set up the State, women can rule – but they are not to marry. In the *Laws* women marry. As their husbands' property they cannot govern.
[4] Making maternity women's function and their eroticism only 'for man' (Irigaray 1985b: 23–33, 68–85).

For Sartre, the frustration of encounter arises from how what exists for itself relates to what is, in itself. The presence of another *as a subjectivity* has eluded his conceptual grasp. We have seen how he evokes an image of reciprocity that vanishes under the combined weight of rigid concepts and descriptive seduction. I have already displayed this conceptual fixity in relation to Sartre's treatment of the 'Other', though so far the diagnosis only suggests a remedy. The seduction of Sartre's examples and stories has to be met, as Wittgenstein would remind us, by a wider array of images and stories. Sartre admits there is a moment of love, when each accepts and regards the other as for themself and for the other, as, indeed, something in itself that has achieved this being for itself and for the lover. Sartre reminds us too often, however, with too few alternative possibilities, of how the project of love tends to degenerate into either fixed or oscillating sadism (making an object of the other) or masochism (consenting to be an object for the other). Any reader has been involved in some phase of what Sartre describes. Thus, with no prepared alternative conceptual strategy, the reader of the Sartrean text feels angrily trapped in what s/he does not want to believe, and uneasy at being merely pious in espousing more 'positive' 'life-enhancing' postures and opinions. Beauvoir has more room to manoeuvre around the impasse because she observes some of the mechanisms by which the 'other' we need is turned into an 'Other' who can do nothing but threaten us. First she describes more thoroughly the damaging way in which 'woman' is made to solve the conundrum of each person's need of the 'other' than threatens rather than vindicates their consciousness. 'Woman' is conjured out of the bodies of women, ready-to-be-free, a renewable resource that are a living semblance of an impossible relationship of reciprocation with another, beings who can be relied upon to confirm the consciousness of just one party to the contract:

> This dream incarnated is precisely woman ... She opposes him with neither the hostile silence of nature nor the hard requirement of a reciprocal relation; through a unique privilege she is a conscious being and yet it seems possible to possess her in the flesh. [Thus] there is a means for escaping that dialectic of master and slave which has its source in the reciprocity that exists between free beings (SS, 172).

Beauvoir's critique of the 'Other subverts the 'feminine mystique'. Women are bulwarks against angst because men control the concepts:

> the categories in which men think of the world are established from their point of view, as absolute: they misconceive reciprocity, here as everywhere. A mystery for man, woman is considered to be mysterious in essence (SS, 286).

In these closing pages of the section on myths, Beauvoir distinguishes this 'mystique' of woman as esoteric yet 'inessential' Other, from the constant 'mystery' that any conscious being remains, as a being whom one cannot fully grasp. The elevation to mystique as 'inessential Other' is a function of economic (or other) power:

> It is noteworthy that the feminine comrade, colleague, and associate are without mystery; on the other hand, if the vassal is male, if, in the eyes of a man or a woman who is older, or richer, a young man ... plays the role of inessential object, then he too becomes shrouded in mystery. And this uncovers for us a substructure under the feminine mystery which is economic in nature (SS, 286–7).

Beauvoir on Sexual Consciousness and the Feminine Mystique

Refusing Communality

Beauvoir's work, some six years after Sartre's, has begun to shift the field of our thought, experience and preoccupations. The look that objectifies achieves its effect because of a real or assumed power differential between observer and observed. Sartre was on the brink of fully recognising this in his discussion of 'we' and 'us' at the end of the third Part of *Being and Nothingness*. He had reminded us how chance events can produce a shift from individualist indifference or antagonism to communal solidarity:

> I am on a pavement in front of a café; I observe the other patrons and know I am observed ... the most ordinary case of conflict [between] the Other's being-as-object for me [and] my being-as-object for the Other. (There is) a slight collision between a jeep and a taxi. Immediately ... I experience my self ... as engaged in 'we' ... [T]he slight conflicts have disappeared ... 'we' look at the event, 'we' take part (BN, 413–414).

Sartre has evoked more than he would countenance theoretically, and he throws the philosophical taxi into reverse. Like the effect of the collision, that of the textual action is immediate. When 'we' speak, Sartre stammers, there is only an 'I' which co-opts the word:

> it is clear that the 'we' is not an inter-subjective phenomenon ... the 'we' is experienced by a particular consciousness (BN, 414).

Having then minimised this communality that he evoked so well, Sartre, as we shall continue to observe, finds objectification in face-to-face encounters inevitable. In contrast, Beauvoir, by first taking in Hegel's analysis of the 'master and servant' and then surpassing it, has placed herself in a position to describe what refused to stay in focus for Sartre. First, she casts in a positive light what emerges as only trauma in Sartre:

> It is the existence of other men that tears each man out of his immanence and enables him to ... complete himself through transcendence, through escape towards some objective, through enterprise (SS, 171).

She lays out the Hegelian story of conflict that Sartre had absorbed:

> But this liberty not my own, while assuring mine, also conflicts with it ... each separate conscious being aspires to set himself up alone as sovereign subject ... by reducing the other to servitude (SS, 171).

Then she declares the difference from Sartre that she had argued out with him during the period of his writing *Being and Nothingness*:

> It is possible to rise above this conflict if each individual ... regard[s] himself and the other simultaneously as object and as subject in a reciprocal manner. But friendship and generosity, which alone permit [*concrètement*] this are not facile virtues, they are man's highest achievement, and through [it] he is to be found '*dans sa vérité*' (SS, 172).

Now, Sartre's belittling of communality is preceded in *Being and Nothingness* with a cynical or farcical account of the generosity love requires. Perhaps to pre-empt Beauvoir he writes:

> How good I am to have eyes, hair, eyebrows and to lavish them away tirelessly in an overflow of generosity ... Whereas we ... had felt ourselves 'de trop', we now feel that our existence is taken up and willed in its tiniest details by an absolute freedom which ... our existence conditions and which we ... will with our freedom. This is ... the delight of love ... we feel that our existence is justified (BN, 371).

Sartre cutely evokes the narcissism disguised in love's opening moment − '*How good I am to have hair, eyebrows*'! Beauvoir herself does not blink at the difficulties that lie ahead:

> [T]his verité [in recognising each other] is that of a struggle unceasingly begun ... unable to fulfil himself in solitude ... success [in his relating to his fellows] is never assured. [For] he ... aspires ... both to life and to repose

... he knows ... that the price of being near to himself is his distance from what he is conscious of but he dreams of ... an opaque plenitude ... endowed with consciousness (SS, 172).

In Sartre's very dawn, the light fades from delight as love declines into a 'project' of 'justifying one's existence'. This *'real goal of the lover'* is going to *'provoke a conflict'*.

The Inessential Other

It will turn out that the *'wondrous hope that man has often put in woman'* is a very special conceptual arrogance supported by various arrangements of power. A sexual relationship as providing the reality (or sustained illusion) of 'possessing' another consciousness but still as free, has a quite particular status in Beauvoir's as in Sartre's, (dialectical) analyses of the search for a freedom compatible with secure possession. In Beauvoir either an angry or a satirical tone mostly prevails. Perhaps such a one will fancy that he can *'fulfil himself as a being by carnally possessing a being* (while) *confirming his sense of freedom through the docility of a free person,'* she writes. In this search, a woman must appear *'as an abundance of being in contrast to that existence the nothingness of which man senses in himself'*. Now, one would think that *any* 'Other', being regarded as the object in the eyes of the subject, is regarded as therefore as a being ('en-soi'). However, by a quite special magic, *'in woman is incarnated in positive form the lack that [he] carries in his heart'* (SS, 173).

Beauvoir proceeds to diagnose the urgency of the misogyny caught up in this mystification of sexual involvement as a special kind of *possessing*, a mystification that surpasses the cliché of 'possessing a woman' in intercourse towards the dream of possessing a 'freedom'. Material and social conditions are at odds with the indefinite perpetuation of the myth. Intimate involvement with a woman leads a man, not to some perpetuated high life of spirit, but into the particularities of physiology, society, economics and obligation. Thus 'woman' becomes a double symbol. She raises man to his true reality while degrading him to be a servant of necessity, in reminding him of his origins in impotent dependency on 'her'.

[M]an ... sees himself as fallen god ... fallen from a bright and ordered heaven into the chaotic shadows of his mother's womb ... The contingency of all flesh is his own to suffer ... in his unjustifiable *gratuité* ... Because he is horrified by *gratuité* and death, man feels horror at having been engendered (SS, 177).

And so we find a cycle of horror and desire. The 'horror' of being engendered that goes with a sense of being cast adrift into a world not of his choosing, becomes motive, not merely for sex as one of life's diverting pleasures, but as an antidote to the very complaint that it has engendered. '*His normal sexuality tends to dissociate Mother from Wife*', and in his dream of '*the erotic release, man embraces the loved one and seeks to lose himself in the infinite mystery of the flesh*' (SS, 183). But because, while '*feel[ing] repugnance for the mysterious alchemies of life*' he still desires them, he looks towards an idealised '*Venus newly risen from the wave*'. So man requires from a sexual relationship '*[not] only a fleeting pleasure*', but '*to conquer*' the woman in a vain attempt to make her fit the ideal (SS, 183).

For Beauvoir, the inflated expectation of what can be revealed of a person in a sexual encounter is explained in the dynamics of the cycle between the materiality revealed in sexual intimacy, and the momentary release from a sense of material bondage that is discovered in 'erotic release'. There is also, of course, the post-Hegelian theme of self-recognition in the recognition of and by another:

> Man discovers woman in discovering his own sex ... and inversely woman is redoubtable in that she incarnates sexuality ... What I fear or desire is always an embodiment of my own existence, but what happens to me comes only through what is not me (SS, 193).

But the usual pratfall that follows hard upon Hegel's *Spirit's* release from 'illusion' into 'understanding' takes on new colour in Beauvoir's descriptions and experience:

> [T]hat organ by which he thought to assert himself does not obey him ... unexpectedly becoming erect, sometimes relieving itself during sleep. Man aspires to make Spirit triumph over Life ... but ... finds himself again beset with life, nature and passivity (SS, 194).

Being brought up against his own vulnerability, 'man' may still be determined to live out his original fantasy of 'woman' as a being whose consciousness – and freedom – is something he can possess as it 'rises to the surface' of her body in her sexual relation with him. Sexual connection takes on a cosmic significance – it is made to lie beyond the decorum or proprieties of 'bourgeois' life with its petty materiality, obligations and daily rituals. Beauvoir touches upon a particular fantasy of bohemian life as driven by the same possessiveness as bourgeois morality, citing Henry

Miller who, 'in *going to bed with a prostitute, feels that he sounds the very depths of life, death and the cosmos*' (SS, 223–224).

In the final chapter of this section on 'Myths', Beauvoir brings together, as closely as she dare, her radical critique of these fantasies and the experience that seems to verify them. It is true of real particular women and men that their attempts at a free reciprocal relationship is threatened from within and from without:

> In a way [the] source [of the myth] is in experience. [W]oman is other than man, and this is felt in desire, the embrace, love; but the real relation is one of reciprocity; as such it gives rise to authentic drama. Through eroticism, love, friendship, and their alternatives, deception, hate, rivalry, the relation is a struggle between conscious beings each of whom wishes to be essential, it is the mutual recognition of free beings who confirm one another's freedom ... the transition from aversion to participation (SS, 283).

And yet, despite these creative possibilities, perhaps it is simply the relentlessnes of the struggle that leads men to deem that

> Woman is the absolute Other without reciprocity, denying against all experience that she is a subject, a fellow human being (SS, 282–283).

For Sartre this tendency is written into the very business of being conscious of another conscious being. The fact that 'woman' is a 'mystery' to man whereas to woman, man is merely puzzling in his obtuseness, is neither recorded nor pondered for its reason. The 'mystery of woman', for Beauvoir, is not simply a result of an objectification intrinsic to experience, but a specific capitulation to all that obstructs and occludes free reciprocity. There are reasons – the many whose description fills the hundreds of pages of *The Second Sex* – why this capitulation occurs, but the 'making mystery' of woman is as much cause of woman's objectification as its effect. And if there is a 'mystery' to woman beyond the fantasies that proceed from their convenience to the power and self-satisfaction of men, it is one that finds a universal echo in experience that does not depend at all on the myth of woman. It is what some writers would call the 'mystery of being' itself:

> [W]oman is ... 'mysterious as is all the world', according to Maeterlinck. Each is subject only for himself; each can grasp in immanence only himself, alone: from this point of view the other is always a mystery (SS, 286).

Beauvoir proceeds to develop this 'sense' in which existence itself is a 'mystery' that poses limits to our understanding. This acceptance of an horizon that recedes as we approach motivates development of understanding, in fact. *This* 'ontological mystery', far from serving complacency is a permanent challenge to it. And yet this salutary sense of something that always lies beyond one's grasp, whether it is conscious or not, is exploited, degraded, in 'men's eyes'. It then appears as a mystery about women, for men, at the very point where concrete understanding is urgently required, and is perfectly feasible, if a challenge:

> [T]he opacity of the self-knowing self, of the pour-soi, is denser in the other who is feminine; men are unable to penetrate her special experience through any working of sympathy: they are condemned to ignorance of the quality of woman's erotic pleasure, the discomfort of menstruation, and the pains of childbirth (SS, 286).

Tension now emerges between Beauvoir's *ameliorism* and her *fatalism*. 'Ameliorism' – '*yes, things are bad, but with a little good will on both sides a great deal can be achieved*'. 'Fatalism' – efforts at reciprocity founder on myths that entrench self-centredness. Though, as she says, it has been rare for a man to enter into a woman's life closely enough to realise much of '*the quality of woman's erotic pleasure ... the discomfort of menstruation*' and so on, she too is liable to be '*in ignorance of the male's erotic feeling*'. But there remains an essential and damaging asymmetry:

> [T]he categories in which men think of the world are established from their point of view as absolute: they misconceive reciprocity. A mystery for man, woman is considered to be mysterious in essence (SS, 286).

The subsequent work of Luce Irigaray that stresses women's 'difference' is now commonly read as antagonistic to Beauvoir's 'feminism of equality'. Beauvoir herself presses on into this question of 'mystery' in a way that invites an interesting comparison with Irigaray:

> [T]he 'mystery' is not subjective solitude ... nor her secret organic life. [The 'mystery'] implies a stammering presence ... [N]ot that she is silent, but that her language is not understood ... [In consequence] it may be imagined that ... a fundamental ambiguity marks the feminine being: [that] she is even for herself ... a sphinx (SS, 286–287).

But these words are part of a phenomenology of a form of life that Beauvoir is in process of deconstructing. We must recall the bracing words that had already put to flight the idea of a 'mystique' especially connected with femininity as such:

[T]he feminine comrade and colleague are without mystery; on the other hand, if a young man ... plays the role of inessential object for a man or a woman who is older, or richer then he too becomes shrouded in mystery. [T]his uncovers ... a substructure which is economic in nature (SS, 287).

In fact, Beauvoir moves back and forth between bringing the 'mystery' down to earth, and an informed 'sympathy' of sexual vision that does recall a metaphysical aspect of the issue:

[T]he Feminine Mystery ... in mythical thought is a more profound matter ... implied in the mythology of the absolute Other ... If reciprocity is to appear as impossible, the Other must be an other for itself ... This consciousness ... would be ... Mystery in itself since it would be Mystery for itself; it would be absolute Mystery (SS, 288–289).

It is against the walls of race, power, and prejudice that Beauvoir deflects Sartre's cry of a hopeless struggle against the mystification of the Other:

[T]here is mystery in the Black, the Yellow ... when considered as the inessential Other ... [T]he American citizen who baffles the European, is not, however ... 'mysterious': one states that one does not understand him. And woman does not always 'understand' man, but there is no 'masculine mystery'. Mystery belongs to the slave (SS, 289).

The first volume established how myths mask men's self-flattery:

[T]he myth is in large part explained by its usefulness to man ... Through ... religions, traditions, language, tales, songs, movies, the myths penetrate even into ... [harsh] material realities [so that] everyone can sublim[ate] his drab experiences: deceived by the woman he loves, one declares that she is a crazy Womb ... still another enjoys his wife's company: behold, she is Harmony, Rest, the Good Earth! The taste for eternity is at a bargain; a pocket-sized absolute [to be] shared by a majority of men. The smallest emotion ... becomes the reflection of a timeless Idea (SS, 289–290).

The exposure of these myths as farce allows Beauvoir to look towards being free of them. This is neither an attack on 'poetry, adventure, happiness or dreaming' nor a puritanical attack on erotic love. Indeed, stories that are more creative may arise when the old myths disintegrate as women find their place in public life:

[I]t may be disturbing to contemplate woman as at once a social personage and carnal prey. For a woman to hold some 'man's position' and be desirable at the same time has long been a subject for more or less ribald joking; but gradually the impropriety and the irony have become blunted, and ... a new form of eroticism is coming into being – perhaps it will give rise to new myths[5] (SS, 290–291).

Sartre's Enforcement of Objectification

Sexual Consciousness as an Escape from Objectification

We have observed Sartre's ambivalence between finding an escape from the traditional self-centredness of philosophical vision in being exposed to the 'Other's' look, and his co-option of this 'Other' by returning their gaze in counter-objectification. The co-option is not only a moral but also an ontological disaster. Sartre has rightly attacked the dualist's vision of the relation between one conscious being and another, as enforcing a doubly unbridgeable chasm between them:

> [Dualistic] realism has not been concerned with establishing an immediate reciprocal action of thinking substances upon each other ... The Other's soul is ... separated from mine by all the distance which separates first my soul from my body, then my body from the Other's body, and finally the Other's body from his soul (BN, 223).

Sartre is searching to describe a reciprocal relation between us that is not the 'external' one of simple spatial proximity, nor the Idealist's conception of a relation between two internally connected series of pure ideas. The Idealist no less than the dualist picture means that '*my relation to the Other must ... be in the mode of indifferent exteriority*'. This would have the consequence that the '*Other (could) not act on my being by means of his being – [that] he can reveal himself to me [only] as an object to my knowledge*' (BN, 231). And yet, as we have observed repeatedly in the preceding chapters, Sartre finds his own system producing its own version of this very effect. The system makes it seem that in being aware of another I make them 'object', not 'conscious subject' for myself.

It is in the chapter that deals with 'Concrete Relations with Others' that we should expect to find whatever solution to this problem that Sartre has been able to discover or contrive. Sartre explains again why the '*upsurge of the Other touches the for-itself in its very heart*'. In so doing he explains that what exists 'for itself' is '*foundation of all negativity and of all*

---

[5] Perhaps, for the twenty-first century, the (U.K.) T.V. series '*Attachments*' might be taken as exhibiting the sort of shift in sexual dynamics Beauvoir prophesied -- exhibiting our contemporary mores, also, as easily falling back into the old structures that she lampooned.

relation' simply in that to exist for oneself simply is this '*flight toward*' – this flight as both '*fleeing and pursuing*'. As we recall, to be for oneself is to 'nihilate', and to 'nihilate' is to fly from what exists only as in itself and to fly towards '*an impossible future [of being] in-itself-for-itself*' (BN, 362). But I think that Sartre gives the wrong reason for the correct proposition that the Other touches me in my '*very heart*'. It is his saying the right and perceptive thing for the wrong reason that entraps and confuses us as readers. And yet, at memorable moments, Sartre begins to give the right reason why the Other touches me in my '*very heart*'.

The wrong reason is the false idea that in the eyes of another I exist only as an 'in-itself', like the flying arrow in Zeno's paradox that is transfixed because at each instant it is precisely *at* the point it occupies. It is true that my conscious doing, expressing and refraining – as evident to the one who observes me – becomes something that I cannot recapture for myself. This lack of congruence remains, no matter how sympathetically and finely they tell me what they see of me. But neither logic nor grammar forbids that another can see me *in my freedom* – that another is taking note of the *conscious manner of approaching things* that is quite peculiar to me and that I am therefore not being transfixed in my free flight. It is only the assumption of the very dualism that Sartre attacks so effectively that prevents one saying that another *sees* me in the free pursuit of my conscious ends. It is not inevitably because of some objectifying look that I seize up in what I am doing. It may be for lack of courage, of internal wit, or most likely of bruised ego that I lose my free 'flight towards' when I become aware that I am being observed.

To insist that the differing regard of another is *bound* to freeze my free possibilities is reminiscent of the attitude from childhood that if the others won't play exactly as I had arranged then I won't play at all. The other does '*touch me in my very heart*', as Sartre says, and as Beauvoir has enunciated yet more descriptively. This does mean that the other has disconcerting aspects. Nevertheless, this effect need not be read as an alienating – because objectifying – effect of the other. This reading would confuse the distance between my point of view and that of the other, with the distance that exists between what exists for itself and what exists in itself. This 'distance' may be creative and generous, as much as it can be malicious or destructive of my freedom.[6]

But what of the specific idea that in sexual intimacy there is an unparalleled immediacy of consciousness of each to each? Sexual activity with another may involve little intimacy, of course, and, in the case of prostitution, no sexual reciprocity, and in the case of rape no reciprocity of

---

[6] Beauvoir shows how some *particularity* of another's acts destroys my freedom.

any kind. Even as commerce or even as violence, sexual connection with another conveys a good deal about the client or the attacker's 'inner nature' – more revealing than when he buys groceries or casually thumps someone who annoys him. In the case of prostitution his conduct says at least that he cannot, for whatever reason, gain satisfaction with someone he would have to love and with whom he would have to be open. He is saying that he accepts that another should make their body available on the basis of a financial contract. More could be said about this – about what is implied by his prepared to undress, to state or demonstrate his sexual needs before a stranger. And that analysis leads the imagination on to what the rapist must reveal, in his effort to short-circuit, by violent domination, not only intimate reciprocity but the recognition of the mentality and needs of another that is implied in the financial negotiation of prostitution.

It is vital to place these areas of sexual activity in the foreground, even if temporarily and in these brief and partial notes. Prostitution and rape tend to be left only to moral and legal philosophy, which is scarcely surprising. But one is confronted by Sartre and by Lévinas, to take two notable examples, with an ideal image of sexual relationship as involving, uniquely or even, simply, most intensely, a kind of intimacy of one conscious body with another. It then seems urgent to frame their idealistic pictures within these everyday facts of commerce and of violence. The immediate physical contact and exhibition of the exploiter's sensation in prostitution or rape does not amount to an intimate communication of feeling, merely on the basis that it is sexual in character. And, on the other side, immediate physical contact and demonstration of sensation and other feelings loses nothing of intimacy when, in the case of friends, children, and parents and guardians of children, these expressions have no sexual agenda.

I have emphasised these points in order to counter the way in which Sartre attributes a special status to sexual intimacy. But this is not to mock the idea that sexual activity with another reveals consciousness in ways that cannot be disguised, whether in the commercialised use of a 'sex worker' or in the horrific crime of rape.

The reader may laugh at the suggestion that Sartre's is an *idealised* picture of sexual connection, and observe, too, that even Beauvoir, in attacking the mystique of 'woman', still sticks to some of his sexual 'engluement'. After all, Sartre, certainly, sees an inevitable and rapid degeneration of the project of sexual love into some forms, perhaps mild and socially commonplace, of sadistic and masochistic feeling and conduct. So, his view is not morally idealistic. Nevertheless I suggest that it is idealised, even if to the point of cynicism. While implying nothing about his moral attitudes, I would point out that his phenomenology of sexual connection makes no distinction between sexual love, prostitution and rape. He is carried away, seduced even as he seduces the reader, with the metaphysical intensity of a picture of sexuality as intimacy. As usual, the other side of idealism's coin is cynicism – a remorseless objectification of the other in order to escape love's 'bonds'. Certainly, we feel the other's immediate 'touch to the heart' in reciprocated sexual love, but reciprocity requires that we resist making of this an impossible ideality.

For the most part the differences between Beauvoir and Sartre about sexual connection as an ideal of intimacy could not be greater. Sartre sees an ontological necessity, beyond our powers, at work in the degeneration of love's dream. Beauvoir sees an initial fantasy – usually by the man – about what sexual connection can achieve and mean for him, turning to cynicism as dreams hit the daily reality of complex bodily, social and economic needs. Positively, she describes some of the many ways in which children grow up to be sexually differentiated, and to conceptualise their sexual desires. Sartre uses 'he' as a universal subject and thus falls awkwardly into the grammatical appearance of homosexuality when attempting to describe heterosexual intimacy. In contrast, Beauvoir takes the possibilities and meanings of heterosexuality and homosexuality as explicit themes. The ill effect that remains in Beauvoir's writing, all the same, is that sexual feelings and conduct emerge in the text only at an impersonal level. These are the abstractions that she shared with, borrowed from, or lent to Sartre.

The first six pages of Sartre's 'Concrete Relations with Others' reinscribe within its explicit theme the structures of consciousness already established. I 'look at' another to objectify them in order not to be objectified by being looked at. I seek to 'fly' from what exists in itself (which would include my own body or the body of another, each considered at the level of being 'in itself'). At the same time I 'fly' towards the receding horizon of existing for myself, but with all the solidity and reliability of what exists in itself. That structure is then imprinted upon the hopefully new theme of *concrete* relations with others – the specific bodily ways in which we are involved together. There is no particular reason given why the discussion then veers towards the topic of love, and sexual love in particular. Indeed, to speak of love appears to be a sort of euphemism for sex. So the discussion elides the possibility that love between friends, siblings, children and parents might be equally, or more usefully, a site of release from relations of aggression and contest. Forewarned by Beauvoir's subsequent work and a half century of renewed struggle and work regarding the position of women we may fairly suspect from the outset that the text lurches, summarily, towards sexual love because it is the traditional site of domination and possession for a masculine narrator.

For all the force of this critique – so easy for us to make now – Sartre evokes how sexual love does tend to undo itself, as do other forms of intimacy. And his paragraph on 'generosity' shows how close to satire is his story of love's decline. To read his account of seduction as a means of avoiding being entrapped is to arrive at part of the truth about reciprocal observation, feeling and involvement. Beauvoir's critique, then, shifts phenomenology's linguistic register rather than changing Sartre's logic.

The Lover's Failure of Generosity

Consider the desires Sartre attributes as at the heart of his *lover*'s projects:

To assimilate the other, gaining for myself the substance they see in me.

To become my own foundation.

To *be* the whole world for the one I love.

To *make* the one I love freely act and feel with love towards me.

To escape my shame and uneasiness in experiencing 'being-for-another'.

To escape the look of the one I love into a world revealed in terms of
     myself.

To seduce the one I love rather than reveal my subjectivity.

To risk of making an object of myself in the process of seduction.

To treat people with indifference, to escape the danger of their regard.

To ensnare another in their sexuality, to 'skim off' their consciousness.

In the detail of text from which these observations are made – whether on the level or in dark irony – it is plain that the descriptions are set against 'fall' – of the sort that Camus describes – from a quite different ideal of love. The text is composed of repeated insistences on these ineluctable tendencies that make an impossibility out of love, and of any other attempt as in indifference, masochism, sadism and hatred to achieve a relationship with others that is in any way successful and satisfactory. This repetition serves to turn the spotlight upon the ideal of love that is being proclaimed impossible, rather than undesirable.

Sartre has earlier (in the previous chapters of this same Part Three) argued cogently against the dualistic spectre of one's relation to one's own body and to that of others. He says that the spectre is conjured up principally by taking our *knowledge of* others, rather than our modes of *being with* others as the primary issue. This promising suggestion lies behind the emphasis – perhaps an overemphasis as argued above – on being with another sexually as a mode in which, pre-eminently, each may cease to objectify the other. Sartre's analysis of the sexual situation, more nuanced than one might have expected, is itself strewn with claims of the necessary failure of sexual love to achieve its aims. Having analysed the attempt to be with another in love as leading, in its failure, to a form of masochism in which I try to turn myself into the object that would satisfy and please the one I love, Sartre takes up the possibility of indifference. This attitude might seem to promise at least a practical stability in dealing with others.

The study of indifference and of its failure leads without warning on to his study of sexual desire. The connection becomes clearer in light of the failure of indifference as a stable policy because it results in my permanent uneasiness in the face of my need to *maintain* indifference. The problem of a painful sense of freedom – of mine in being indifferent, and of theirs as requiring my tactic of indifference – reverts entirely to myself without any possible support from anyone else. Generalised and permanent indifference can be maintained only by a passion – 'fanaticism' might be the word – for indifference. And so indifference as a general strategy to avoid the threat of the other deconstructs itself.

Here it is that Sartre reintroduces love in the guise of desire, which is to say in his context, sexual love. The structural reasons for the failure of this desire to achieve its aims are predictable. What is interesting is some detail of phenomenology that emerges, and that suggests some more open possibilities. It is only after ten or twelve pages of sexual phenomenology that the project – if 'project' is really the word here – is made to appear as impossible. Sartre argues that sexual desire can succeed only if it takes the form of seduction, 'enchantment' or 'fascination' of the other. But in seduction I have to exhibit myself as 'seductive' or 'fascinating' object, and thus fail to be with the other, and, in the process of sexual resolution of desire, I change my aim from the non-objectifying 'caress' to the appropriative act of penetration. There are thus chasms in the phenomenology itself. Under the demands of describing heterosexual relations without patent absurdity the language has shifted from the universal 'he' to 'he' and 'she'. But it seems to lie outside the imaginary of *The Second Sex* to object that a woman in a reciprocal relationship does not regard herself as merely 'penetrated' but as taking hold of her partner (Gatens 1991: 198). And, if it were simply 'penetration' that 'appropriated', then a woman's sexual love would be incapable of appropriating a man. We shall find that Sartre suggests something very different from this in the final Part of *Being and Nothingness.*

At the same time, Sartre's introduction of 'penetration' is perfunctory, as if the reader is to understand that it stands for the general failure of sex to bring people together as reciprocally free and conscious beings, when it comes to the point of consummation. A distinction Irigaray makes (Irigaray 1985b: 23–33) exposes one image of heterosexual intercourse as 'penetration' *simpliciter*, and thus as a violation of the ambiguously dual/singular labia. She says that women may, it will be insisted, feel pleasure though in this role of 'being penetrated'. But, she asks shrewdly, do they thus take pleasure in their pleasure?

It is hard to find a reason why the non-appropriative non-exploitative character of the caress must change into an *opposite* character when caress arouses passion. Certainly, Sartre does not assume that all thought of the other is lost in sexual passion. Hands helpfully guide parts together, and so on. And what is the point of saying that 'pleasure is the death of desire'? Certainly, there is a pause, minutes, hours, days, before the desire for such pleasure is renewed. Scarcely 'death'. Or let us grant the old cliché of *'un petit mort'*. It does not have the implications that Sartre would draw. In a sweet profusion of confused metaphors, Sartre himself says, 'the caress aims to impregnate the body with consciousness and freedom'. Chiding his male readers whose sexual aims have lapsed into wanting nothing but ejaculation, he claims that in sexual desire one *'seeks consciousness'*. But when 'we' are finished, 'I' am left holding nothing but an object, Sartre alleges. He says this not in the spirit of a daring allegation, but as drawing the reader's attention to the obvious.

Now Sartre may be writing about these matters as if to investigate the consequences of the assumption that being with someone sexually can achieve – in its reciprocated forms – a kind of immediacy of one consciousness that is unthinkable in any other mode of intimacy. In that case, tautologically, the end of the sexual encounter is the end of that immediacy. And, to be fair, we can see the quite common, false, hope that he exposes here the hope that in achieving reciprocal sexual pleasure, each then 'knows' the other intimately in some more general sense. We quickly learn that this is not the case. The same misunderstandings, the same irritations, the same intolerance remain, almost or completely unchanged. What this means is the simple truth that being intimate and happy with someone in one mode does not amount to intimate understanding or enjoyment in any other. As if an ecstatic shared enjoyment of a concert might better inform a couple's difference of taste and method in cooking.

Certainly part of the success of Sartre's writing about these, as with other matters that are commonly fraught with confusion and disappointment, is to exhibit the exaggerated aims and expectations that are written into our desires. But, since the 'excess' that he describes is of desiring impossibility, we need not feel that in avoiding his conclusions we are settling for something a little more prosaic and perhaps dull. We can recall Beauvoir's words at the end of 'Myths', that love and erotic feeling does not die along with the failure of fantasies that have embodied, after all, nothing but megalomaniac attempts at total domination. More creative stories of love and desire have room to flourish in their place.

Sartre signals more than the doom of the 'aim' of sexual love in particular. He has claimed that sexual desire *is* just the desire to get hold of another's free subjectivity through their objectivity for me. The failure of sexual desire (in this respect one ought to say, in fairness) is then just an instance of the general failure to 'get hold of' another's free subjectivity by any means whatever. What I would argue here is that, again, Sartre has not fully played out the hand that he and Beauvoir hold between them. He makes headway in describing, along the way, the very thing he is decreeing, when all is said and done, to be impossible in the end.

The Possibility of Generosity – Free Consciousness in Desire

Some of what Sartre describes while on the way to show the 'impossibility' of love and desire suggests different possibilities:

The body is desired as revealing not only life, but consciousness.

Desire is a 'troubled' surface of consciousness, like 'troubled water'.

Desire is not only of the other's body, but the 'final consent' to one's own body.

The caress, as a 'studied' action, reveals the body's 'web of inertia'.

Sexual possession ('connection') appears as a double reciprocal incarnation.

Sexual desire radically modifies what exists for itself, 'clogging' its facticity.

Desire aims at enchantment – ensnaring the other in this facticity.

I catch the consciousness of another as one might 'skim cream off milk'.

We can discount as beside the point, Sartre's tedious objection to desire – that it is extinguished in achieving satisfaction. Only a desire for eternal life could pass the implied test of adequacy. And we can set aside any implied idealisation of the sexual encounter when we accept that the desire for full and free reciprocity is one of the numerous forms of sexual desire. A particularly interesting question then 'rises to the surface' in Sartre's discussion, freed of these encumbrances. Sexual desire for another as a form of reciprocity can succeed, even if at some remove from certain ideals. We know this from experience, and Sartre's own descriptions provide at least one framework for conveying that experience. We can agree with Beauvoir that to escape from cycles of alternating appropriation and submission requires a generosity of spirit not always available or forthcoming. Placing her hopes alongside Sartre's formulation of a position she avowed she shared with him, we can then see how it can be worked 'operatively' to accommodate the reality of this generosity.

On Surpassing Ontology by Generosity

Intimate and Immediate Experience

Beauvoir has observed the myths attending excessive expectations of sexual encounter, and has appealed to 'generosity' to break the cycle of submission and domination. Sartre himself, as we have observed, records a moment of delight when it appears that 'our existence is justified', that each knows the other's 'secret of existence' and, moreover, that each is more than content with it, and that the other should know of it. There are various reasons why Beauvoir has placed herself in a better position to take on the possibility of observing and relating to another without 'objectification'. She has worked her way through Hegel more thoroughly than did Sartre. She takes on, not just as an *aporia* on which to place a signpost, Hegel's account of the conflict that arises between one being and another as each becomes aware of the other's consciousness. She then sets out in a somewhat more hopeful fashion to use Hegel's realisation of the need the 'dominant' consciousness has of the one dominated. A conscious being has no option but to exist 'for others' as much as 'for himself'[7] and his realisation of himself cannot have any validity greater than that of the observations and dealings others have with him. So he requires being involved with at least his equals, and, indeed, with others who have some qualities of perception and judgement that supplement his own deficiencies

---

[7] It is anachronistic – and hides the bias – to change Hegel's 'he' to 'he or she'.

in those respects. In a 'free and reciprocal' relationship, if that can really exist, he will make his contribution in other respects of skill and perception.

Hegel's 'spirit' travels in drama discovery and disappointment in its ways of dealing with these necessities of reciprocity – whether there is any 'solution' offered by Hegel depends on one's reading, and credence towards his evoking of an 'absolute' spirit, with 'absolute' knowledge. It would be rare for any contemporary thinker to see the move towards an 'absolute' as, at best, one more temporarily useful illusion that sustains exploration prior to its disillusionment. And certainly Sartre and Beauvoir, equally, describe the tendency towards an absolute as the product of failing to realise the conflicting demands of self-confidence in one's own consciousness of things, and open vulnerability to the consciousness of others. Life must be a struggle since life must involve others and there can be no simple, harmonious and permanent resolution of differences with others – without the differences others would not be 'other', and one's existence as for others would remain unfulfilled.

That we recognise others as 'other' is right and proper, for Beauvoir. The deplorable condition is that of being, or making another to be, an 'inessential other'. We can recall her shrewd observation of how, with a traditional division of the sexes, a man is certainly perceived by women as 'other' than them, but not as mysterious. If feared, it is because he is implacable, cruel, unjust or ignorant, not because he is incomprehensible. And as to Sartre's sense of an intrinsic necessity of objectification as overtaking attempts at intimacy, it is for assessable reasons that the 'other' (and for the sake of argument let her be a woman) is 'threatened' by a desiring look. The 'look' already carries a threat of objectification that she is supposed to endure. Either she is not in a position of equal power – whether economic, social or of status – or the look automatically regards her as 'coming with the territory' of gender no matter what her powers and status.

Bodies of Women

Some two hundred pages after the studies of 'concrete relations with others', as he draws the immense work to a close, Sartre returns to the themes of possession – knowledge itself is represented as a kind of *possessing*. And, unexplained but with an air of inevitability, the discussion reverts to sexual encounter as infected by the desire for possession, for achieving the stability of what exists *in-itself*, while yet in the mode of existing as *for-oneself*. But now, the promised encounter with a body that would free its lover from the cycles of objectifying and being objectified has its 'revenge'. It threatens to reduce 'him' to what exists 'in itself'. The description of the female body proceeds from a masculine narrator's voyeurist vision. The air of detachment might speak of disgust.

As Sartre had observed,[8] someone with a passionate or loving attitude to another sees, not a 'body', but a bodily *someone*. But here Sartre describes the perceiver as alienated from the woman he looks at. There is nothing intrinsically unpleasant in the regard of the body that Sartre describes. Formally, it might be the regard of a painter, a child, or a lover who observes with pleasure the outlines of the body in its various dispositions. Sartre's narrator has an interest that is, however, ambiguously erotic and clinical, and this creates a sickly description. The imposition of abstract metaphysics upon an individual exposed figure means that the description is neither detachedly clinical, nor unselfconsciously involved by some passion. The narrator's description of 'the flattening out of the full breasts of a woman who is lying on her back' has an effect of burdening the body with metaphysics. The philosopher, here, has found himself unable to effect a transition from what lives for itself, to what exists purely in itself, and the result is an invasion of privacy. While she is in repose, the text loads up her body without her consent; her body is lumbered with a task the theoretician cannot solve. As male, the narrator might have described his own detumescence as the 'collapse of the for-itself into a 'deflated' in-itself.

Le Dœuff resolves what she finds repulsive in Sartre's description. The metaphysical theory that is made to produce bodily description is thick with paranoid feeling. I would observe, also, that Sartre's procedure unfairly gives a bad name to the 'visqueux' itself. It is not the association of the 'visqueux' with a woman's body that is repulsive. For either sex, sexual love includes the sticky and the slippery. There ought to be no offence in these associations. It is *fear* that converts the deliciously 'slippery' into the repulsively 'slim*y*'. Le Dœuff precisely diagnoses the fear that '*there is a possibility of what exists in itself absorbing what has being for itself*'. Or, as she puts it again, that '*what is, in itself, should lure what has being for itself in its contingency, in its indifferent exteriority, in its baseless existence*' (Le Dœuff 1991: 80). A number of fears run together here. The fear of a loss of 'ego' in sexual involvement – a loss of the image of what one is for oneself – that is a long-standing observation. The unnecessary fear is that I will exist only as something that exists 'in itself' – in coming to live, in part, 'for another' I shall lose, along with part of this image I have 'for myself', my very being as living for myself.

---

[8] In 'The Body', and in 'Concrete Relations with Others'.

It is true that in coming to live for another I lost some of the life of fantasy about self and other. I must therefore begin to live closer to material necessity. In living for another, and for and with myself, I am more subject to the demands of how things are 'in themselves'. The fear of what the other will do to life my for myself concerns the reduction of living for myself to this 'indifferent exteriority'. This is the ascetic's fantasy that the materiality of sex as 'mere carnality' excludes 'spirituality'. There is, however, no need to revive spirituality, whether humanist or religious. Materiality need not alienate us from our personal and intimate ways of feeling about, and dealing with, each other. It is our medium of exchange.

PART IV

FINDING OURSELVES
IN TECHNOLOGY

9

Lost in La Motte-Picquet-Grenelle

To go from the subway station at 'Trocadero' to 'Sèvres-Babylon', 'They' change at 'La Motte-Picquet'... If I change routes at 'La Motte-Picquet' I am the 'They' who change ... In this subway corridor there is only one project inscribed a long time ago in matter ... I insert myself into the great human stream which has flowed incessantly into the corridors of the station 'La Motte-Picquet-Grenelle' (BN, 424).

I am not reduced to 'a someone or other' in the passageway of the métro 'La Motte-Picquet-Grenelle' if I walk towards you [à toi]. My interiority, my intention, remain with me contained and close, despite the crowd)[1] (Irigaray 1997: 72).

Irigaray's 'Other'

Wonder

There is an apprehensive mood to Sartre's discussion of regarding and being regarded by others. What Irigaray evokes on the same topic is in striking comparison. In 'Wonder:[2] A Reading of Descartes' (Irigaray 1993a), she writes of the need to avoid an oscillation of 'acceleration and braking' when dealing with both things and people. She warns of the machine's threat to 'destroy us through the speed of its acceleration'. Then

---

[1] All passages cited in English from *Etre Deux* are the present author's translations.

[2] 'Wonderment' better conveys Irigaray's *L'admiration*. 'Wonder' suggests a less discerning state of mind. '*L'admiration*' does not translate exactly into 'admiration', which is listed as only one of various senses of '*l'admiration*'. Uses more akin to 'wonder' occur in idioms that translate as 'lost in admiration'.

The *Petit Robert* clarifies the reasons for the complications. Standard meanings for '*l'admiration*' are '*étonnement devant qqch. d'extraordinaire ou d'imprévu*' – 'astonishment at something unexpected'. Or, '*sentiment d'épanouissement*' – 'a feeling of opening out, or blossoming'. Close synonyms are '*émerveillement*' – 'wondering', 'marvelling'; '*enthousiasme*' – 'enthusiasm'; '*ravisssement*' – 'rapture'. Still, that one can use 'admiration' for '*l'admiration*' indicates that it more strongly suggests judgement and appraisal than does 'wonder'.

she writes on a more hopeful note: '*... unless there is wonder? Can we look at, contemplate, wonder at the machine from a place where it does not see us?*'. She proceeds with a possible allusion to Sartre's 'observer as observed':

> Still, the other – he or she – can look at us. And it is important for us to be able to wonder at him or her even if he or she is looking at us. Overcome the spectacle, the visible, make a place for us to inhabit, a reason and a means of moving, a way of stopping ourselves, of going forward or backward through wonder (Irigaray 1993a: 74).

A paragraph later, in an expression which parodies Sartre's fraught recognition, she writes:

> Before and after appropriation there is wonder. It is set apart from rejection, ... [t]hat which precedes suitability has no opposite. In order for it to affect us, it is necessary and sufficient for it to surprise ... not yet assimilated or dis-assimilated as known. Still awakening our passion, our appetite (Irigaray 1993a: 74–75).

Irigaray explores the relation I have to what I observe in wonderment:

> Attracting me ... wonder keeps me from taking and assimilating directly to myself. Is wonder the time that is always covered over by the present? ... Where I am no longer in the past and not yet in the future?[3] A separation without a wound, awaiting or remembering, without despair or closing in on the self (Irigaray 1993a: 75).

Sartre describes a destruction of morale as intrinsic to one's being the object of regard. In contrast, Irigaray conveys the pleasure and enlargement of mind of finding oneself in a world with beings and dimensions beyond one's own. Certainly we recognise Sartre's point when he dramatises the shift between *being-for-oneself* – being the observer of things, and realising one's *being-for-others*. There is a hazard in allowing myself to be 'seen'. I cannot ensure that I will be accepted. Even when I am regarded with admiration, another may co-opt me by their values rather than confirm me in my own. Nevertheless, Sartre's apprehension of destruction of one's mode of consciousness when subject to another's regard is hyperbolic, like Descartes' own 'hyperbolic' doubt.

---

[3] The passage persists with a provoking metaphysics of time and space: '*The point of passage between two closed worlds, two definite universes, two space-times or two others determined by their identities, two epochs, two others*'.

Irigaray is concerned with a loss of a connection between a philosophical vision of the world, and the picture that the sciences present. It is against this loss that she would reinstate *l'admiration*. Traditionally, the philosophers '*always accompanied their metaphysical research with cosmological research*'. She claims that 'it is only lately that this grounding of research has been abandoned', resulting in a lack of connection between philosophical and scientific vision.[4] She exposes the dualism in Descartes, in the *Discourse* and *Meditations* in particular.[5] She shows how it threatens our capacity to sense that we are the one being who thinks and feels, intends and recalls, and also is observable in personal, social and scientific contexts. Parallel to this dualism is the new 'scission between the physical sciences and thought' which, Irigaray thinks, '*threatens thought itself*'. If we think of ourselves and of the world around us exclusively in terms of the physical sciences then we '*[split] our life, our bodies, our language, our breath into several worlds*'. The reaction to this split may be some sort of Idealism. We raise up an ideal ego 'as if that were our true nature, and return to 'religiosity, slogans, terror, etc.'. When religion's ideal of spirituality looks at the threat of the 'real world' that world has to be derogated by slogans. When the slogans don't work, 'terror' is the final remedy.[6]

In this return to religiosity, there are only '*passively experienced emotions in which the subject is enclosed, constrained, deprived of its roots*'. Religiosity's vision of 'something more than science' includes '*no window, no remaining open on, or with, the world, the Other, the other*'. 'Scientism', exploiting the success of the scientific method, proposes the world as an affect-less array of pure facts, but religion offers no richer texture of concepts. 'It is '*in terms of the passions*', rather, that we can see what is lacking both in scientism and in religiosity. She relates the loss of the passion of wonder, to the dividing of self from the body – and thus of oneself from others. This phase concludes with an astonishing proposition and half-question:

> Wonder is mourning for the self as an autarchic entity; whether this mourning is triumphant or melancholy. Wonder must be the advent or the event of the other. The beginning of a new story? (Irigaray 1993a: 75).

---

[4] Irigaray's analysis applies with a peculiar force to 'Anglo-American analytical philosophy' as it seeks to centre itself on the scientific outlook. This philosophy swings back towards idealism when its mechanistic (electron-istic) reduction fails. There is no reciprocity of scientific and philosophical thought.

[5] Descartes' *Passions of the Soul*, discussing wonder, is both dualist and reductionist.

[6] The emotional action in the 'right to life' campaign illustrates this.

The meaning of this emerges as Irigaray takes up the phenomenon of being stupefied by an excess of wonder. Setting herself against the cliché that the two who form a couple should 'suit each other' she reminds us that

> wonder goes beyond that which is or is not suitable for us. We would ... have reduced the other to ourselves if he or she suited us completely (Irigaray 1993a: 74).

She concludes with the image of excess, over and above such conformity:

> An excess resists: the other's existence and becoming as a place that permits union and/through resistance to assimilation or reduction to sameness (Irigaray 1993a: 74).

It is in this context of *resistance to assimilation* that the theme of *mourning* had first emerged. Now, in the context of wonder, we can read the 'astonishing' remark that '*wonder is a mourning for the self as an autarchic entity*'. Wonder is such a 'mourning' because to learn from another requires me to wonder at them; to wonder means to forego mastery of my own limits. Both Sartre and Irigaray recognise that, '... *whether this mourning is triumphant or melancholy*', in my recognition of the other as a separate consciousness I suffer loss. Whereas in Sartre this registers as anxiety and terror, however, for Irigaray it emerges as 'mourning'. The 'mourning' can be 'triumphant' – the loss of self-definition of reality is a thrill, and releases the self to the other. It can be 'melancholy' in lamenting the departure of one's perfect narcissistic friend. In either case, *wonder must be the advent or the event of the other*. The other becomes an 'event'. The other *happens* to me. Thus arises the new possibility, Irigaray's half-question – '*the beginning of a new story?*'

Irigaray analyses the character and sources of the fear expressed in Descartes' insistence on the *hazard* of wonder. He warned of the danger of being open to that same emotion which, earlier, he had praised. She revives the reader's confidence in wonder. It makes change possible – wonder '*interrupts the flow of time*'. She expands this in a grammatical figure: Wonder is '*not yet frozen in a predicate which would split the world in two*' (Irigaray 1993a: 76).

Grammar and Domination

Grammar can signify a way of dealing with the world. Irigaray reconstructs the Sartrean grammar of domination. If each person can 'wonder' at the other, there will be 'two-way predication'. In the traditional grammar, the 'subject' of the sentence is what determines the topic to be discussed – the 'thing' about which things are to he said – about which they are 'predicated'. Thus the 'subject' 'dominates' the sentence, as Sartre's observer dominates the object s/he regards. The 'subject', like the observer, is the one who speaks and who introduces the topic. He has introduced the topic, so he 'dominates' (Ferrell 2000: 100–114).

When this situation obtains, conversation is displaced by, at best, an alternation of domination. In Sartre this is the alternation of 'looking' and 'being looked at'. In terms of speech there would be an alternation of 'speaking' and 'being spoken to' in which each seeks to dominate the area of discourse. On this critical basis Irigaray discusses, in physical terms, Descartes' speculation on wonder. Descartes associates wonder with the 'rarity' of a thing, and the 'force' with which impressions are conveyed into and fixed in the brain. Irigaray welcomes his emphasis, but remarks upon inadequacies in his picture. As Descartes depicts wonder and its operations, '*it would not change anything in the heart or the blood*'.

To counter this she develops his discussion, using the physiological characterisations of mind and emotions common in his century. She would not 'dominate the subject' herself by using a physiology unavailable to the one with whom (historically) she converses.

A Critique of Descartes and a Parallel with Sartre

Irigaray suggests that in claiming that 'we have only wonder towards those (things or people) which appear but seldom', Descartes' principal inadequacy appears. Though wonder is a valuable impulse towards knowledge, it '*can take away or pervert the use of reason*', he thinks. We must replace wonder by exact knowledge and understanding that will '*free us as much as possible* (from this) *passion of youth*'. In contrast, Irigaray means to recall wonder at what has become most familiar. Wonder at sexual difference and the very 'otherness' of the inanimate world, made of the same stuff as us, and yet immeasurably different. Not to be horrified at technology, nor alienated, nor holding it in contempt, Irigaray would 'wonder' at the difference from us of the 'machinery', the 'electronics' that we tend to fear.[7] Irigaray connects the capacity for wonder with the capacity for love and for knowledge. We continue to love what is most familiar, and continue to come to know what we know most intimately. This is possible only if we can retain wonder at what is most familiar.

---

[7] We tend to idolise technology itself. The 'wonder' – *admiration* – which Irigaray summons up would displace that as much as it counters 'fear and loathing' of technology.

Irigaray thinks that Descartes may have not distinguished properly between *astonishment* that paralyses, and *wonder*, which encourages attraction to something and impels us to come to know it. Wonder's impulse to come to know, escapes the logic of the *'dominating subject'*. Knowledge as owned by the one who dominates what they know, she suggests, has controlled our picture of how science replaces superstition and religion and finally, even common sense and the common heart. Irigaray concludes in the utopian mode with which she began 'Sexual Difference':

> Wonder would be the passion of the encounter between the most material and the ... most metaphysical ... neither one nor the other (Irigaray 1993a: 82).

Yet, though neither one nor the other, this is not to say that we are dealing with the neutral or neuter. Wonder, she is proposing, is

> the forgotten ground of our condition between mortal and immortal, men and gods ... creatures and creators (82).

These words are written to produce wonder. She speaks of bridging the 'mortal and immortal'. Rejecting 'religiosity', how can she speak of a relation between men and gods? As in *'Sexual Difference'*, in coupling *'creatures and creators'*, she describes as within the world those aspects of the ordinary which religious thought has placed beyond it. In traditional religion, the 'Creator' is beyond the created world. Irigaray finds the 'wonder' of creation and the created *amongst* people and in the space between them and the inanimate world itself. This 'wonder' arises at the creative relations between us, and is found in our creative relations to technology. These things we create, and the 'world of nature', have their creative powers over us. We *create* what we invent and use and, in turn, are the *creatures of* our science and technology.

The Crowd and Us

Being Done with Vain Pursuits

The passage (cited at the outset) from Irigaray's *Etre Deux* continues:

> This interiority safeguards my mystery as yours makes you a mystery for me.
>   I am protected in three ways from being transcended by the 'someone or other':

– I am sexed; I am not a 'they', neuter, anonymous;
– I am moved by intentions towards the other ... towards you [à toi] and not determined unequivocally by the world which surrounds me;
– I am a mystery for you [pour toi], as you are for me, and our inter-subjectivity is protected from ... an external and anonymous world whose end-point is to address a 'they' 'no matter who' (Irigaray 1997: 72–73).

Sartre perceives an 'I' that is swallowed up in a crowd as it attempts to form a 'we'; Irigaray appeals to an intimacy between *toi* and *moi*.[8] In one respect, engaged in a detour that began with the publication of *Ce sexe qui n'en est pas un* (*This Sex which is not One*), she agrees with Sartre. One cannot dissolve a primary antagonism between 'I' and 'Other' by submersion within a primordial 'us' or a 'we'. Although 'my' being part of 'us' is a real phenomenon, it relies upon a 'third' party. The bond she is interested in *lies between* us. Irigaray would note with Sartre, too, that the more active 'we' who act as such, are bonded only in a pre-technological 'rhythm' of labour or custom, or in an anonymous participation in mass culture. And, since *Ce sexe qui n'en est pas un*, she has been constructing detours around the site of 'I' and 'Other' which had mis-defined each other by negation and antagonism.[9] In *Etre Deux* she has now turned her attention to Sartre's way of dealing with the irreducible difference between one person and another that she has always approached through the fact and symbol of 'sexual difference'.

In *Fille et Femme*[10] Irigaray claims that '*Sartre attempts to situate the bodily tie with the other, in a horizontal dimension*'. Within her vision of people and philosophy, this contrasts with a possible 'vertical' dimension which we 'divine', of which we plumb the depths while knowing we cannot reach any bottom, foundation, secure base.[11] In writing, '*the primary connection with the other is a bodily one*', she sets out from Sartre's own position, but her terms and style shift the accent of his images and stories. She writes, as Sartre would not, of an 'interiority' that 'safeguards' a *me* who can meet another, intimately, in the crowd at La Motte-Picquet. The difference is of emphasis rather than opposition, nevertheless. Like Sartre, Irigaray opposes both idealism and any materialism that was suspicious or exclusive of consciousness.

---

[8] I leave the French 'toi' since public and intimate uses of 'you' are not marked in English.
[9] *Sexes and Genealogies and I Love to You*, culminating in *An Ethics of Sexual Difference*.
[10] The second chapter of *Etre Deux*.
[11] Irigaray uses a verb to disturb a complacent noun. In *Divine Women* and in 'Sexual Difference' (*An Ethics of Sexual Difference*) she writes of 'divining' the other. It is this unfathomable but human activity which provokes the error of a 'religious divinity' that would guarantee one's knowledge of another.

Sartre is in two minds about the relative priorities of body and of consciousness. While the self as an *object* of consciousness must be bodily (thus the risk of objectifying the self), the relation of 'body to body' is subtended by the 'nihilating' work of consciousness. Irigaray's stress on 'interiority' rather than 'nihilation' requires that Sartre resolve his dilemma of 'being a subject who observes' or 'being an object who is observed'. Why not stretch the categories towards *seeing the other as subject*? And what about involvement? I may see another *as a subject* while involved with them. We can disturb this simplified concept of a *subject* that has been made to bear too much of the weight of *interiority*. The '*more-than-objecthood*' to which Sartre constantly alludes has to be worked out in a manifold of concepts and images. We might even recover the intimacy of objectivity and objectity themselves (Deutscher 1983: 221–271).

Like Sartre, again, Irigaray sets out from the domestically familiar. As with Sartre, the familiar is made metaphysical even while the metaphysical is made familiar. '*The first other I encounter is the body of the mother*', she says, with the promising possibility that

> In as much as they are different, in body and history, the one and the other can re-integrate, in their interiority, through the primary relation with the mother and thus escape the infinite repetition which estranges all present relationship (Irigaray 1997: 57).

This reference shifts the balance towards the initial relationship of '*body to body with the mother*' (Irigaray 1993b: 7–22). This relationship is formed prior to my responsibility and initiative in 'nihilating' this and that, to subtend a significant world. This dependency is upon something always already within the domain of 'making something of' and 'making nothing of'. The mother initiates the relation in response to the gestures, expressions and incipient attentions of the new child. The idea of a time of dependency prior to one's power of autonomous 'nihilation' is the idea of a time of interchange. One is immeasurably more knowing about the scope of the world than is the other. This time of interchange, part mythic, part real, is a time before the desire or need for self-assertion against the other. For her own sake and in order to care for the child, the woman who is a mother must be able to maintain a sense of her own desires and needs. Though in reality and symbolically the child is the site of infinite demands, these are prior to their being construed as demands conflicting with her needs. The conflict of those demands with her needs lies outside the scope and meaning of the infant's cries and smiles.[12]

Irigaray challenges Sartre's presumption that the *for-itself* founds its own attitude to the body, and links it with the impossibility he finds in securing a relation with some specific person *as a conscious being*:

> For Sartre, the tie with the other is like a flight towards an impossible future: I must flee before the other, gaining for myself the in-itself-for-itself, making of myself a defined ['propre'] substance, a body born of my awareness (Irigaray 1997: 58).

This is a sharp observation by Irigaray. Sartre's 'flight towards a future' has an 'impossible' goal because it does not allow me to rest in some later moment, to take satisfaction in success. When that moment arrives, my meaning is still a project in which I 'take flight' towards what is 'future'. By the same logic the 'Other' is held perpetually at a distance. If I approach someone in the park whom I had recognised as a centre of their own world, their reaction to my intrusion *is* liable to 'objectify' me. As object of my approach the other ceases to be subject; as subject myself I am not discernible as such to the other. Each of us is a 'subject' only in the role of transfixing the other's subjectivity. Alternatively, as merely regarding their existence there is no objectification, but also no encounter. So, Sartre's promise of an encounter in which each apprehends the other as conscious is never fulfilled.

Irigaray proposes a different appreciation of the distance between one person and another, which promises a 'different future'. Instead of a struggle of the *for-itself* to transcend its objectual status, the *for-itself* as a gift from one's relation with the mother[13] is already more than mere *objectity*. Irigaray points out that Sartre already recognises this to some extent:

> In that I belong to a gender, my body – my 'in-itself', as Sartre would admit in some fashion – already comprises a for-itself. It is not a simple factuality or facticity; it is already awareness (Irigaray 1997: 58).

This *for-itself* is not 'given in advance'; already it is in a 'flight towards' an in-itself which awaits my power to lend it form. Irigaray insists upon what Sartre also requires – nothingness cannot found being. The *petits riens* of everyday life are functions of a lack that nihilates a given facticity. This

---

[12] Compared with a newborn baby, a toddler demands attention *in that* the parent is interested in something other than the toddler himself or herself.

[13] Irigaray likes to deal in these simplifications of the parental situation.

nihilating *for-itself*, already a *factuality*, owes debts to the in-itself. Sartre's 'nothing-ing had better be the act of an already legible body upon an always articulated world.

Bravely launched into space, hopefully aloft or in despairing free-fall, Sartre's *flight* was always *from* something. Irigaray's counter-proposal of a *'return towards myself … to myself, to cultivate that being which I am'* may seem too simple. Domestic? Sartre's perpetual *flight towards a future* as from a *failed previous venture of making the for-itself coincide with an in-itself* is no heroism, though – it is merely to skedaddle. Irigaray's 'return to oneself' counters the pressures of philosophy, language, and society in turning the child away from its bond with the mother. This 'return' differs from any new mystique of motherhood that would, in sanctifying it, diminish the sense of a bodily tie. In domestic terms, too, that sanctification de-registers from the employment list, women who have children. Their work is a 'pure labour of love', requiring no other recompense. 'The greatest job in the world', etc. According to the mystique of motherhood, it is built on self-sacrificial love. It is the *'bad mother'*, the *'suffocating woman'*, who *'will not let go of her tie with the child'*.

Irigaray exposes these fantasies of woman who as 'bearer' of a child, compensating for her own lack of development and recognition, has to 'live through' the child. It is not the woman who treasures her bodily relationship with her child who dominates the child by living through it. When we accept the bodily tie as originary and continually sustained, the 'difference' emerges in an always renewed 'wonder at' the other (*'admiration de l'autrui'*).

Irigaray does not write about the creation of a bodily bond between father, foster parent, family friend[14] and child – it is for them to articulate this. Nor does she write about abusive bodily contact. Sexual and other physical abuse enforces proximity rather than creating a bond. In Irigaray's terms it would be contact that is enacted without that 'wonderment' on which she centres her dreams and rigorous demands. Contact as physical abuse is contact without respect for difference, without reference to *interiority* – that irrecoverable distance which intimacy recognises between those who are most close.

Affection in the Bodily Tie ['lien']

Irigaray is aware that what she says may appear too 'empirical':

---

[14] Such a phrase now evokes the *abuse* of children, too. The *stepmother* was traditionally 'wicked'; the *stepfather* will be the first suspect as abuser in the absence of the father. In the face of this, the 'abusive mother' over-controls the child for the survival of her self-image.

The desire of the other in being connected to an awareness of a defined and possessed body ['corps propre'] and, differently, of its own history, is still not considered as a philosophical question, neither by Sartre nor by the latest Western philosophers. Desire as it is for me, a woman with a different awareness and belonging to a body of an other gender, remains a blind task. Still, today, to confront such ontological problems is scarcely recognised as philosophical work. This dimension of human being is relegated to an unsophisticated empiricism (Irigaray 1997: 67).

Irigaray has an exaggerated sense of isolation. Many feminist philosophers experiment with similar ideas, but their need to do this lends support to her claim about the resistance of philosophy to such ideas. One may be embarrassed by Irigaray's suggestions about irreducible sexual difference, a *'different awareness, as belonging to a body of an other gender'* and seize upon the profoundly important feminism of fairness, equality and material opportunity as the only reasonable voice. Irigaray, however, plans to upset thought patterns that rely on some 'one voice', implicit or explicit, and could never accept *one essential feminine voice* as signifying *difference*. (In writing this, *I* should take account of my voice as embodied, as of a male body, inscribed in cultural biology and biological culture as *masculine*. But this is not to identify my voice with that of all men, joined as *essentially masculine*. After all, many philosophical men pillory the idea that one's voice is embodied. *'We'd appoint a broom stick if that were the best philosopher'*, as one put it aggressively, apparently unconscious of his phallic imagery.)

In arguing against Sartre's picture of domination, Irigaray conveys the most traditional of images – the look of affection from mother to child, and the child's delight in being recognised.[15] Her 'empirical' observation that raises a question about Sartre's system of concepts is an idyll that does not hear the incessant screams of a baby, and the exasperation, desperation and resentment that mix with love. Paintings and sculpture, exploited as icons in politics and religion, exhibit this same idyll. For all that, they register a true moment.

From Irigaray one might explain how Sartre's distortion of the relation of *'for-itself'* to *'in-itself'* arises. Her 'exchange of delight in each other's presence' occurs between an adult and an unselfconscious infant. If (as Freud suggests) the delight of adult love is its recovery of infantile bliss, then it is bound to degenerate into patterns of domination and acceptance. When spontaneity occupies the field of adult love, either or both play the delighted and delightful infant. For adults to live out this fantasy beyond its

---

[15] Always Irigaray risks being identified with conservatism about sexual difference.

moment, produces the ugly side of dreams – they force each other to conform to an imaginary possibility. Thus, Irigaray's appeal to a renewal of *l'admiration*. By work, we can remain true to what is remarkable in the infant, and the infantile state of being. Infants say what they think and express what they feel, and it is in order to 'grow up' that they learn to inhibit this. Then it requires, in adulthood, the *work* of candour, honesty and art not to be stifled and stifling in reticence and its ensuing hypocrisy (Ryle 1949: 181–5). Irigaray writes of sexual difference itself as a kind of *work*. To recognise the mentality and specific intent of others is also a kind of work, a virtually *divine* work of *divining* the 'other'. Like all work, it may simply occur, or we may have to practise, initiate, and devise strategies to make it happen. Irigaray claims that when we fail in *l'admiration* we cannot maintain loving perception face to face. Such 'wonder' is possible because

> in the very presence of my body there is already an intention towards the other ... first at the level of genealogy ... [E]ven if [my parents] raise me with little love or skill, I am always inscribed within their 'intention' ... My body is never simple factuality or obduracy; at the very least it can never ... nullify these intersubjective relations that have marked it since infancy (Irigaray 1997: 60–61).

If there is no certain route to *l'admiration*, at least we can learn ideals of intellectual practice which do not erase it. A kind of 'reason' would *'triumph over this bodily, affective infancy of ours'*, in the name of *'an abstract and solipsistic universe'*. This is what produces Sartre's sense of *'a nullity of existence in which a pre-ordained life become[s] a flight towards an impossible future'* (Irigaray 1997: 61). From infancy, by intimate bodily involvement with my mother (and other carers), intentions towards me and from me are inscribed. Irigaray is saying that (in Sartre's terms) this inscription is a successful *in-itself for-itself*. Just the state of being which Sartre had claimed was an 'absurd' passion. My bodily involvement has being *in itself* since it has a factualness, and obduracy upon which I can rely. It has being *for itself* since it is always at work in what I am *for myself*, and *for others*. Without an intelligible project of an *'in-itself for-itself'*, my life would be directionless – only a set of projects that leave me always in need of another task into which I can flee. Sartre cannot describe how I can rest in an accomplishment of something that is satisfactory *in itself*. To rest is not *to be* in bad faith (Deutscher 1983: 248–271).

There is a similar structure in Irigaray's implicit argument for sex and gender as another *in-itself for-itself*. That my body is inscribed from birth (and no doubt before it), creates a form of being in *'relation-with me, my gender, with the other gender'*. This will be true whether my adult sexual relationships eventuate as homosexual or as heterosexual. My relations with others of the same sex still are amongst my ways of relating to the other sex:

> [L]et us imagine a contemporary utopia: a woman engenders another woman, living in a community of women ... [She] would have to think her identity as woman as an identity in relation to the other [sex], at least at the level of an intention to achieve her own (Irigaray 1997: 64–65).

The 'Passive' and the 'Active'

Desire and Possession

Irigaray's strategy is to relieve the pressure of the masculine-feminine division by working against the division of *activity* and *passivity*. Sartre's consciousness as an active *for-itself* working upon a passive *in-itself* implies that women and men, being conscious, are equally active (BN, 254–255). His persistent identification of the image of the *in-itself* with the feminine, however, results in a picture of man making himself a *for-itself* in the very struggle of escaping femininity. Like the *in-itself* of which it is a trope, this 'feminine' now appears everywhere – within his own *in-itself*, within the feminine in other men, and in women. Irigaray points out how Sartre's allegations about *desire* achieve these identifications:

> What is desired according to Sartre, is that the other make of itself an in-itself, or object-objectness for me as subject. Also I must transform myself into an ideal in-itself, absolute, for him. I should thus become a visible ideal by which his regard can allow itself to be fascinated (Irigaray 1997: 66).

Irigaray loosens the conceptual bonds between desire and *object-ity*. Like Wittgenstein in his method of 'reminders' (Wittgenstein 1953, 1958), she works by describing what has been forgotten.[16] She diagnoses not just a simple lapse of a philosopher's memory, however, but his un-examined *desire*:

> [H]is attention is not taken by *'I love you and I desire you because you realise the becoming of your gender, inscribed in your body'* (Irigaray 1997: 66).

---

[16] Wittgenstein practices philosophy as a series of 'reminders'.

Irigaray is right to allege that '*it does not concern Sartre [that] I can look at the other, contemplate him as body and as thought*' (Irigaray 1997: 66), but she overlooks Sartre's lyrical descriptions of the other as body and as thought (e.g. BN, 254, 255, 295). It is when he attempts to describe 'being approached by the other' that he loses the sense of this coexistence.

Existing in Co-ordination: Existing in Irreducible Difference

In her Wittgenstein-like insinuations about the darkness of contemporary times[17] Irigaray equals Sartre in her deferral of describing these desired encounters. Her gestures in summoning up utopias veer towards the vapids:

> Philosophy would have to recast itself in terms of the existence of two different[ly sexed] subjects ... That would imply a revolution in thought towards an anti-capitalism and spirituality by the acceptance that awareness, truth, ideality, are each two-fold (Irigaray 1997: 67–68).

But how are we to understand this unity of body and thought, and how achieve a social and political world that encourages difference within a co-operative unity? There is a more provocative challenge in her idea of '*awareness, truth, ideality [as] each two-fold*'. Is this the ideal of separate 'feminine' and 'masculine' sciences, mathematics and forms of writing, and a split between scientific or cultural institutions? We may prefer to be more open – even vague – about differences in the ways men and women approach knowledge. Irigaray's idea is not, however, of two utterly distinct and irreconcilable different genres or genders. She hopes to describe how one conscious being recognises another *in their difference*, without loss of interiority on either side. She sets out to explain how irreducible elements may make an irreducible couple:

> Such a 'two' does not signify 'trouble' ... 'equivocality', 'ambiguity', terms used by some philosophers to speak of a connection between two subjects in which each loses its irreducibility (Irigaray 1997: 68).[18]

Irigaray has long elaborated a logic of 'neither one nor two'.[19] Her morphology of 'lips' as neither one nor two might be a model for the sexes themselves. Perhaps the 'couple' of the two sexes does not bifurcate into two incommensurable units. An irreducible difference of outlook between

---

[17] See the preface to Wittgenstein's *Philosophical Investigations* (Wittgenstein 1953).

[18] Irigaray is indicating something other than the 'trouble' of 'double' systems of thought, an 'equivocality' of two distinct meanings, or Merleau-Ponty's 'ambiguity'.

[19] Beginning most explicitly in *This Sex which is not One*.

any woman and any man rests on no essential 'one-ness' of being masculine or of being feminine. The difference Irigaray proposes does not entail *two* systems of physics[20] since the 'two' of the 'two sexes' is not the result of a '1' + '1'. Irigaray sketches this irreducible difference of non-essential identities in terms of a logic of community, giving some content to a 'new politics of anti-capitalism'. She criticises *'the effacing [of] the primary tie between two awarenesses, which would transform each into a zombie, a neutered individual'*, for this would make an impossibility of *'the concrete encounter with the other, the entrance into the fleshed presence with the other'* without which we cannot be *'parts of a community'* (Irigaray 1997: 60).

In a couple as in community, we count ourselves as 'neither one nor two'. This 'neither one nor two' is not a vagueness that might be eradicated by clarifying terms. Nor is this 'neither/nor' merely the penumbra associated with every ordinary or scientific term. And it is not a matter of ambiguity – whether of careless expression or of intrinsic quality. An ambiguous term oscillates between two meanings that may be recognised separately. 'Bank' is ambiguous between 'a centre of finance for commerce' and 'the edge of a river'. The ambiguous 'duck/rabbit' figure oscillates between two well-defined recognitions. An ambiguous remark shifts between kindness and insult. In comparison (to develop Irigaray's concept), the *ones* of some couples are not separate and do not add up *separately* to a *two*. Such couples may include lips, lovers, *'being body'* and *'being conscious'*, the parties to an ethical contract, and the relation of being joined with another in a fused intention. In some such couples each *one* may be irreducibly different from the other and may be capable of changing so as to exist separately from the couple with which they had partially fused. We might think of lovers, parties to an ethical contract and those joined in a project with a fused intention. The members of such couples can exist, changed, after break up, though remaining marked in disposition and memory by having been part of the couple. Other couples – *lips*, and *being body and conscious* – do not resolve into their separate elements without radical and irreversible change in those elements, though the elements were always distinguishable from each other.

Desiring Others in their Difference

The desire of the other in being connected to an awareness of an owned and defined body ['corps propre'] and, differently, of its own history, is still not considered as a philosophical question (Irigaray 1997: 67).

---

[20] Sokal's *Intellectual Impostures* contains an instructively gross misreading of Irigaray.

It is as if Sartre has come *so close* to a solution. He describes the conundrums of human desire and shows how they arise from fantasies, but, insisting on desire as possession, his own account of relations between people spins out into space. He responds to difference in terms of his philosophical project that declares each person 'absurd' and yet inextinguishable. What he lacks is a phenomenology of *desiring the other in their difference*.

Irigaray's use of 'sexual difference' acts as a synecdoche for an array of differences – male/female, homosexual/heterosexual, same nation/different nation. None of these pairs can be made essential to 'difference' – heterosexuality, for instance, is no guarantor of respect for difference. Irigaray exposes the ways we would guarantee permanence by institutional means. The two of the 'couple' are made 'equal in the sight of God', 'made one flesh'; they are 'one and the same in the eyes of the State'. Such traditions construct one sex as 'lacking what the other has'. The love affair of Church and Fascism with 'woman as wife and mother' converts partial description by relationship into definition of essence. It makes of *wife* the one who does *not* have the power to lead or to negotiate on equal terms. As *mother* she is 'inseminated', then 'bears', is 'container for' what is already spoken for as a 'child'. This 'child' is already the child of her husband and of the church's god, the god's church. Even the accolade 'mother of God' only values her intermediary function. Amazing that God can condescend so far – '*Lo, he abhors not the virgin's womb!*'.

So, '*philosophy will have to recognise that two subjects exist and that reason must confront the reality and the being of these two subjects, in their horizontal and vertical dimensions*' (Irigaray 1997: 67). Irigaray explains this 'reality' in terms of sexuality considered as a 'framework for a new interiority'. To refuse a sexuality of difference is to refuse interiority along with the significance of bodily exteriority.[21] To refuse sexual difference is to define one sex as what it lacks by comparison with the other. This treatment of sexuality generates the traditional structures: '*respect for parents*', '*cult of ancestors*', '*love of children*'. To substitute these 'structures' for sexuality distorts their form, converting them into rigid structures. Such sublimation cannot replace a relationship with a specific individual, Irigaray claims.

Perhaps Irigaray exaggerates the 'revolutionary' quality of what she recommends. Is it 'only now' that such a thing can be thought? Michèle Le Dœuff has constructed a critique of feminists whose 'avant-garde' outlook occludes the history of women's struggles and achievements (Le Dœuff

---

[21] Irigaray criticises Freud for using the 'masculine' as the reference point for a 'lack' in women, but takes up and reworks his *repression* as what she calls a 'refusal of difference'.

1991, 1998). In its lack of historical specificity, Irigaray's style takes on an apocalyptic tone – a leap to a place whose description is available only 'after the revolution', as it were. (Irigaray herself would define romantic love as having just this sort of 'apocalyptic logic'. Woman is defined 'away from herself' as 'that which makes possible a man's pleasure and liberty'.) Irigaray would wish, rather, to conceive of a woman (or a man) each as existing in their interiority. Each retains, maintains, this sexual self-possession even as their interiority is changed in sexual encounters and relationships.[22] More specifically, Irigaray writes:

> This new interiority [beyond a fixation on ancestors, parents, children] can exist in the framework of a sexual relation, and only thanks to it (Irigaray 1997: 68).

The description of the sexual relation reminds us of the variety of relations that exist within a recognition of sexual difference. Sexuality and sexual difference as the framework for a deconstructive relationship need involve no overt sexual activity.[23] Rather, the recognition that *'because I am not you, I can open a space within myself, a space of interiority'*(Irigaray 1997: 68). Not a romanticism of *fusion*, of loss of limits and identity, but discovery of a more rigorous interiority to which each returns.

There are limits that condition *'my presence in the world, in the face of the other, of others'* – limits that confine my presence and make it possible. First, I am bound to my *'adherence to a genre [as "kind" and as "gender"]'*. Where Sartre places my not being you as the elemental negation at the heart of my alienation from you, Irigaray sees it as securing the space for each of us to *'return within'* ourselves, to *collect* ourselves. It does not divide me as 'a subject who observes' from 'you as an object observed'. Therefore it does not, as Sartre fears, make me your object when you observe me.

Being an Object of Consciousness

Transcending Egocentricity

Irigaray would set limits to genre and gender; she welcomes the 'irrecoverable' distance between one person and another. This setting of

---

[22] Though 'sexuality' is the framework for liberation, Irigaray differs from Marcuse, Laing or Reich, who replaced 'woman' as 'wife and mother' with a 'hommo-sexual' narcissism.

[23] The tragic farce of Clinton's 'not having had sexual relations with that woman' stirs thinking about a sexual *relation* as more than a sexual gesture.

limits safeguards human awareness from a reduction to a Sartrean *'pursuit of an impossible future'*. Sartre's quest for an other who becomes 'object' as the immediate consequence of his being aware of them, is an *'impossible autism'*. It is a quest for an autism either of *'one sole subject'* or of *'one sole people'*.[24] Such a quest is flawed, too, in imagining the search for being as occurring within an *'in-finite space and of an in-finite time'*. These 'in-finites' are not wonderful alternatives to inadequately finite things. They are amorphs – projects constructed to place their objects always one step ahead of their pursuer.

Irigaray's *'irrecoverable otherness'* marks a contrast to these autistic plans. To recognise difference *'give[s] me the present [and] presence'* and *'the possibility of being in myself, of trying to cultivate the in-stance and not only the ek-stase'* (Irigaray 1997: 69). Irigaray does recognise, though, the force of Sartre's insistence that any encounter is *'at least in the modality of object-ness'* (BN, 252–253). There must be an admission of any encounter's *'factuality or facticity'*. To deny this is to refuse the bodily character of consciousness, and to refuse this bodily character is to refuse the implicit sexuality of consciousness. Irigaray's *'entry into presence, or being-in-the-presence-of, two different subjects'* excludes a reduction to 'factuality or facticity'. Sartre reads too rigidly the *aporia* in knowing another in their interiority and their knowing you in yours. For him, though I know you are an 'unreachable interiority', when I *perceive* you only as an object, I accept you as a conscious being only as I myself become object.

Irigaray, in contrast, reads the otherness of another's interiority as a catalyst not an obstacle. Another's interiority does not enter into the reaction as ingredient or result, but enables the reaction to occur in conditions otherwise inadequate to initiate or to sustain the reaction:

> This barrier [arrêt] before the other gives me back to the present, to presence. To stop before the other is recognition but also it is desire, and a call to overcome the interval (Irigaray 1997: 69).

The point is to overcome but not to remove this *arrêt*. The difference remains an 'irrecoverable' distance between one and the other.

Using a Kind of Magic to Traverse the Distance

If we can neither remove nor deny this 'interval', how is it to be 'overcome'? Sexuality is involved, but Irigaray locates falsity in the

---

[24] Like Kristeva in *Strangers to Ourselves*, Irigaray likens the personal autism we cherish as 'autonomy', with our fantasies of perfect national boundaries.

promise of a 'liberated' sexual life in which we rely on *'instinct, impulse, sexual attraction'*. In any 'simple resort' to sex, we 'abuse' it as a means of crossing the distance between us. This is to *abuse* sexuality.[25] The 'abuse' is 'unethical' in refusing the 'ontology' of sex – cutting short its possibilities as a 'way of being'. Something more a *'simple resort'* must *'elaborate the attraction and construct a relation'*. Repetition of an initiating condition does not amount to elaboration. The ontological question about relating sexually to others, whether implicitly or explicitly, is whether we consume the other and ourselves. *L'être deux* ('being-a-couple') should *'return us to ourselves in our interiority'*.

Irigaray is critical of the 'proper' ways that we suppose will elaborate our sexual 'being with' each other. These means attempt to supplant sexuality. These means to propriety 'sew up' the sexuality of women, and mystify that of men. A religious emphasis on sex as a means only as bringing forth children within the family faith, fails to 'elaborate' the initial attraction between the sexual couple. Unless the partners offer each other more, each leaves the other in a state of incomprehension, which they may hope that love for their children will supplant or reduce. Irigaray's ethical and ontological critique prompts specific social criticism. Children born within such a misunderstanding become the hapless mediators of their parents' distress.

Some will reject religion and still look for 'elaboration' of their sexual attraction, but, not recognising they cannot comprehend the other's interiority, will be inclined to *'raise up constructions which claim to overcome sensibility'*. In this class of intellectual constructions we would find, I think, the various kinds of reductive materialist theory. 'Cognitive science' may be represented as such a reduction, though, in itself it is simply a cluster of investigations into how we perceive and know the environment. Only a refusal to place feeling and sensibility within that perceiving and knowing causes it to lapse into ideology.[26]

Irigaray is alert to the usual ways of short-circuiting the aporia of interiority. *'Dialogue'* is not enough. It may help *'ward off alienation and* [mere] *fascination with the constructed world* [monde fabriqué] *which surrounds us, preventing a community of "entre-nous"'*. The limitations of 'dialogue' emerge, however, when we look at Sartre's account of life as 'we-subjects'. He articulates how we live within a world of manufactured objects and means of doing things, and points out that we recognise them not as 'mere objects' but as expressing our common humanity. But 'dialogue' is too bland to cure the lack of any eruption of individual

---

[25] 'Ab-use' – to use something 'away from' its principal or intended possibilities.

[26] Thus the joke – 'Cognitive science is where philosophers go when they die'.

feeling. I could share my participation in 'dialogue' with any stranger as '*I insert myself in the great human stream which ... has flowed incessantly*'.

I Run into You [Toi], in the Crowds

As Sartre had described the situation I achieve a genuine communality, but

> my immediate ends are the ends of the 'They', and I apprehend myself as interchangeable with any one of my neighbours (BN, 424).

Irigaray takes up Sartre's theme here, expressing in her terms what is involved in being part of such an inadequate 'we':

> To be part of a social and cultural movement can create diverse forms of empathy, of sympathy, of solidarity between individuals, but those are generally determined from the exteriority of the shared world ... I am not attentive to the other, to others, but I do as they do out of passivity, out of egoism, in a certain sense. Thus I become [merely] an individual 'someone or other' (Irigaray 1997: 72).

Caught within 'the great human stream', Irigaray's narrator is rescued in meeting someone she knows. Sartre's narrator, too, would be rescued from anonymity, but at the price of such conflict that his 'I' might prefer to remain within the stream, for long as I am caught up within it, my sharing in technology is an escape from loneliness. Returning perhaps from the subway to opening a can of preserves in my empty room, the can opener fits my hand and still reminds me of a common world of people who work to understand each other's needs. Or have I opened a can of worms? I might get the impulse to go out and find myself amongst this common mass. I might run into someone I knew; I might shrink from the contact, for, as Sartrean 'I', who is to be the controlling observer? In the struggle, each of us will lose our sense of interiority – of 'my' own, and of the other's. I will be left in loneliness. A worse isolation than when I was alone in conversation with remnants of past encounters and myself.

So how does this Luce's garden grow? No more than Sartre, does Irigaray entertain the fantasy of knowing another 'in their interiority'. 'I' can not convey my own interiority to 'them'. What remedy then? Suppose we transport the word of Sartre's *look* into her world. In the world she constructs each of us accepts the 'irrecoverable' interiority of the other as the point from which to deconstruct the impasse. It is in accepting this 'irrecoverable interiority' that we leave the paralysing loneliness of an empty room, while hoping for something better than an erasure of loneliness within the 'corridors' of a technologically mediated humanity.

Irigaray looks for more than Sartre does in these impersonal corridors, however. She reminds us of a 'look' not envisaged by Sartre. She would 'walk towards' you in those corridors of the metro,[27] but free of that effusive show of feelings by which I affect to turn my interiority inside out while still preserving its inner 'sincerity'.[28] Irigaray writes in a mood reminiscent of Saint-Exupéry's *Petit Prince*, *'qui marche tout doucement vers la fontaine'*. She says:

> Je ne me réduis pas à un <<on quelconque>> dans le couloir de la station de métro … si je marche vers toi' ['I am not reduced to a 'someone-or-other' in the metro corridor, if I walk towards you'] (Irigaray 1997: 72).

In the crowded *couloir* of the métro, a public demonstration of feeling will only resemble the actions of the public in public, reducing me to a cliché of 'showing my individuality in the crowd'. You've seen the movie-shot too often. Irigaray's version of the Paris-metro-movie, though, is of a couple intimate with each other, each intimate with himself or herself, whose *'interiority*, [whose] *intention remains with* [them] *contained and close, despite the crowd'*. That I can not 'recover' this interiority (whose containment is a condition of intimacy) is what *'safeguards my mystery as yours makes you a mystery for me'*. Irigaray makes this use of 'mystery' partly to combat another cliché – the 'loneliness of the crowd'. As only a member of a crowd,[29] knowing no one better than another, I am alone, my interiority unregistered.

For Irigaray, everyone 'alone in the crowd' knows everyone *all too well*. *En masse*, we announce our conformity at every point of movement and dress. Each is secure in the knowledge that there is nothing more to be known – as if there is nothing *to be known* beyond the banalities they might exchange with regular co-travellers on the train home. It is not simply technology that displaces interiority. Technology itself might revive *l'admiration* – critical and inquiring wonderment – not a mute and stunned astonishment at novelty. We need to recollect what is not seen in what we see, what is not heard in what we hear, what is not felt as we brush by against each other. But we have to read, *tout doucement*, this 'unseen', this 'unheard', this 'unfelt'. Otherwise we shall have returned to a classical dualism that mechanises the body,[30] or else to 'idealism and religious

---

[27] Sartre's man 'passes by', the woman 'approaches me', the beggar cries out his appeal.

[28] The typical style of actors in giving an acceptance speech for an Academy Award.

[29] To work as one of the 'philosophical crowd' is to sacrifice one's sensibility'; harsh doctrine hides the loss.

[30] See *Perçevoir L'invisible en toi*, which succeeds *Fille et Femme* in *Etre Deux*.

terror'. This 'interiority which protects me' is not ineffable. It is a bodily matter:

> I am sexed; I am not a 'they', neuter, anonymous and interchangeable: I am moved by intentions ... towards you [toi] and not determined unequivocally by the world which surrounds me (Irigaray 1997: 72).

Being sexed does not, as such, distinguish me from all others of the same sex. To be brought into the field of sexual difference is to be brought short against one's specific interiority – what one will do with one's sexuality or any other aspect of one's interiority. No longer one of a crowd of 'men-and-women' dressing and behaving according to the appropriate codes, memories of one's intimate past may be revived. I am 'moved by intentions *vers toi*' – towards 'you' as an intimate. I have to choose how I will approach and respond; I can not make assumptions about your 'interiority'; nor ignore the fact of it.

In Irigaray's language (Irigaray 1993a; 1993b: 55–72), each has to 'divine' the other, and each proceeds on the basis of their sensibility – observing, guessing, inferring, taking chances. Approach and response is possible, and while complete comprehension is beyond reach, the other is not an *occult* mystery. As Sartre says concerning the immediate 'upsurge' of someone as a conscious being, we are dealing not with mystical communion of souls but with an everyday interchange. To 'divine' the other as existing in their interiority is to know another as a being that is always in the process of being known, and thus to know of the 'irrecoverable' difference between us. I may treat another as a purely observable object of which I may accomplish my knowledge. Or I may venerate them as an ineffable spirit beyond experience. Either way I refuse their presence. To consider that I have accomplished the knowledge of another is to refuse their difference and their interiority. To consider them as an ineffable spirit keeps them at precisely the same distance. It is to refuse the immediacy of their presence and approach as a bodily subjectivity.

10
Divining Others

Seizing Others

Subjects and Objects

In the chapters immediately before and after 'Fille et femme', Irigaray's 'respect' for the difference of the other begins to make a mystery of it. Things begin well in 'Les noces entre le corps et la parole' (Irigaray 1997). She marks a difference[1] between two clusters of relations. She wants to emphasise the priority of relationships

    as between subjects
    to the other sex
    à deux

Sartre (and others in what Irigaray calls the 'Western' tradition) prefers to emphasise relationships

    as between subject and object
    as between subject and object by instrumental means
    between one and many – à eux rather than à deux

Irigaray criticises Sartre, not for connecting the person too closely with the body, but for treating the body-of-the other as only 'facticity'. The other becomes only 'what I can see or touch'. Yes, says Irigaray, I can see and touch the other, as against what idealist or dualist pictures imply. Sartre's error lies elsewhere, in his reductive assumptions about what kind of seeing and touching, what reading of vision and touch is in question. What kind of perception of the other will leave room for recognition of awareness – of self, for self, of the world and of the body? Sartre did not set out to be reductively materialist. He emphasised one's being as a *for-itself* whose mode is marked by a transcendence of facticity. He never loses sight of this

---

[1] One might not agree that this 'difference' is special for 'woman' and 'man'; still, intimate relations with others might have priority in revealing consciousness.

dimension. The problem of what the Other can be for me arises from his image of perception in all its forms as objectifying what I perceive. The problem thus becomes how I can *desire* the other, since I direct my desire towards the other as *for themselves* – a body transcending its facticity. Sartre's attributes the impasse over this question to humanity itself. In his famous phrase, 'man' is a 'useless passion', but Irigaray looks towards what Sartreanism lacks in theory and experience.[2] Her question is how there is a bodily relation with another if one's desire for them is in relation to their 'transcendence'. She challenges Sartre's depiction of perception of the other as bound to objectify them.

Sartre does show how we have bodily desire and why it is bound to be frustrated. A person achieves 'transcendence' in and through their bodily being. Hence, one might expect that in bodily intimacy one would be closest to them, as transcendent. As we recall, 'transcendence' is not an existence on a spiritual plane apart from the body, but consists in the ways in which *I* '*exist*' *my body*. I desire to know or to experience another in their transcendence. I do not thereby attempt to break through from their body to their immaterial soul, nor to a Cartesian mental substance. I am trying to relate to another in their way of regarding and deploying their body. Even without Sartre's insistence that desire for something must take the form of an aim to *possess* it for oneself, the quest smells of impossibility.

Sartre's preoccupation with possession as the form of desire casts his story in the mould of bafflement. In bodily desire I desire what comes to hand, for instance. If it is someone whom I desire, than my desire is to be in contact with them as a 'transcendence'. In consequence I desire that they 'come to the surface' of their body, that their awareness could be 'skimmed' – '*prise*' – from the body, as cream is '*prise*' as it comes to the surface of milk. As if '*the for-itself of the Other [might] come to play on the surface of his body [so] that I [might] touch the Other's free subjectivity*' (BN, 394).

Sartre's desire to escape a dualist vision of being conscious struggles against tendencies towards a reductive materialism that would degrade the difference between the desire for someone and the desire for an ice cream. Yet might I not desire that the other 'rise to the surface' in their bodily intention without aiming to *possess* them? It is only 'possession' that Sartre demonstrates to be absurd in sexual desire. Irigaray challenges Sartre's preoccupation with desire as the wish to possess, but leaves untouched his model of how awareness can exist in bodily form as available to another.

---

[2] Le Dœuff challenges Sartre differently. She demonstrates the ordinary prejudices at work in a text whose abstract and metaphorical quality serves them up as theoretical necessities.

We shall have to see whether her alternative model leaves in place nothing but the untouched mystery of the other's existence as interiority.

Sartre cites the traditional figures of erotic desire as the intention to fascinate, to 'bewitch' the other. The desire is to *'caus[e] the other's awareness to descend into the body, to affix liberty in the facticity of the body'* (Irigaray 1997: 37). Irigaray's desire is to represent the possibility of the other's awareness flowering in their body. She denies that this must result in Sartre's *engluement* of liberty and body. Unless we assume such an impassable dichotomy of awareness and body, a congruence of awareness and bodily freedom is a possibility to consider. Like Le Dœuff, Irigaray points out that 'Jean-Paul Sartre' produces a bizarre picture of sexual or other bodily encounters by failing to specify the sex of the 'other'. Sexual difference remains 'unthought'. This unthought dimension produces irreality in Sartre's theory as in his imagery. For Le Dœuff, Sartre's failure to recognise the sex of the 'other' is a strategy to dominate the other's conscious freedom. For Irigaray the lack of specific recognition means that he takes no account of the 'lived sex' of the other. We observe and objectify *'elle'*. We meet and deal with only *'il'*. Sartre suppresses the feminine.

In his description of desire, Sartre refuses to recognise the unknown in what we desire. Irigaray ties this to his lack of recognition of sexual specificity. The other is 'sexed', I am 'sexed'; the assumption is that we understand each other pretty well. Irigaray proceeds, in turn, to tie this implicit homogeneity with the insistence on *possession* as the object of desire. Within the frame of possession each would-be lover has found neither their own freedom nor that of the other. The 'flesh' of the other reveals not what is other to me but what exists only as 'for me'. We wake not in freedom but in fright and nausea. Fright because the other has regained their freedom. What now? Nausea at having been reduced, or having the reduced the other to something 'glued down' to their body rather than having operated with a new freedom. 'The awakening lovers are graceless, stuck down, thickened *(empâtés)* in the facticity of the body', she says. A tacky event.

Irigaray begins to tackle the question of perception as objectifying what is perceived. *'J'aime à toi'*, she suggests. The intimate you (*'te'*, *'toi'*) is made the dative instead of the direct accusative of love. The 'you are neither me nor mine' that is to typify non-possessive desire goes with a grammar in which my desire is 'as towards' the other. This is a grammar or relationship without possession. The form could signify a different form of perception, too, which would not objectify the other as an object directly grasped within one's regard. To go in her direction we would invent, thus,

'*Je perçois à toi*' rather than '*Je te perçois*'. We are to maintain the sensuous, sensible nature of someone we can know and love, and also the impossibility of reducing that sensibility to a simple sum of qualities. I love, I perceive *towards* you ... you are not an ensemble of qualities that makes you simply perceptible by me.

Sartre's use of a capital 'A' for 'autrui', the 'Other' signifies a related error, according to Irigaray. The recognition of irrecoverable difference between another and me is not the elevation of them to another plane; it is not a magnification of them nor of the problems of knowing them.[3] The big 'O' (in French, 'A') speaks Sartre's distorted kind of transcendence of the body and thus of the other. His transcendence, she says, is '*au-délà de toi*' in a way that abolishes the possibility of (properly addressing you as) '*tu*' in a phrase we could construct as '*tu-autre pour moi*'. It is from this point that Irigaray's language begins to move from 'respect for difference' to 'the mystery of the other's being' (Irigaray 1997: 40). Irigaray constructs the bridge between *difference* and *mystery* by experimental declarations produced for the reader's philosophical meditation. She closes the paragraph with this flourish: '*I will never comprehend you, never grasp who you are; you will always hold yourself beyond me ... for the 'verb' takes its own bodily form in you [toi] – and in me too, but differently*' (Irigaray 1997: 40).[4]

I can hear these expressions in many ways. First, these confessions of my limits are expressions of intimacy. They are not what I would say to an employer whose motives are hard to assess. 'Comprehend' is an important word to the point of the declaration. To comprehend something is to be able to contain it within my system of perception, imagination and powers of inference. This recognition of non-comprehension is one of the recurring themes of a live relationship.[5] '*I will never comprehend you [toi]*' is neither a premise, a conclusion, nor a disguised principle of inference. It is not a settled statement of fact which each gets to accept with equanimity as the known state of things. That would signify only a lack of interest in each

---

[3] Throughout Irigaray's discussion there is a question whether 'knowing' is the appropriate concept to describe someone's relation to their (intimate) other.

[4] I worked from *Etre Deux*. There is now an English translation (Irigaray 2000). With regard to some phrases it flattens Irigaray's prose – perhaps to sound acceptable to the anglophone ear. For instance, '*Le verbe en toi s'est fait chair*' becomes the religious cliché 'the word is made flesh in you' (Irigaray 2000: 18). But in Irigaray's hands the religious 'divine' becomes a humanly active 'divination', so the primary sense of 'verbe' as 'verb' (and not just any 'word') is vital to her deconstruction of religious language. Philosophically, too, sexual difference is a *work* – a 'verb'.

[5] To react with *in*comprehension is a different matter! To let matters remain in that state is a refusal of intimacy.

other. That neither will ever 'comprehend the other' is not something that either of them *knows*. It is something each *grants*. Its expression evinces the continual surprise at the other as a being irreducibly different from the one who makes the declaration. '*I will never comprehend you [toi]*' might be said in wonderment, in irritation, as a challenge to the other to make some attempt to explain themselves. You can know a good deal about what you cannot comprehend.

Can *any* thing, from the simplest inanimate object to the most creative being, be comprehended? I may comprehend statements about such things. Even so it is risky to look closely at concepts. One becomes philosophical, deconstructive: '*The cat sat on the mat*'?? A cat may look at a king, but does a cat *sit*? Squat? In using everyday sentences it is best never to look or to think closely. Irigaray proceeds with these trial declarations:

I will never grasp who you are [*Je ne saisirai jamais qui tu es*] (Irigaray 1997: 40).

Is she just teasing? We can hear many different performances. A promise: '*I will never seize*[6] *you*", meaning that I shall approach you more gently. Or it is a caution: '*The way you are, I will never [be able to] grasp you*', meaning '*Are you sure you want to maintain such a barrier between us?*' It might be a confession of proper limits: '*Though I may grasp you it will never be you as you are yourself*'. If it is in their 'essential being' that someone exists in an unreachable interiority then indeed I shall neither seize, touch, caress, or think of you 'as you are'.[7] There are more of these de-mented[8] test runs of language:

You will always hold yourself beyond me [*toujours tu te tiendras hors de moi*] (Irigaray 1997: 40).

What is this? An instruction? What if I do not comply? A recognition? A regret at the other's 'modern narcissism'?[9] An ontological necessity? If so, how can the other *hold themselves* 'outside' me? Under necessity they would have no option. If I hold myself back or hold myself in I don't stay

---

[6] 'Saisir' might be translated as 'seize' – 'grasp' tends to weaken to 'understand'.

[7] We shall see that Irigaray, finally, is prepared to countenance this limit.

[8] It is this old word I mean to ab-use, not Irigaray. To be 'mented' is to be mindful, to grasp with the mind. Irigaray brings us back to how the way we relate in intimacy, though demanding knowledge and understanding, is also *de*-minded.

[9] The phrase is from Le Dœuff's *Genèse d'une catastrophe* (Le Dœuff 1986b). She attributes the quality to Adonis, who is more interested in keeping his soul as an untouched inner citadel than in reciprocating love with Venus.

'back' or 'in' when I let myself go. In reading these Irigarayan declarations of the demented ontology of intimacy we have to deal with inflexions of necessity, entreaty, promise, forbearance and metaphysical imagery.

Irigaray is arguing, on the very basis that intimacy is partially de-mented, for the necessity of *speech* (la parole) between us. The recognition that I cannot 'comprehend' another in the fashion of surrounding them with my body or mind, is not a plea for silent incomprehension. It is *'not to be 'I', 'me', or 'mine' that makes speech possible and necessary between us'* (Irigaray 1997: 40), she says. To recognise that I cannot 'comprehend' or 'seize' what I desire is not to recognise defeat. I should understand that *'no question of desire is worth anything unless it carries the silent question 'Who are you [tu]?'* I must ask the question on the understanding that I can hear it, understand each word and yet shall never comprehend it as grounded in the other's being. I listen to you, recognising that you *'transcend me even if I touch you ... you will never be me or mine'* (Irigaray 1997: 40):

> [F]or the 'verb' takes its own bodily form in you [toi] – and in me too, but differently' [*car le verbe en toi s'est fait chair et aussi, différemment, en moi*] (Irigaray 1997: 40).

Irigaray's language disrupts the religious cliché, 'the word is made flesh'. In her hands *'le verbe'* remains 'the verb' - not just any 'word'. As we saw in the previous chapter, the religious 'divine' has become a humanly active 'divination'. In the same manner, the primary sense of *'verbe'* as 'verb' is vital to her deconstruction of religious language. Philosophically, too, And when Irigaray alludes to bodily, and sexual difference – *'the verb takes its bodily form ... differently in me'* – we should recollect her thesis that 'sexual difference' is a kind of *work* – a 'verb' (Irigaray 1993a; 1993b: 57–72).

Irigaray concludes this part of her theme on the ambiguities of 'grasping' others by attending to the nuances of my 'perceiving' them. To 'perceive *towards* the other', I must treat the other as the very being I perceive. The *'towards'* does not elevate them to an unapproachable level, nor remove them to obscure depths. The other is not the merely 'outward show'[10] of the body as object, nor a spirit on another plane. I must bear the tension of their difference, of their interiority. I must bear it in mind, eye, ear and hand. Irigaray uses sexual difference as a synecdoche for this

---

[10] From the de-mented Hamlet, arguing with his mother about his father, and Ophelia. His mother says *'Why seems it so particular with thee?'* Hamlet replies, *'Seems, madam! Nay, it is; I know not "seems" ... I have within which passes show'* (*Hamlet*, I, 2, ll. 75–86).

ontological difference. She sails close to dualism's wind. '*Beyond the colour of the eyes etc. etc ... there is a subjectivity which I can not see, neither by sense nor mind*' (Irigaray 1997: 41).[11]

Differing from Merleau-Ponty and Lévinas

Merleau-Ponty prides himself on having improved upon Sartre's vision of the intimate relations that are possible between one person and another. Irigaray points out that '*his connection between shame or modesty* ('pudeur') *and shamelessness* (impudeur) *recalls Sartre on bewitchment* (as the means of securing the other), *and possession* (as one's aim in doing so). Merleau-Ponty's suggests that in erotic sight and touch the body of another, or one's body for another, becomes *ambiguously* consciousness and 'flesh'. This, no less than Sartre's alternation of domination by perception and submission to perception, has 'echoed' in the 'collective conscious'. Irigaray is doubly dissatisfied with Merleau-Ponty's direction. On one side of the ambiguity, Merleau-Ponty appeals to my desire to 'capture' the other, to 'possess', to 'have them available at last beyond question'. In his desire to take another as a conscious being, yet in the very mode of their consciousness he is still very like Sartre. I may be particularly unguarded, spontaneous and vulnerable to another in intimate contact. This fact encourages such an idea. On the other side of the ambiguity, the 'flesh' is, when all is said and done, flesh. It is the body; it is object. I am subject to being made object no less in Merleau-Ponty's schema of perception than in Sartre's. My status is *ambiguously* that of object for a subject, and my 'flesh' is *ambiguously* also a mode of awareness. This 'ambiguity' does not lessen the force of the patterns of domination and submission in Merleau-Ponty's picture of things. Irigaray quotes Merleau-Ponty (*The Phenomenology of Perception*), to good effect:

> Shame and immodesty, then, take their place in a dialectic of the self and the other which is that of master and slave: in so far as I have a body, I may be reduced to the status of an object beneath the gaze of another person, or else I may become his master and, in my turn look at *him* (Irigaray 1997: 41).

Merleau-Ponty turns away from the psychologically informed observations with which he began, towards considerations of 'metaphysical

---

[11] This is an allusion to Descartes' argument (*Second Meditation*) that he can know of the nature or existence of mind only by the mind. Another's difference from me in their sexed interiority is, for Irigaray, available neither to my 'rational thought nor to my senses'.

significance'. As he does so, this ambiguity seems to harden into the original subject-object dichotomy he had intended to displace:

> Saying that I have a body is thus a way of saying that I can be seen as an object and that I try to be seen as subject – that another can be my master or my slave. Thus, shame and shamelessness express the dialectic of the plurality of consciousnesses, and have a metaphysical significance. The same might be said of sexual desire (Irigaray 1997: 41–42).

In his declarations about how things stand between one person and another Merleau-Ponty aims at a softer, more moderated tone than Sartre's. As Beauvoir makes clear in 'Merleau-Ponty et le pseudo-Sartrism'(Beauvoir 1955), much of what he says is in counterpoint to *Being and Nothingness*. The last sentence of 'The Body in its Sexual Being' is evidently meant to correct Sartre's famous conclusion to his thesis that '*Every human reality is a passion ... that projects losing itself so as to found being*':

> But ... we lose ourselves in vain. Man is a useless passion (BN, 615).

Merleau-Ponty, considering how we 'found our being' in a sexual relationship while also losing our self-containment, responds with

> No-one is saved and no-one is lost (Merleau-Ponty 1962: 171).

Irigaray would say that Merleau-Ponty's vision is still imprisoned like Sartre's by '*the effort to capture, not just the body, but a body animated by awareness*'. They share in an effort to find a language that recognises awareness without producing a dualism. In this effort, each is distracted from a shared failing. They are still intent upon 'capture' of another, and that this desire produces the wrong kind of rapprochement between body and awareness. As to the achievement of objectivity in the eyes or touch of another, Irigaray would remind them that

> as belonging to a gender my body is already an objectivity for me. I am not simply a subjectivity in search of an object-other. Within me there is a dialectic of subjectivity and objectivity (Irigaray 1997: 42–43).

This ought to be recognised by the male author who should accept the objective subjectivity of the position from which he writes, as does the woman who writes in opposition. This is not all. Irigaray continues,

> The subject/object dichotomy depends on the way of conceiving of sexuality itself. For Merleau-Ponty the 'ambiguity' (of sexuality as

involving body and awareness) concerns not only the body but also life generally (Irigaray 1997: 43).

This might seem an attractive idea, ceasing to make a fetish of sex in favour of recognising a more dispersed sensuality. Irigaray insists, however, that

> Sexuality as thus conceived puts no premium on intersubjectivity but involves rather a duplicity in subjectivity itself such that all actions, feelings and sensations are equivocal, troubled, and cannot speak to the other as such (Irigaray 1997: 44).

The movement of thought that Irigaray criticises here is like the one that Le Dœuff discerns (Le Dœuff 1989: 138–170). There is a structure Le Dœuff calls a 'chiasma', in which the specific difference between one thing and another is denied at its point of most intense distinction, and rediscovered, in attenuated form everywhere else. Merleau-Ponty

> has forgotten the function of sexuality as a 'relation-towards', and the role of perception as a means of access to the other as other (Irigaray 1997: 44).

Irigaray does not want to generalise or to homogenise the specific nature and role of sexuality as a mode of perception and as a mode of 'speaking' (*s'addresser*) to the other. Nevertheless, her alternative to Sartre and Merleau-Ponty's view of how I may relate to another involves a capability in perception that is not limited to sexualised perception. Let us suppose she is correct in her criticism that '*our tradition is not interested in the culture of felt perception* (la perception sensible)'. It is the capability of this 'perception sensible' that interests her as showing how I can 'speak to' another, love and perceive 'towards' another, while seeing their difference as beyond my possession. At this stage, she says no more about this *felt perception.* She reminds us of the familiar bifurcation of intellect and emotion, sensation and understanding, which is part of the 'tradition of western philosophy' – whether real or legendary. She appeals to the need for a '*culture of sensibility [which would] be true to the reciprocity in touching and being touched, whether in perception or speech*' (Irigaray 1997: 48).

Irigaray's appeal to this 'culture of sensibility' oscillates between attentiveness familiar in the everyday, and a revolutionary demand for something scarcely heard of in the 'western' tradition. Thus her first appeal is for an attitude lost only in an excessive intellectualisation of life. On the one hand, for Plato (or Plato's Socrates?) the search for truth in the *eidos* is a '*night of the senses, a transmission of speech and of truth without putting them to the test of daily perceptions*' (Irigaray 1997: 44). She makes an approving reference to the Buddha's attention to a flower, and develops this remark to show how perception of it as not possessed as 'my' object of sight, leads us to think of its whole world, in its seasons, growth and roots, and for its beauty. This is at least a hint of the model of what she has in mind. Her desire is for a 'culture of sensibility' in perception that would take it beyond sensation. This is some clue to what she means in saying, '*we have to learn to see each other, what is within each other*' (Irigaray 1997: 46).

The appeal to 'everyday life' (*la vie quotidienne*) is inviting, but she is asking us to put a favourable 'spin' on the phrase,[12] without which the 'everyday' could not do the work she desires. In daily life people treat each other as functionaries. We distance the other as raised on a pedestal, or short-circuit understanding by an attempt at immediate contact. To use Irigaray's word the other becomes a means to 'sensation'. Yet is she right to lay this alternation of high-mindedness and erotic solipsism at the door of the intellectual? While the intellectual theories typically show a lack of sensibility, there is no need to mystify everyday life as a source of spontaneous reciprocity of innocents who recognise each other's unplumbed depths.

Irigaray's case studies are well focused, however. Lévinas' language of the 'caress' exhibits the faults of a romantic who disguises his narcissism. Irigaray quotes a telling section from his *Totality and Infinity*. Evidently his language interests Irigaray in its emphasis, like hers, that '*the caress consists of not seizing anything*'. She criticises Lévinas for writing as if about erotic love and knowledge in general, while describing it from the point of view of a man who approaches a woman. The distortion far exceeds that of the male writer's pre-disposition. How else would the desiring lover be led, inevitably, not only '*à la virginité*' but to feminine virginity (*la virginité, à jamais inviolée, du féminin*)? '*La virginité féminine*' can be read either as *feminine* virginity, or as *virginity*'s being feminine in aspect. Perhaps the elusive, therefore *untouched* nature of the object of desire is what is meant by its perpetual 'virginity', its 'femininity'. Lévinas persists in a unilateral emphasis on the female figure as what is sought by the male, a figure who keeps herself hidden nonetheless. He inscribes the feminine '*L'aimée*' just where it might have been a man loved by a woman, or by a man.

The textual effect is not only that of the distortion towards 'man the lover', 'woman the loved'. There is a phenomenology only of the lover. This is a man, the writer's a man; he makes no play with the sexed voice of his philosophical narrator. The narrator has no place from or within which

---

[12] See Lefèbvre 2000 and Michel de Certeau 2000 for brilliant critiques of 'ordinary life'.

to subtend the phenomena of being loved. The masculine narrator has the voice of one infinitely careful not to arrogate the feminine other to himself. This is the attraction of Lévinas to strategists who would displace possession from the primary lexicon of love. The one loved becomes a mystery, however. Ergo the feminine is a mystery. (Clasps forehead! Where *have* I heard that before?') Not only *not, never, fully known.* Not only *always, ever, to be approached as if to be known.* Sexual contact emerges yet again as *profanation* – a profanity a woman escapes by inner self-possession, maintaining an 'untouched virginity':

> The profanation which entwines itself within the caress makes its appropriate response to the originary status of this dimension of absence ... In the bodiliness of tenderness, the body surpasses its status as a being. The Loved one [feminine – *aimée*] is someone you can take hold of who is at the same time un-touched in her nakedness. She is something beyond the object and facial expression. Thus she is beyond the status of a being; she is self-possessed in virginity (Lévinas, cited in Irigaray 1997: 49).

Fantasies are at work here, working with and against each other to produce a phantasmagoria. In this show woman appears as threatening profanation, as an infinitely vulnerable figure man guiltily profanes, as a mysteriously inviolable and thus invulnerable figure. Across some decades, Irigaray has thrown more than a spanner or two into the works of this traditional loom. She makes a caustic remark about Lévinas who describes bodily love solely in terms of a man's intention towards a woman. The 'sexual masculine' is made still fishier than that. Enough already. There are other sprats to fry. A bodily relationship, a sexual *rapport* can be reciprocal.[13] If it is to be reciprocal then to be familiar with the phenomena of being approached is important, like those of the sensitive *approach.* No one in a Lévinasian scenario has much idea of what they are doing in approaching another. No one has any idea of what their approach would be like for the one who approached. No one even dreams of what to feel or do if someone approached them. So far as the man who sets off this mysterious episode of sexual love is concerned,

> She loses herself in a being which disperses without will and even without resistance, as in an impersonal dream; a passivity, an anonymity at once animal or infantile, as if to the very point of death (Lévinas, cited in Irigaray 1997: 49).

---

[13] That much is now available in magazines in dentists' and hairdressers' waiting rooms.

As in the fairy tale, with dawn everything disappears. Now Irigaray does not wish merely or even totally to mock this romance. She does not wish to replace it simply with the banal factuality of a magazine's commercial offer of information about 'how we can understand our partners'. She uses *'mystère'* in relation to what each recognises in the other, not when each does not 'know' the other, but most particularly when each knows the other. It is when each knows the other as within a long period, and in a most intimate moment that each recognises the irrecoverable mystery of the other's being, and thus of their own.

Renovating Mystery in the Old Sites of Dualism

Irigaray wants to renovate the 'mystery' of human existence. She uses a strategy familiar from her earlier writings. She had reformed 'God' into a need for human and textual genres. 'Divinity' had become the need to 'divine' each other rather than merely to observe and make inferences about each other as empirically given objects.[14] On the one hand the 'mystery' of human existence is the vulnerability of behaviour and expression to another person's reading of it. What is another person prepared to find, and what is that person prepared to deal with? On the other hand it is the sheer 'interiority' of each person's existence. She shares with Sartre an acceptance of this category – of its moral and of its ontological force. She shares with Sartre (and with Ryle too) a rejection of the Cartesian interpretation of that interiority. In particular she emphasises one's own profound unknowing about one's inner life – an unknowing from which one can depart only by intimate connection with others. Nothing could be further from a 'Cartesian' division in which I know this mind simply in that it is mine. And as to the mind of another – for Descartes as dualist just as for Berkeley as idealist – only by the grace of God can I speak of knowing such a thing.

To the extent that one knows and understands interiority, it arises for 'the one who knows' and 'the one who is known', in reciprocal intimate encounter. Since reciprocity is a *sine qua non*, each who forms the couple is in the process of becoming both 'knower' and 'known'. In her representation of this situation Irigaray places sexual difference and sexual intimacy at the heart of such knowledge, and of the need for it. I have no motive to displace her own imagery. I intend, rather, to broaden the scope of intimacy without further ado. Using terms that are currency in the ethical

---

[14] I would deconstruct 'mystery' rather than oppose it full-frontally, locking us into the 'dualism/materialism' debate. The advantages should become apparent.

commonplace, Irigaray criticises the cultivation of sexual freedom as enough to answer fully the need for intimacy between the sexes. She writes of the need to develop sexual relationships into conversation and co-operative action if they are to maintain recognition of the *difference* between us. To maintain this recognition within the demands of everyday life is to retain our sense of the *mystery* of the interiority of the other, and that of oneself. To speak of this interiority as a *mystery* is to speak of it as what each must divine within another, allow to be divined within oneself, and to divine within oneself for oneself.

Incomplete understanding remains between people in their intimacy with each other. The greater the intimacy the greater the awareness of the extent of it. There are two reactions to this 'mystery'.[15] I may posit a mysterious link of body with an unobservable mind. This degrades to banality the need for each to divine the other. Each of us would have to accept our inert inclusion within an occult arrangement. Gilbert Ryle has pointed out how such an arrangement is no less mechanical for being a *para*-mechanics (Ryle 1949: 19–23). The other reaction – romanticism – uses sexual intimacy as a mode of *bewitchment* of the otherwise unreachable other. Seduction or bewitchment induces someone to 'come across' from the commonplace of separate existence, into sexual intimacy. This confuses each about what each knows and, worse, the level of what each does not know about the other. It is bad enough that I do not have to understand you, nor that you need understand me. More dangerously, each of us, as party to the magic, has the experience of being in close, intense and reciprocal involvement. We can find it hard to believe that 'nothing more than sex' was involved. More was involved since awareness was brought to the surface of the bodies. It is 'brought to the surface' only to be 'skimmed off', Irigaray complains, by the one who has the conceit of manipulating the magic.

A reciprocal awareness of the need to divine the other in what they express may occupy a site of impossible comprehension. This, at least, is what Irigaray proposes. To be brought to that site by bewitchment is to be brought blindfolded by the other. The blinded one will not know how to return under their own control. They will not know how to leave. 'Where am I to go from here?' is the cry, unanswerable since if the liaison began reciprocally the question would have the basis for the form 'Where do we go from here?' Worse still emerges from this analysis of the predicament thus wrought.

If 'I' blindfold 'you' in dazzling you, bring a desire to the surface, this desire surfaces without expressing an intention including 'me' within the

---

[15] I should state that the ensuing remarks are entirely my own responsibility.

direction you were inscribing within your life. If you cry out 'But where do *we* go from here?' I cannot reply. I may be smitten by sexual conscience but that leads me nowhere. We each came across the line between object and subject; if bewitchment was the mode now there is a cost. 'You did not compel 'me' to understand where you stood nor to know what place you occupied. 'You just don't know where I am coming from' reduces 'me' to silence.

Lévinas made an effort to recognise the unknown dimension of the other which intimacy reveals. In changing his slant, Irigaray sets out to surpass banality without recourse to bewitchment. Reciprocity is to be possible even though what it reveals is the 'mystery' of the other.[16] In its *not reaching* the other, Levinas describes only a fumbling groping caress. It 'searches', it 'rummages' (*'fouille'*). Irigaray might agree that the caress should not aim to 'uncover', but she would not be happy with his alternative of *'recherche'*. If I perpetually 'search' for the other in the interiority of their own difference I have crossed the border of being irritating, into the territory of harassment. This fumbling, groping, hopeless searching 'expresses love in a certain sense', claims Lévinas. Irigaray is not so sure.[17] Levinas is right to recognise that the attempt must fail, but that does not make something holy of his attempt at capture.

As with Sartre, Lévinas' impetus is that of possession, and Irigaray shifts language towards *'J'aime à toi'* and *'je perçois à toi'* to signify that the impetus of love is to offer it – to offer one's perception to the one you would love.[18] Lévinas's line of thought becomes still more dubious here. He supposes that his 'grasping after' someone who escapes in the act by which he attempts to take hold of them, 'expresses love'. It gets worse. His lover also suffers from an incapacity to speak: his grasping *'exprime l'amour, mais souffre d'une incapacité de le dire'* ['expresses love, but suffers from an incapacity to speak it'] (Lévinas, cited in Irigaray 1997: 48). Irigaray better articulates the attempt to express and to reciprocate love. 'I' offer my speech across the space of a difference that 'we' reciprocally recognise, not needing the (hopeless) intention that this speech bring the life and consciousness of the other within my own.

---

[16] Irigaray wishes to rehabilitate 'God', 'divine', 'mystery' while subverting them to new ends, but the words carry heavy baggage. If the words cannot be ignored, perhaps we should use them 'sous rature' – under erasure.

[17] When she quotes his *'La caresse cherche, elle fouille'* [The caress *searches*, it rummages], she interpolates after *'cherche'*, *'et j'ai envie d'ajouter: celle de l'homme Lévinas'* [and I feel like adding: that caress of the man Lévinas].

[18] Think of Plato's *Lysis*, which exhibits how it is arrogant, not friendly, to say that I am someone's friend unless they reciprocate. In contrast, I may love someone who does not care for me – to love is to make that person's interests paramount.

Reciprocation, Difference and Mystery

Having sketched her 'phenomenology of the caress', Irigaray proceeds to the more detailed critique of Sartre on love and possession that we examined in the previous chapter. Then, in 'Percevoir l'invisible en toi' ('To perceive what is invisible in you'), she returns to the 'mystery' which must be recognised within the difference between *je* and *toi*. Her phenomenology declares the reciprocity each lover desires. She challenges us – this reciprocity is possible because from time to time we achieve it – and simply sets out before us the phenomenology of its practice:

> The caress is an *éveil* – a dawning, and as dawn awakens us, an arousing. It is a dawning arousal then, *à toi, à moi, à nous.*[19]

> The caress is a *réveil* – a wakening or summoning call to my body, skin, senses, muscles, and to those nerves and organs which I most often inhibit and make subject to my will in the 'world of needs, work, and the imperatives or restrictions necessary to everyday living in a community.

> The caress is an *éveil* to intersubjectivity, to a touch between us which is neither passive nor active, an *éveil* to gestures, perceptions which are at the same time actions, intentions and emotions. These gestures and perceptions are not therefore ambiguous, but attentive to touching and to being touched, and attentive to the two subjects who touch each other.

> The caress is thus an *éveil* to another life than that of daily labour. It is a call to return to you [toi], to me, to us: as living bodies, as two, as different and as co-creators.

> The caress is joint activity and work, irreducible to activities that serve individual or collective obligations. [20]

Irigaray also analyses the category of the 'caress'. It is like a 'speech-act' which 'clears' the horizon or 'clears' the distance of intimacy with the self. ('Clears', both as one 'clears' undergrowth, and as a horse 'clears' a fence.) This is reminiscent of Sartre, on how the appeal of another, and my actions towards them, should 'get me out of myself'. But can this be done, and how is it to be achieved? Irigaray is determined to create a phenomenology that

---

[19] *Etre en éveil* – to be on the alert, on the 'qui vive'. *Donner l'éveil* – to give the alarm. *Mettre qn. en éveil* – put somebody on the alert. The constructions *à toi, à moi* are Irigaray's own. The transitive verb *éveiller* [to arouse etc.] would become *éveiller à*. This would parallel her conversion of the transitive *aimer* into the intransitive construction *aimer à*.
[20] A free translation of a paragraph of Irigaray 1997: 50.

recognises some force in what Sartre, Merleau-Ponty and Lévinas said about the tendency to objectify the other, while radically inflecting their words. Her strategy is to challenge them:

> Isn't this something you recognise as within the powers of you and someone else? Isn't it only the grip of love as a 'desire for possession' which makes Sartre's phenomenology a nightmare from which we cannot awaken. Doesn't that 'great echo of the collective conscious' of which Michèle Le Dœuff writes reverberate from that?[21]

In '*Les noces entre le corps et la parole*', Irigaray rejects the sense of 'bewitchment' and subsequent 'nausea' which by which Sartre typifies sexual love. She rejects, too, Merleau-Ponty's sense of a bodily 'ambiguity' intrinsic to bodily intimacy. She refuses Lévinas' 'equivocal' nature of the female body, and of the feminine. This 'bewitchment', this 'ambiguity', and this 'equivocalness' each signify the same error. Those writers think in terms of a couple that manifests at the same time the existence and the absence of two subjects and of intersubjectivity. We don't have to countenance a loss of the difference between two different subjects in order to recognise a full intersubjectivity. So Irigaray argues.

Irigaray explains her version of conscious awareness as a 'mystery in broad daylight'.[22] This 'mystery' is the difference between *je* and *toi* that neither party can traverse. By perception of the other and expression of my desires I can be aware of myself, of another, of another as aware of me, and of us as aware of each other. Neither *je* nor *toi* is unknowable *tout court*. Each moves from impersonal ways of relating based on reference to objects or functions they have in common. Intimacy, intimate *knowledge*, makes each aware of what neither can comprehend of the other. Hegel – and Sartre in his Hegelian mode – is right in refusing Descartes' way of setting up the 'mind/body' difference.

For, it is not that I know myself perfectly in being myself, being deprived only of a parallel knowledge of you. I know myself in essential part by the responses I provoke in you, by how you look at me, by the ways in which you describe me. This realisation can lead as easily to demoting the other as to installing them as necessary. You may become only one more functionary, if a metaphysically poignant one. I need you, but only because I will not know myself otherwise. Hegel's and Sartre's concepts produce the consequence that one's love for another cannot exceed one's

---

[21] This is my imagined expostulation, of course.

[22] The most relevant chapters of *Etre Deux*: 'Percevoir l'invisible en toi' [To perceive what is invisible in you], 'Transcendants l'un à l'autre' [Transcendents to one another], 'La mystère qui illumine' [The mystery which casts light].

need for them. One's desire falls back to a desire for what one gains from the relationship. Sartre's phenomenology of love epitomises this distortion. Love appears as a 'desire to be the whole world for the one I love'. Generosity in love might suggest the desire to *give* 'the whole world'! Such a desire *for* the other is be ruled out as a metaphysical impossibility. Sartre orders the scene: One must perceive what one desires. To perceive something is to make an object of it. It is impossible, then, to perceive the other as a subject, and not only in *'the modality of object-ness'*. Thus it appears to be ethical posturing in the face of conceptual limits to suggest the possibility of a more generous perception by which one discerns another's subjectivity.

Sartre would protest, *'I cannot perceive the other's interiority'*, and Irigaray would agree. To 'perceive the other's interiority' would reduce interiority to exteriority, reducing the relation of *je* to *tu* – and that of an *il* or *elle*, to a *lui*, where gender has been homogenised. It is a more subtle attention to the possibilities in perception, however, which she attempts to sustain as an alternative. I can stir from a passive level of sensation to a perceiving which is part passive, part active, and also beyond the difference of passive and active. When I budge from the quasi-solipsistic stasis of sensations I gain from another's presence, actions, images, I perceive the 'mystery' of another's being, and, as unnecessary bonus, that of my own.

The present writer rather than your now familiar narrator who bears opinions his author may not share now feels impelled to speak. *I* do not relish writing down 'mystery'. *I* want to rush to disclaimers of all kinds – of *my* own for *my*self, of *mine* for Irigaray, of Irigaray's for herself. *I* content myself with only one. The rest will appear between and in the lines as the discussion continues. 'My' not being able to comprehend the other in their difference is not the Cartesian division between an always-doubtful knowledge of another and a perfect knowledge of myself. It is in like fashion that to admit the mystery of another's being is not to perpetuate the 'mystery' of how consciousness can appear in an otherwise merely material world. Mystery mongering about the world elevates our ignorance of its processes to an occult status. *'These things are too much for us'*, say the priests, along with McGinn[23] and those with ouija boards. The mystery of being is not of that sort. We perceive with the utmost 'clarity and distinctness' that not everything can be explained. To explain is to refer something to something else not identical with it. To explain is to defer the need to explain what we appealed to by way of explanation.

---

[23] McGinn (1991) defends a 'mystery' of mind antithetical to Irigaray's divining' others in their difference while not grasping them. Many forms of metaphysics 'echo in the collective conscious' in riding over our perception of this possibility.

Scientists in their philosophical moments are none too clear about the terms of their quest for a 'holy grail' when they seek a 'theory of everything'. If it is a system of principles which unites all presently articulated principles of operation and functional dependence, then it is coherent as a quest, however enormous in ambition. The ambition can overpower a certain canny awareness:

> We can ask of any theory of 'everything' why the theory itself obtains.

The dilemma is clear. If the theory *does* explain everything else, there is nothing else to explain the theory. It must remain a 'mystery', if this means something we shall never explain. If it does *not* explain everything else, it is not a theory of everything. A theological tradition would escape this dilemma by asserting there is a divine being whose existence and nature explains itself. Accordingly, an enterprising philosophical scientist might suggest that the 'theory of everything' explains itself.[24] This would be, not the final explanation, but the ultimate mystery. No theory *appears* to explain itself. It simply states that things are *thus and so*. It states that quantities are functionally related *in this way* and not in some other. If a physical theory 'explains itself', it does so in a way that remains a mystery.

The 'mystery' of the other's being is the 'mystery' of one's own. It has a form like the 'mystery' of existence itself. Only by *not* explaining all of existence can any existence be explained. Only by *not* regarding everything about me as something to be set up as an object of knowledge can I know anything about myself. As Ryle wrote:

> To try ... to describe what one ... is now doing, is to [make a] comment [which] is not ... the step on which that commentary is being made. Nor can an act of ridiculing be its own butt. [M]y commentary on my performances must always be silent about one performance ... and this performance can be the target only of another commentary. Self-commentary ... and self-admonition are logically condemned to logical penultimacy. Yet nothing ... is privileged ... to escape comment or admonition forever (Ryle 1949: 195).

Such reflections reverse the Cartesian order of thought. They expose the illusion of perfect knowledge of oneself. By intimate acquaintance I am too close to myself to know everything of myself. Thus arises the suspicion that strictly, I do not 'know' anything about myself. I am myself, but the perfection of that 'intimacy' means that I have no distance from which to gain knowledge. I imagine a distance. I imagine myself 'as others see me'.

---

[24] Perhaps it is some awareness of the need for this which produces the metaphor of such a theory as the 'Holy Grail', whose value would be self-authenticating.

Thus the doubt, 'How can I tell that this effort at imaginative self-detachment is anything but a self-deception?'. No. It is the others whom I can know. Thus the excesses of clinically detached observation in psychology and in medicine.

From this point of view we can understand Irigaray as demonstrating a 'logical penultimacy' to 'my' knowledge of another, a penultimacy like that of 'my' knowledge of myself. It won't do to give up on the effort to know myself for myself. If I do not take that seriously, I will be incapable of distinguishing prejudiced or malicious observation of another from fair-minded and generous estimates. Yet, I cannot know myself without experiencing that I am known by another. This means that interiority can be shown to another. Since I am the 'other' for another, I can not consistently regard the other as beyond my knowledge and experience simply in being another. Just as I am the 'other' for another, the 'other' is an 'I' for themselves. So I can not properly regard the other simply as an object to be known. That is something I know. I know it as well as I am likely to know anything beyond the solipsistic simplicities of arithmetic and sensation.

Irigaray would regard the significant intentional life of another as '*to be found here, now, between us*'. In her effort to restore confidence in this idea, she leans hard into the concept of *perceiving*. She '*reject[s] the separation between the visible here and now, and the invisible in the beyond*' (Irigaray 1997: 79). If the 'visible' is what can be known in simple sensation then the 'invisible' itself is part of the *basis* of what we say and know about the invisible. What we can *perceive* in another must always already surpass what we might try to distil out as given in 'simple sense'. We succumb to the banality of the blindingly obvious? We know the 'invisible' of someone in their '*interiorities [and] futures*' on the basis of the 'visible' as what is sensed? This interiority, then, will never find its own conceptual place. Irigaray challenges the dichotomy of 'I' as subject and 'other' as object of perception. It is this prejudice that produces the conclusion that 'I' cannot know the 'other' as subject:

> Objects as such, whether concrete or abstract, sensible or mental, are not necessary to perception.[25] I can see another living being in respecting them as a subject (Irigaray 1997: 76).

In 'respecting them as a subject, they remain, for me, a being

that corresponds to an object-like perception with me, furthermore who

---

[25] Sartre insists that they are necessary to *observation.* Etymology colours present usage. One speaks of scientific *observation,* not of scientific *perceiving.*

remains a stranger to reduction to an object, who remains on the side of the other: a history, a becoming, an interiority (Irigaray 1997: 76).

Irigaray begins to *explain* this kind of 'knowing the other' though s/he is a 'stranger' who cannot be (fully) *explained*. People are a stranger to the object-status that would make them fully accessible to knowledge by observation. One's partial knowledge of the other as partly beyond what can be sensed has its explicable sources. The partial incomprehension of each person by anyone (including themself) is the partial inexplicability of existence – of being itself.

There are more specific 'invisibilities' too. Someone I meet is present to my perception in their manner, words, tone of voice, bodily disposition and yet I don't 'know them'. To counter Descartes' world as haunted by an unknowable other, Ryle stressed the 'invisibility' of one's history. He lampooned the image of man as a machine animated by a ghost. Irigaray's 'mystery' of interiority is congruent with Ryle's criticism. Descartes' dualism lacks *tact*. If you lay in a Cartesian space you would be out of touch. It is only

> what touches me [that] can teach me how to sustain your becoming, how to approach you … in wonder (Irigaray 1997: 85).

Reciprocal contact implies that you, as intending, can be perceived within what I can sense. Only this reciprocal contact prevents me appropriating the other as my interiorised image. Irigaray cautions the lover and the theorist:

> I cannot use what I receive from you without your involvement. Thus I can not use your image only to be seduced by it. I can not appropriate what you propose to my sensibility without my intention towards you. There must be a dialectic between us if each is to [remain] sensible to their own being and that of the other (Irigaray 1997: 85).

If *Je* and *toi* let each other 'be' in our difference we recognise our shared 'mystery'. The ideal of perception is thus '*to let the other be, not to possess them in anything, to contemplate them as an irreducible presence*' (Irigaray 1997: 85). Irigaray is strong in stating ideals. She knows what threatens these ideals; she has some idea how to implement them, and her choice of words conveys the immediacy of the other's presence to our senses. But any theory that we might construct has to build upon these hints, these implicit suggestions. As I 'let the other be' in their difference, I *savour* ('goûter') them. As thus I 'taste' the presence of the other, I perceive their presence as 'in-appropriable'. '*I see, hear, touch them in knowing that what*

I perceive is not mine', realising the incomplete comprehension in *perceiving* the other 'in their difference'. I realise this incompleteness *à travers* their presence to me in sense. My recognition by sense and perception of a 'mystery' in the other, requires me to take a certain attitude:

> Experienced by me, he remains other nevertheless, never reduced to object or instrument ... Almost no trace of exteriority remains in such sharing. This [absence of exteriority] is to be assigned in part to a faithful memory and, perhaps, an alliance (Irigaray 1997: 86).

I take an *attitude* of respect for difference in *perceiving* what you do. These conditions strengthen each other. By intelligence, memory and knowledge of your history and hopes I surpass living only in sensations of you. I have to negotiate with you yourself even as I make an image of you:

> To perceive you is a way of approaching us. What I perceive and what I offer [of myself] to be perceived has to be considered. It remains to give a perspective to perspective itself, to put you into relation with you in the space of my thought, in my heart (Irigaray 1997: 86).

Here, Irigaray reintroduces her sense of the 'spiritual' – '*It remains to give a spiritual measure to my sensibility, as if I looked at you with one eye and evaluated you with the other*' (Irigaray 1997: 86). It is in this way that she constructs a kind of description of seeing the invisible in the visible. She means to describe how someone appears as an intentional being *in* their visible and tangible 'flesh'. What is thus accessible to sense and perception is always in excess of what appears:

> When it happens, the look can fit in as one [*s'harmoniser en un*]; I contemplate in you the union of corporeal and spiritual nature. Thus you make me see the invisible. The invisible is here. You are visible and invisible. The invisible shows across and through you, but also it remains gathered in you ... It appears and subsists (Irigaray 1997: 87).

In demonstrating that I perceive another as conscious in their bodily action and disposition, Irigaray proceeds by means of description rather than metaphysical argument. Description can establish actuality, and thus possibility. Description does not explain this possibility but, nevertheless, to describe vividly how we experience a 'spirited body' is to lessen the force of an opposing metaphysics. The 'mind' may be 'body and brain' but still, we 'wonder' at this being, for the interiority of the other lies there. It is as visible that we deal with the invisible, and yet it is the body itself that is 'invisible' in its history, interiority, and its future. There is a performative dimension to this, too. In respecting you and myself in our intimacy,

> I must also maintain a reserve. In my intention of appearing to you must subsist that of remaining invisible, of covering life and love with the shadow of mystery. The eyes are a bridge and gestures express a wish, but that itself is shown in being hidden ... My body is not reduced to a simple naturality. The desire to love remains still and always a woven garment, as much by me as by you, of earth and of sky, of night and of light, of shade and of sunlight (Irigaray 1997: 87).

Readers will differ in their response to this poetry. It may sound like a coy romanticism bound to traditional femininity, or perhaps the postures of the 'new man'. We may read it in a more friendly fashion, recalling how it is those we know and love best who choose most thoughtfully what to portray of themselves.[26] At one pole lies deceit and restraint but at the other, disregard 'lets it all hang out' under the banner of true feeling. We live between these extremes. We 'exist our bodies' in a space where reciprocity's demands for simple candour are contested by the resources of art and of artifice. In all of this, the self-centredness of honest sensation pleads its hearty case against the *perceiving* that might lead us to finer, perplexing, feelings.

---

[26] It was only God the Father who knew us 'in the recesses of our hearts'.

11
'The Great Echo ... in the Collective Consciousness'

Might not the great echo which Sartre's philosophy found in the collective consciousness arise from the fact that, far from displacing the models of social relations, it recycled their subjective quintessence using language in which they were unrecognizable? (Le Dœuff 1991: 195)

Le Dœuff's Critique of Sartre's 'I' and 'Other'

'Objective Signs' of States of Awareness

Le Dœuff satirises the way that Sartre, who affects to read consciousness as a bodily mode, erases sexual difference. In distinguishing the 'objective' *body-for-others* from the *body-for-myself* Sartre risks ignoring the body itself as part of the facticity with which the *for-itself* must negotiate. If we were to recollect Sartre's general structure of thought as from the very commencement of *Being and Nothingness*, we would dare to say that considered 'in itself', *being* possesses no negativity, and thus no difference. Therefore, if the role of what exists *for-itself* is to create significant form upon what exists *in-itself* – so as to 'raise up' a body, as it were, then this existence 'in-itself' cannot be male or female, woman or man, masculine or feminine. What exists as *for-itself* raises up these differences as terms of its nihilation upon *being in itself*. Sartre *reads* consciousness as what exists, actively, for itself, and this is to operate as a *no-thing* that *nothings*. We have observed how the action of what exists purely *for itself* thus falls towards being unintelligible. And yet, we *do* understand something as existing 'for itself' because its being is never purely 'for itself', and what can be perceived or spoken of as existing in itself is, thereby, not purely 'in itself' either. Thus we lend each phrase contextual sense.

Earlier[1] I tracked the unresolved tension between the *absolutely free* and the *material* character of the *for-itself*.[2] Such an abstract metaphysics takes form in a picture of the *for-itself* as *nihilating* any given *in-itself* into any one of an indefinite array of plastic alternatives. At its extreme this picture would seem to permit me to include a sketch in which 'I' nihilate into masculinity or femininity the *in-itself* that is my own body.[3] (A whole philosophy of gender, sex, and the plasticity of the body forms around these possibilities.)[4] There is a coefficient of adversity; there is the facticity that provides a field for the operation of freedom. This 'being responsible for one's own gender' *erupts* in the text, simply because Sartre does not make a theme of it. Le Dœuff has observed some of the usual points of neuralgia (Le Dœuff 1989: 3). The 'tender points' of the theory where imagery has to do the work that theory cannot accomplish. There is more than this at work, too, in the way both the imagery and the metaphysical figurativeness carry the reader through thickets of text. Sartre has inscribed one's position as perceiver of another who thus objectifies them, with all that implies. Doing violence to another by one's 'look' becomes a necessity of theory. Who can then be ashamed of doing it? Who can complain of having it done to them? Le Dœuff voices a general suspicion about the (onetime) widespread, if inarticulate registration of what Sartre was saying in his language of objectification by perception:

> To what extent is the monopolistic violence which ... is structured around the position of the writer ... unconnected to other ... less literary forms of violence, such as ordinary domestic violence? Might not the great echo which Sartre's philosophy found in the collective consciousness arise from the fact that it ... recycled [prevailing] models of social relations, using language in which they were unrecognisable? (Le Dœuff 1991: 195).

Le Dœuff observes how the assumed 'il' for *whoever, whether man or woman* has unintended effects when Sartre produces graphic descriptions of a sexual encounter. Sartre's uncritical grammar deems that the one whom his narrating 'I' caresses shall be a 'him'. Sartre should have decided whether he had set out to describe homosexual relationships. Le Dœuff observes, also, that when an eroticised body is the object of the

---

[1] Particularly in chapters 3 and 4.

[2] This 'materiality' is read in by making *being* that from which *nihilating* emerges.

[3] One can 'exist the body' in various modes without a sex change operation.

[4] E.g. Butler 1980, Butler 1993, Gatens 1996, Deutscher 1997.

narrator's perception, by some miracle it immediately *becomes woman*.[5] A decision about the sex and sexual orientation of his narrator was required in the first place. Le Dœuff cites these passages, amongst others:

> Sartre discourses at length about 'my flesh' and 'the Other's flesh' and 'the joyful ease of flesh against flesh', but with practically no reference to sexual difference between flesh and flesh. His words are sufficiently general to be ... [of] a relation which is that of neither a man and a woman nor two women nor two men, but which is the common denominator of all such relations ... or of two partners who fall short of sexual difference (Le Dœuff 1991: 63).

When it comes to theory, we are thus '*using the greatest imaginable abstraction .... given that ... to mention 'flesh' is already to accept a fairly weighty adulteration*' (Le Dœuff 1991: 64). When it comes to stories and images, Sartre gives us the greatest possible specificity of sex, just when theory should make it irrelevant.[6] Le Dœuff shows how this is part of Sartre's device for giving his tacitly masculine narrator a god's-eye view into female or other characters expected to be submissive. While the sexual bias demonstrated in the narration falls between two extremes this does not show that the theory is *so* flawed that is must be used in a biased way. At the same time, it does exhibit more than an accidental lapse in how Sartre places figures in his philosophical tales. The biased image enables Sartre to say something that his theory will not permit. The narrator has to be represented as 'knowing' the real state of awareness of successive figures. First there is a woman who denies her sexual pleasure though she shows objective signs of enjoying it. Then we are shown a woman who is sexually interested in a man though she shows no overt signs of that to him. Finally there is the feminised '*in-itself*' that represents the threat of pure immanence for a man, evoking the sexual nature of that fall.

In the last example, theory says that, as conscious, a woman and a man are perfectly alike in being a 'pure freedom in relation to facticity'. Without that premise Sartre could not impute 'bad faith' to the woman in the examples of 'feigned' frigidity and 'feigned' lack of sexual interest. We have already traced some of these conflicting tendencies in Sartre's narrating and theorising. Another person erupts as a conscious subject within my conscious life. When I perceive that person do they become no more than a perceived object for me, whose own *being aware* lies beyond

---

[5] See Le Dœuff's critique of Sartre's depiction of the female body (Le Dœuff 1991: 79–83).

[6] The critique here has been developed in the second and third chapters of this work.

the limits of my perceptions? Earlier, I attempted to demonstrate how Sartre interiorises the 'other' as fast as 'he' or 'she' erupts.[7] The 'ambiguity' emerges in the passages to which Le Dœuff pays close attention. She asks how Sartre, who lays such emphasis on the freedom of every conscious subject to interpret any phenomenon, can speak of 'objective' signs of sexual pleasure. A sign calls for interpretation. She cites a critical response to this objection of hers:

> Sartre has a theory of precisely the immediate readability of emotional manifestations, or what he calls expressive behaviour. According to him, such behaviour is immediately comprehensible because its meaning is its being: it refers to nothing beyond itself and in no way indicates a hidden affection or one experienced in secret by some psyche (Le Dœuff 1991: 68).

Le Dœuff dismantles this idea of 'objective sign'. Yes, there are situations we read – a pallid or a flushed face, a clenched fist – nevertheless something is a sign not just in itself, but in our being able to read it. Le Dœuff aims her remarks very precisely against a casualness in Sartre's expression that would disarm critical thought. The tone of 'evident common sense' in Sartre's reference to supposedly 'objective signs' of feelings seems to place his recycled observations as beyond the dubious realm of philosophical scrutiny. Le Dœuff points out that in reading behaviour as expressing anger we perceive the person as *clenching*, or *having clenched* their fist. We do not perceive the simple object *clenched fist*. Thus the sign as we read it is more than the object. We read the sign within a *'portrait of the angry man [which] shows him whole and entirely involved in what he does'* (Le Dœuff 1991: 69).

Le Dœuff highlights those 'symptoms' we read in another's body that form part of an intentional nexus. We might want to point out, in addition, that someone's simply going pale, or becoming flushed – not intentional actions – are other signs that we read. But, if these are 'objective' signs, they are not something we can read directly *as* anger. It is only the intentional nexus ('stammering', 'clenching the fist') which places anger as present in its 'symptoms'. Sartre mixes more or less intentional acts ('frowning') with distinctly non-intentional symptoms ('trembling hands'). The (sometimes) immediacy of one's perception of the mentality of another's behaviour is, I should say, a product of familiarity in which both intentional and non-intentional behaviour perceived in its congruence – or

---

[7] This work is done in Chapter 7.

its dissonance as when a non-intentional set of the eyes betrays the falsity of an intentional smile.

Mentality and Behaviour

The mentality of behaviour is neither necessarily occluded, nor simply present and fully given in any particular form of behaviour or expression. That we have to read both intentional and non-intentional 'symptoms' supports Le Dœuff in arguing that Sartre displaces the problem of *reading* symptoms by the spurious use of 'objective sign'. For, let us agree with Sartre that anger is not an intrinsically hidden interior event.[8] Even so, what I know by observation permits me to challenge but never simply to override the person's own sincere avowal. Furthermore, even when my observation and the person's avowal are congruent, I have to 'divine' the other person (to use Irigaray's figure). The person has to divine his or her own state of mind, too. It is not 'given' wholly, simply and transparently to anyone. So consider afresh Sartre's picture of an immediate 'upsurge' of the other as a conscious, let us say as an *angry*, being. It is not on account of some infallible observation of 'objective signs' that this *angry person* is a *being* for me. Whatever it is which puts them beyond the realm of the merely *epistemic* must have to do with what arises *between* us.

The Evanescent Body

Le Dœuff has succeeded in exposing 'macho' assumptions in the way Sartre treats the relation between a powerful and a submissive figure in his stories of one person interpreting the awareness of another. She has shown up inconsistencies between Sartre's interpretative phenomenology and his descent into a language of 'objective signs'. What can we say then about how a being as conscious is related to that being as observable? What can we read from Sartre's problems and from Le Doeuff's critique, and from Irigaray's criticism that Sartre does not respect the distinct difference of the 'other'? Certainly, we can observe that all of them – Sartre, Beauvoir, Le Dœuff and Irigaray – in their differing ways – tend towards an ontology that would not divide person from body. Such ontology of an observable bodily consciousness must then take care to respect the interiority of a

---

[8] It *may* be secreted within, though there will be symptoms beyond the person's control. But it is anger no less when public – in its uninhibited manifestation.

person's life as something always only partly known and understood – whether by themselves or by another.

Sartre has it that 'being-for-oneself' is not a different being from that (the body as object) which has 'being-in-itself'. To be conscious is to *void* what has being in itself, not to add substance to it. Conscious being still remains one with bodily being also, in that I, in the mentality that I count as most intimate to me, find myself observed and thus observable by another. The other has seized me-myself. I cannot flee, to leave what this other has laid hold of, as if it were a mere 'outer tattered garment', to summon up one of Sartre's telling phrases from early in his work.

Now, it would be a rich project indeed to place Le Dœuff's own (often implicit) views on the relation of the self as '*I who think, feel, intend*' and '*I who hold bodily sway in the world*',[9] thus to become observable and accountable to others. One would gather evidence from texts as far apart as her essays on Thomas More, on some speeches by Shakespeare's characters, and her critique of existentialism and the 'unique speaking subject'. In 'Du Sujet' she raises a crucial and revealing question about the relation of 'individual' to 'universal' subject, followed by a diagnosis of how one tends to slip into the other:

> [I]sn't there something in the whole concept of the human person as subject which tends to run together the individual subject with the Absolute Spirit – that is to say, to make it lose its status as an individual among individuals, to gain the advantage of a certain uniqueness – to be the only subject in the world – indeed to be the subject of the world? ... This text [*Venus and Adonis*] allows one to think, perhaps, that ... just as soon as I define myself as a subject, I tend to define myself as being absolute Spirit' (Le Dœuff 1986a: 24–25)

The emphasis is on 'define'. I *am* a 'subject' but to define myself as such is to lose my grip – to slide towards thinking of myself as a 'unique' or 'absolute' subject radically distinct from my 'empirical specificity'. For Le Dœuff, reciprocity is the principal key to ethics, and the position of 'unique speaking subject' is its antithesis.[10] So it is not Sartre's acceptance of the accessibility and thus the at-least-materiality of the conscious self of which Le Dœuff is critical. It is not as if he is merely too brutal a

---

[9] A typical and striking expression of Husserl's (Husserl 1970b).

[10] See her critique of a common reaction to Sartre's promiscuity (Le Dœuff 1991: 186). Also, the connections between Venus' self-definition and her 'corps morcelé (Le Dœuff 1986a).

materialist. Her suspicion about the long currency and status of his ideas is, rather, a hunch that his intellectual system raises up a specific male voice as if it were 'unique' or 'absolute'. The effect is to rationalise a verbal violence towards others, including women, congruent with common domestic violence.

Irigaray's Critique

Irigaray, too, though criticising Sartre for making objectification seem inevitable, sides with him in requiring no different *being* from what exists in itself, in order to explain the consciousness of the body for itself. On her view, we reject a mind/body dualism, while maintaining wonder at one's own consciousness, and that of another. We maintain a wonder at what is bodily, too, and towards machines and the systems of technology. By perceiving in all these modes of existence a difference that we cannot co-opt, we decentre our narcissism. We know another in their expressive materiality. But when we go towards someone whom we know intimately, picking them out from a crowd, our sense of *knowing* them *is* our sense of knowing how they lie beyond our knowing, beyond our picture of them – beyond the reality of our own feeling by which we hurtle towards them.

One might surmise, therefore, that Irigaray would half-sympathise (as Le Dœuff would not) with Sartre in feeling that in just *observing* another we find them there only as object. What Sartre neglects, for Irigaray, is 'divination', which I read as the working of imagination, empathy and active informed guesswork upon close perception, recall and retention of what has been said and done by and with the other. In naturalising her risky term *'divining'*, we might also think of the figure that used to stand at the bow of a boat taking *soundings.* These had to be taken rapidly, taking account of the fact that the vessel advanced all the while that the soundings were being taken – by the time one had taken a depth one was already in process of taking the next. There was no time to sit down in a detached way to measure the length of cord that had spun out – the knots that marked its length had to be counted, by familiarity, as they slid past the fingers. And the depth was known only for a moment, then passed over, as new soundings were taken just ahead of the vessel's direction. Fixed charts[11] might be made from the series of readings – but later.

To respond in a less sympathetic way to the reverberations of Irigaray's 'divining' is to think of her as invoking an image of the water 'diviner',

---

[11] In the form of either common-sense, or systematic psychology.

who 'feels the divining rod twitch' when there is a well of water below him. Such talk of 'divining' rouses reasonable suspicions. We have no conception of any means by which water might make a piece of twisted wire twitch. And since the diviner assures us that *he* did not make his instrument move what part does the diviner really play? He has to regard himself as at least a conduit for the mysterious force that emanates from subterranean water – he must accept that it is his hands, then, even if moved by water, that moved his wire. But he likes to think of himself as feeling the wire *being twitched by* the water.

Irigaray is not the kind of philosopher to take up this matter of examining the figure of a 'diviner – it is no use whining about such limitations in her writing. Such provocative philosophy as hers prompts the reader into their own work. The picture I have sketched of 'soundings' is of an alternative, natural, and comprehensible source for her metaphor of how we know another in knowing them yet more intensely as unknown. To understand 'divining' as sounding someone's depths speaks of the risks we take in coming to 'know' them. The *more* intimately we 'know' someone, the more intensely we are aware of the partiality, the provisional status, and the conceptual inadequacy of our understanding of them.

Working on from Sartre and Beauvoir

In continuing to read Sartre and Beauvoir and in employing their ideas and language in contemporary thought, I have used the frame of Le Dœuff's critique of the limitations of their conceptual structures. In order to get the best out of phenomenology, one has to deal with the distortions of 'subject' and 'object' that are endemic to it. And it would be congruent with her critique to develop Beauvoir's proposal about the need for 'generosity' in overcoming Sartre's argument that his 'I' loses its subjectivity in being observed. We have seen how Beauvoir is subverting his phenomenology of an *inevitable* antagonism between 'I' and 'Other', both by an ethical appeal ('generosity') and an importation of issues of economy, social structure and political factors into a philosophical understanding of what goes on in constructing an 'Other'. And, in addition, I have drawn attention to a need to work out a 'naturalised' reading of Irigaray's 'divination' of the other that I began in the previous two chapters.

Despite the criticism that Sartre and Beauvoir's language and method has attracted, they did succeed in clearing a track between a dualism that occludes mentality from view and touch, and a materialism that oversimplifies what *is* available to perception in the body's motions and dispositions. This work is now the common inheritance of all philosophers – 'serious money' in intellectual terms. And for us of this new century, we need to re-invest this legacy from Sartre and Beauvoir's domesticated and sexualised phenomenology. For otherwise we seem unable to find an escape route from the legacy of the last century. The dogged alternatives of extreme materialism, or of a *mystery* in simply being conscious – a dichotomy only exacerbated by 'analytical philosophy'.

Furthermore, there are sections in Sartre on *knowledge*,[12] for example, which could be brought to bear on 'knowing' another's conscious life – and one's own. And within the chapter, 'The Body', that has attracted more attention, there is a complex but neglected discussion of the presence of the 'Other'. We have seen how this Other first disrupts my consciousness as it is for itself, only to install itself within 'my' mind more comfortably, as if to monitor my acts and feelings whether or not anyone is there 'in the corridor' to catch me by surprise.[13]

All of this would repay continuing exact and creative attention. Just as, after much complex discussion, bad faith emerged as an 'evanescent' phenomenon – something that disappeared as one went to get a secure grip on it – so too did consciousness. There is 'no such thing' – it is a nothing, a void, an effect rather than a cause of the sheer fact that as living organisms dealing with a world, we are engaged from the start as 'nihilating' – as making nothing of something in order to make something of something else. Each phenomenon strikes the philosopher as a shock, in writing of these 'phenomena'. Then as we investigate their 'essence' (as Husserl had proposed), we find the phenomena to disappear even as we scrutinise them, only to reappear as we turn away, textually speaking. Then the *Other* makes its discomfiting appearance, only to disappear under scrutiny, then to reappear when least expected – *only* when least expected, perhaps. And finally – well, 'finally' in respect of the philosophical personages that are to appear on the stage of the book – it is 'the body in question'.[14]

Possibilities for the Body

It is true that the 'body' of Sartre's text performs an ontic dance of the veils, taking on the evanescent character that had earlier been attributed to the pure 'nihilations' of bad faith, consciousness and the Other. But as it

---

[12] See the later parts of 'Transcendence', concluding Part II, on 'being-for-oneself'.

[13] See Chapter 7, in particular.

[14] With acknowledgements to Jonathon Miller's T.V. series of that name.

steadies within the mass of text it gains in substance. We should understand that it is not simply the 'imaginary body' that Sartre describes as the *body-for-itself.* Not merely like a 'phantom limb' in which the amputee still feels pain and wants to scratch an itch. The body as something that we 'live' or 'exist', rather than 'inhabit' or 'possess', is physically conscious and consciously physical. Sometimes Sartre uses the phrases that might translate as 'my body' versus 'the body for others', as if to suggest different beings. But he is more liable to speak of 'the body as it is for me' as one of its modes, and 'the (or my) body as it is for others' as another mode. For, as we have seen in detail earlier, this latter distinction is a further construction upon the first elementary one of being conscious, and being a body at no more than the level of *objectity.* That elementary difference consists, of course, between what exists *in-itself* and what exists *for-itself.* And that difference consists not in a *being* that is other than what exists in itself, but in a repetition of 'nihilations' – the making of this body as *in itself* to *lack* being – to be only as a *voidance* of the body. In short, the difference between the conscious and the non-conscious need not involve a difference between one being and another different kind of being.

To read Sartre in this way is to take him closer to Beauvoir's sort of social materialism than is customary. This, though salutary, poses two new problems. One is to understand more precisely what it means to say that these 'nihilations' *void* what exists (merely) in itself. The other task is to relate this distinction of [the body *in-itself* as against the body *for-itself*], with [the body *as-it-is-for-me* and *as-it-is-for-others*]. Sartre has begun to lay out what is involved in understanding the body *for others* – from my point of view and from that of another. Though this is my body as observed 'externally' by others, it does not therefore reduce to the body *in itself.* The body as 'in itself; exists as 'for others', as it does *for me in living it.* My body as perceived and responded to by others is more ready to be perceived by them as a conscious subject than in its 'objectity' as simply bones, blood, eyes-as-lenses, and so on. One certainly cannot (and certainly Sartre does not) identify the 'outside' point of view with that which sees the body only as it is *in itself.*

Despite their intimate connections, there is some autonomy to each of these notions – the *body simply as-it-is-in-itself,*[15] the *body as-it-is-for-others,* and *the body as-it-is-for-me-as-I-live-it.* These 'three' are tightly interconnected and yet autonomous modes of being the one being. No one could suggest (certainly Sartre does not) that there are three bodies – the

---

[15] I have to put aside a discussion of this inviting metaphysical possibility.

body *in-itself*, the body *for-others* and the body *for-me*. To speak of what exists *in itself* and as *for itself* is not in itself a new dualism, as commonly charged by critics. The phrases '*en-soi*' and '*pour-soi*' indicate *modes* of being. And so, as regards these modes, it is not a dual-ism, but a triad-ism in which Sartre (and, implicitly, Beauvoir) is involved. Not a fixed triadism at that. The body *in-itself* is itself the body *in itself as-it-is-for-me*, and *as-it-is-for-others*. And the body *as-it-is-for-others* is also *my* 'body-for-others' as I, in turn, comprehend *their* ways of taking it and responding to it.

Remarks in Departure

In this last Part of the work I have been describing some recent moves in philosophy within the theme of *finding ourselves in technology*. We 'find ourselves' in technology both as one finds oneself 'thrown' into it, as Heidegger would say, and as we 'find ourselves' when awakening in a strange field before we quite remember where and how we settled down there the previous evening. And we 'find ourselves' in coming to terms with our new surroundings and in becoming familiar with them and with each other within them. If I have still emphasised the human body as what is conscious, thus respecting the fact of the continuing tendencies towards some kind of dualism, this need not be read or taken up as the nostalgia of an old humanism. We might still love to think that all would be well so long as we got back to the 'truly human'. But Beauvoir and Sartre's daring adventures in negativity and their searches into the *void* in existence and *les petits riens* in every moment and detail of everyday life are there, still to stir us from that complacency. After Beauvoir and Sartre there have appeared, on the scientific side, discoveries in genetics and newly founded speculations about possible narratives of evolution. In terms of philosophy and its successors in cultural and linguistic theory, we have seen the rise and fall of structuralism followed by the event of that 'de-structuralism' commonly called deconstruction. And, as to feminism, for any Luce Irigaray who would revive a sense of the divine, there is now a Donna Haraway who would say '*I would rather be a cyborg than a goddess*' (Haraway 1991: 181)!

Since that epoch of existentialism and phenomenology the void at the heart of human genre and gender now appears as a radical break between different visions of the problem. On the one hand there are the debates between scientific reductionism in physics and in economics, and the persisting visions based in consciousness and social consciousness – moral and immoral – of reality. An unfriendly critic of those debates would declare a curse on both these block(headed) houses of modernism. The more serious (certainly the fiercest) debates have been those that earned the title of 'culture wars'. These have taken the form of violent and loud attacks by the aforesaid neo-modernists or neo humanists upon the various kinds of 'deconstructionist' and 'post-modernist' writings.[16]

Displaced by the emergence of world wide and deafening events, the culture wars have died down without victory, surrender or truce. That these new catastrophes are actualised in the name of variously tortured metaphors might be claimed as a kind of victory for the post-modernist insight into contemporary society. And yet there is no room for even an ironic salute to a such an understanding. The horror and immediacy of the events will ensure that some other mode of thought will descend upon us, in any case, unless we make the effort to fashion one. Allow me, therefore, in departing this text, a laudatory remark about Beauvoir and Sartre's writing that I make in the face of the recurring tendency to disparage any new philosophy by condemning it as 'fashionable' or 'modish'.

Beauvoir's and Sartre's work is now so far from being fashionable as to be at risk of being appropriated by the conservatism of tradition. But it was the height of 'fashion'. It is the space of a half a century that frees us to perceive the force of their writing, and thus to resist that conservative appropriation. We can be reminded by their adventures that we must 'fashion' philosophy. Otherwise we only hammer at its 'perennial problems'. Beauvoir and Sartre challenge us to keep philosophy open to diverse genres of discourse. We can then take our turn in disrupting the illusion that knowledge and understanding are voiced as if by one, unique, speaking subject. At the same time we can play our part in renewing the sometimes-lyrical power of philosophy's reason.

---

[16] Within this loose assemblage of post-modernists I would mention in particular the work of Judith Butler. Butler set out from her studies on existential phenomenology to supplant Sartrean 'nihilations' of what exist 'in itself' by the problematic of gender as constructed – virtually *performed.*

Bibliography

Principal Relevant Works of Simone de Beauvoir

(1944), *Pour une morale de l'ambiguité*, Gallimard (collections idées), Paris.

(1945), *Le sang des autres*, Gallimard, Paris.

(1948), *The Blood of Others*, trans. Senhouse, R. and Moyse, Y., Knopf, New York.

(1948), *The Ethics of Ambiguity*, trans. B. Frechtman, Citadel Press, New Jersey.

(1949), *Le Deuxième Sexe*, Gallimard (folio essais), Paris.

(1953), *The Second Sex*, ed. and trans. H.M. Parshley, Jonathan Cape, London.

(1955), 'Merleau-Ponty et le pseudo-Sartreisme', *Les Temps modernes*, **10**, pp.2072–2123, repr. *Priviliège*, 1955, Gallimard, Paris.

(1965), *The Prime of Life*, trans. P. Green, Penguin, Harmondsworth.

General and Biographical Critiques of Beauvoir

Appignanesi, Lisa (1988), *Simone de Beauvoir*, Penguin Books, Harmondsworth.

Bair, Deidre (1991), *Simone de Beauvoir: a Biography*, Jonathan Cape, repr. Vintage, London.

Crosland, Margaret (1992), *Simone de Beauvoir: The Woman and her Work*, Heinemann, London.

Evans, Mary (1985), *Simone de Beauvoir: A Feminist Mandarin*, Tavistock, London.

Francis, Claude and Gontier, Fernande (1985), *Simone de Beauvoir*, Perrin, Paris.

Fullbrook, Kate and Fullbrook, Edward (1993), *Simone de Beauvoir and Jean-Paul Sartre: The Remaking of a Twentieth Century Legend*, Harvester Wheatsheaf, Hemel Hempstead.

Fullbrook, Kate and Fullbrook, Edward (1998), *Simone de Beauvoir: a critical introduction*, Polity Press, Malden Massachusetts.

Heath, Jane (1989), *Simone de Beauvoir*, Harvester Wheatsheaf, London.

Jeanson, Francis (1966), *Simone de Beauvoir ou l'entreprise de vivre*, Seuil, Paris.

Moi, Toril (1994), *Simone de Beauvoir: The Making of an Intellectual Woman*, Blackwell, Oxford.

Collections of Critical Papers on Beauvoir

Evans, Ruth (ed.) (1998), *Simone de Beauvoir's* The Second Sex: *New Interdisciplinary Essays*, Manchester University Press, Manchester.

Fallaize, Elizabeth (ed.) (1998), *Simone de Beauvoir: A Critical Reader*, Routledge, London and New York.

Simons, Margaret (1995), *Feminist Interpretations of Simone de Beauvoir*, Pennsylvania State University Press, University Park.

Specialised Studies of Beauvoir's Philosophy

Bergoffen, Debra (1997), *The Philosophy of Simone de Beauvoir*, State University Press of New York, New York.

Lundgren-Gothlin, Eva (1996), *Sex and Existence: Simone de Beauvoir's 'The Second Sex'*, Athlone, London.

Moi, Toril (1990), *Feminist Theory and Simone de Beauvoir*, Blackwell, Cambridge, Mass.

Simons, Margaret
    (1977), *A Phenomenology of Oppression: a Critical Introduction to 'Le Deuxième Sexe'*, University Microfilms International, Purdue.
    (1999), *'The Second Sex': Feminism, Race, and the origins of Existentialism*, Rowman and Littlefield, Lanham, Maryland.

Vintges, Karen (1996), *Philosophy as Passion: The Thinking of Simone de Beauvoir*, Indiana University Press, Bloomington and Indianapolis.

Books Containing Chapters on Beauvoir's Philosophy

Al-Hibri, Azizah and Simons, Margaret (eds) (1990), *Hypatia Reborn* (Part III), Indiana University Press, Bloomington and Indianapolis.

Benhabib, S. and Cornell, D. (1987), *Feminism as Critique*, University of Minnesota Press, Minneapolis.

Deutscher, Penelope (1997), 'The Notorious Contradictions of Simone de Beauvoir' *Yielding Gender*, Routledge, London.

Garry, A. and Pearsall, M. (1989), Part VI, *Women, Knowledge and Reality*, Unwin Hyman, Boston.

Kruks, Sonia (1990), *Situation and Human Existence*, Unwin Hyman, London.

Moi, Toril (1987), *French Feminist Thought: a reader*, Blackwell, New York.

Principal Relevant Works of Sartre

La Nausée (1938), Gallimard, Paris.

Nausea (1965), trans. Baldick, Penguin Books, Harmondsworth.

La Transcendence de l'Ego (1936), Bibliothèque des textes philosophiques, Paris.

The Transcendence of the Ego (1957), (trans. Williams, F. and Kirkpatrick R. Noonday, New York.

L'être et le néant (1943), Gallimard, Paris.

Being and Nothingness (1976), trans. Hazel Barnes 1958, repr. 1976, Methuen, London.

Les Mots (1963), Gallimard, Paris.

The Words (1964), trans. Frechtman, B. Braziller, New York. repr. (1983), Penguin, Harmondsworth.

Critical Expositions of Sartre

Catalano, J.S. (1986), *A Commentary on Jean-Paul Sartre's 'Being and Nothingness'*, University of Chicago Press, Chicago.

Caws, Peter (1979), *Sartre*, Routledge, London.

Danto, Arthur (1975), *Sartre*, Fontana, London.

Grene, Marjorie (1971), *Sartre*, New Viewpoints, New York.

Hammond, M., Howard, J. and Keat, R. (1991), *Understanding Phenomenology*, Blackwell, Oxford.

Lafarge, Rene (1970), *Jean-Paul Sartre: His Philosophy*, University of Notre Dame Press, Indiana.

Manser, Anthony (1966), *Sartre: A Philosophical Study*, Athlone, London.

Naess, Arne (1968), *Four Modern Philosophers*, University of Chicago Press, Chicago.

Richter, Liselotte (1970), *Jean-Paul Sartre*, Ungar, New York.

Warnock, Mary (1965), *The Philosophy of Sartre*, Hutchinson University Library, London.

Wood, Philip (1990), *Understanding Jean-Paul Sartre*, University of South Carolina Press, Columbia.

Specialised Studies

Busch, Thomas (1990), *The Power of Consciousness and the Force of Circumstances in Sartre's Philosophy*, Indiana University Press, Indiana.

Detmer, David (1986), *Freedom as a Value*, Open Court, La Salle, Illinois.

Fell, Joseph (1965), *Emotion in the Thought of Sartre*, Columbia University Press, New York.

George, François (1976), *Deux Etudes sur Sartre*, C. Bourgois, Paris.

Howells, Christina (1988), *Sartre: the Necessity of Freedom*, Cambridge University Press, Cambridge.

LaCapra, Dominick (1979), *A Preface to Sartre*, Methuen, London.

McCulloch, Gregory (1994), *Using Sartre*, Routledge, London.

Morris, Phyllis (1976), *Sartre's Concept of a Person*, University of Massachusetts Press, Amherst.

Natanson, Maurice (1972), *A Critique of Sartre's Ontology*, Haskell House, New York.

Schilpp, Paul A. (ed.) (1981), *The Philosophy of Jean-Paul Sartre*, Open Court, La Salle.

Silverman, H. and Elliston, F. (eds) (1980), *Sartre: Contemporary Approaches to his Philosophy*, Dusquesne University Press, Pittsburgh.

Whitford, Margaret (1982), *Merleau-Ponty's Criticism of Sartre's Philosophy*, French Forum, Lexington, Ky.

Wider, Kathleen (1997), *The Bodily Nature of Consciousness*, Cornell University Press, Ithaca.

Collections Including Chapters on Sartre

Murphy, Julian (ed.) (1999), *Feminist Interpretations of Jean-Paul Sartre*, Pennsylvania State University Press, Pennsylvania.

Howells, Christina (1992), *Cambridge Companion to Sartre*, Cambridge University Press, Cambridge.

Glynn, Simon (ed.) (1987), *Sartre: An Investigation of Some Major Themes*, Avesbury, Aldershot.

Small, Robyn (ed.) (2001), *A Hundred Years of Phenomenology*, Ashgate, Aldershot.

Other Works Cited

Anscombe, Elizabeth (1958), *Intention*, Blackwell, Oxford.
Arendt, Hannah (1971), *The Life of the Mind*, Harcourt Brace, New York.
Austin, John L. (1961), *Philosophical Papers*, Oxford University Press, Oxford.
Ayer, A.J. (1945), 'Sartre's analysis of Man's Relationship', *Horizon*, **12**, 68, August, 101–110.
Benjamin, Walter (1970), trans. Zohn. H., *Illuminations*, Jonathon Cape, London.
Berkeley, George (1972), *The Principles of Human Knowledge*, Collins/Fontana, London.
Blanchot, Maurice (1987), 'Everyday Speech', *Yale French Studies*, 73.
Butler, Judith (1980), *Gender Trouble: Feminism and the Subversion of Identity*, Routledge, New York.
      (1993), *Bodies that Matter*, Routledge, London.
Dante, *The Divine Comedy* (Vol. I), trans. Durling, R. (1996), Oxford University Press, Oxford.
De Certeau, M. (2000), 'The Practice of Everyday Life', *The Certeau Reader*, Blackwell, Oxford.
Dennett, Daniel (1984), *Elbow Room*, Oxford University Press, Oxford.
Descartes (1954), trans. Anscombe E. and Geach P., *Philosophical Writings*, Thomas Nelson, London.
Derrida, J.
      (19820, *Margins of Philosophy*, trans. Bass, A., Harvester Press, Brighton.
      (1987), *The Truth in Painting*, University of Chicago Press, Chicago.
      (1992), *Given Time: 1. Counterfeit Money*, University of Chicago Press.
Deutscher, Max
      (1983), *Subjecting and Objecting*, Blackwell, Oxford.
      (1988), 'Simulacra, feeling and enactment', *Philosophy*, **246**, pp.515–528.
      (2000), ed. *Michèle Le Dœuff: Operative Philosophy and Imaginary Practice*, Humanity Books, Amherst.
Deutscher, Penelope (1997), *Yielding Gender*, Routledge, London.
Ferrell, Robyn (2000), 'Copula: The Logic of the Sexual Relation', *Hypatia*, **15**, 2, pp.100–114.
Gatens, Moira
      (1983), 'A Critique of the Sex/Gender Distinction Allen, J. and Patton, P., *Beyond Marxism? Interventions after Marx*, Intervention Publications, Sydney.
      (1991), *Feminism and Philosophy*, Polity Press, Cambridge.
      (1996), *Imaginary Bodies*, Routledge, London and New York.
Hammond, M.A., Howarth, J.A. and Keat, R.N. (1991), *Understanding Phenomenology*, Blackwell, Oxford.
Haraway, Donna (1991), *Simians, Cyborgs and Women*, Routledge, London/New York.
Hume, David (1967), *Treatise of Human Nature*, Oxford University Press, Oxford.
Husserl, E.
      (1970a), *Cartesian Meditations*, Nijhoff, The Hague.
      (1970b), *The Crisis of European Sciences*, NorthWestern, Evanston.
Irigaray, Luce
      (1985a), *Speculum of the Other Woman*, Ithaca, New York.
      (1985b), *This Sex which is not One*, Ithaca, New York.
      (1993a), *An Ethics of Sexual Difference*, Ithaca, New York.
      (1993b), *Sexes and Genealogies*, Columbia University Press, New York.
      (1997), *Etre Deux*, Paris, Grasset.

(2000), *To be Two*, Athlone, London.

Karpin, Isabel (1992), 'Legislating the Female Body', *Columbia Journal of Gender and Law*.

Le Dœuff, Michèle

(1979), 'Operative Philosophy', *Ideology and Consciousness*, **6**, pp.47–57.

(1986a),'Du sujet', *Cross references*, Society of French Studies, **8**, pp.24–31.

(1986b), *Genèse d'une catastrophe*, Alidades, Paris 1986.

(1989), *The Philosophical Imaginary* Athlone, London.

(1991), *Hipparchia's Choice*, Blackwell, Oxford.

(1998), *Le Sexe du Savoir*,Grasset, Paris.

LeFèbvre, Henri (2000), *Everyday Life in the Everyday World*, Athlone, London.

McGinn, Colin (1991), *The Problem of Consciousness*, Blackwell, Oxford.

Merleau-Ponty, M. (1964), *The Primacy of Perception*, Northwestern University Press, Evanston.

More, Thomas (1989), ed. Logon, G., *Utopia*, Cambridge University Press, Cambridge.

Nagel, Thomas (1974), 'What is it like to be a Bat?', *Philosophical Review*, **83**, pp.435–50.

Plato (1953), *The Dialogues of Plato*, trans. B. Jowett, Fourth Edition, Oxford University Press, Oxford.

Quine, Willard Van Orman (1960), *Word and Object*, Massachusetts Institute of Technology Press, Boston.

Reinach, A. (1982), trans. Smith, B., *On the Problem of Negative Judgement*, Philosophia Verlag, Munich.

Ryle, Gilbert

(1949), *The Concept of Mind*, Hutchinson's University Library, London.

(1966), 'Negative Actions', (1977), *Collected Papers*, Hutchinson, London.

(1964), *Dilemmas*, Cambridge University Press, Cambridge.

Sawicki, Marianne (1997), *Body, Text and Science: The Literacy of Investigative Practices and the Phenomenology of Edith Stein*, Kluwer, Dordrecht/Boston/London.

Schama, Simon (1999), *Rembrandt's Eyes*, Penguin Press, London.

Sokal, Alan D. and Bricmont, Jean (1998), *Intellectual Impostures*, Profile Books, London.

Stein, Edith (1989), trans. Stein, W., *On the Problem of Empathy*, ICS Publications, Washington.

Ricks, Christopher (1974), *Keats and Embarrassment*, Oxford University Press, Oxford.

Shakespeare (1959), *The Complete Works*, Oxford University Press, Oxford.

Smart, J.J.C. (1956), '*The River of Time*', *Essays in Conceptual Analysis*, ed. Pears, D.F., Blackwell, Oxford.

Wittgenstein, Ludwig

(1933), *Tractatus Logico-Philosophicus*, Routledge and Kegan Paul, London.

(1953), *Philosophical Investigations*, Blackwell, Oxford.

(1958), *The Blue and Brown Books*, Blackwell, Oxford.

Index

Page numbers followed by an 'f' indicate that the reference is contained in a footnote.

Name Index

For Product Safety Concerns and Information please contact our EU
representative GPSR@taylorandfrancis.com Taylor & Francis Verlag GmbH,
Kaufingerstraße 24, 80331 München, Germany

Printed and bound by CPI Group (UK) Ltd, Croydon, CR0 4YY
10/06/2025
01898340-0001